DISPOSABLE FUTURES

"Beginning with Primo Levi and ending with Deleuze, Evans and Giroux map the radical transformation that has affected the representation of cruelty between the 20th and the 21st century: from 'exceptional' status, associated with the ultimate figures of state sovereignty, it has passed to 'routinized' object of communication, consumption and manipulation. This is not to say that everything is visible, only that the protocols of visibility have been appropriated by a different form of economy, where humans are completely disposable. To counter this violence in the second degree, and preserve our capacity to face the intolerable, a new aesthetics and politics of imagination is required. This powerful, committed, exciting book does more than just evoke its urgency. It already practices it." —Étienne Balibar, author of *Violence and Civility*

"*Disposable Futures* confronts a key conundrum of our times: How is it that, given the capacity and abundance of resources to address the critical needs of all, so many are having their futures radically discounted while the privileged few dramatically increase their wealth and power? Brad Evans and Henry Giroux have written a trenchant analysis of the logic of late capitalism that has rendered it normal to dispose of any who do not service the powerful. A searing indictment of the socio-technics of destruction and the decisions of their deployability. Anyone concerned with trying to comprehend these driving dynamics of our time would be well served by taking up this compelling book." —David Theo Goldberg, author of *The Threat of Race: Reflections on Racial Neoliberalism*

"Brad Evans and Henry Giroux offer a trenchant analysis of neo-liberalism's ills: its violence, its dystopian vision, its intrusiveness, and its attempt to eradicate all critical consciousness and with it all hope. They diagnose our exposure to disposability in an era marked by the collapse of a vision of a viable future. In doing so, they have laid out the challenge before us. The only question left is, do we have the will, as the authors suggest, to fabricate a nonviolent response to it?" —Todd May, Class of 1941 Memorial Professor of the Humanities, Clemson University

"*Disposable Futures* poses, and answers, the pressing question of our times: How is it that in this post-Fascist, post–Cold War era of peace and prosperity we are saddled with more war, violence, inequality, and poverty than ever? The neoliberal era, Evans and Giroux brilliantly reveal, is defined by violence, by drone strikes, 'smart' bombs, militarized police, Black lives taken, prison expansion, corporatized education, surveillance, the raw violence of racism, patriarchy, starvation, and want. The authors show how the neoliberal regime normalizes violence, renders its victims disposable, commodifies the spectacle of relentless violence and sells it to us as entertainment, and tries to contain cultures of resistance. If you're not afraid of the truth in these dark times, then read this book. It is a beacon of light." —Robin D. G. Kelley, author of *Freedom Dreams: The Black Radical Imagination*

"*Disposable Futures* is an utterly spellbinding analysis of violence in the later 20th and early 21st centuries. It strikes me as a new breed of street-smart intellectualism moving through broad-ranging theoretical influences of Adorno, Arendt, Bauman, Deleuze, Foucault, Žižek, Marcuse, and Reich. I especially appreciated the discussion of representation and how it functions within a broader logics of power; the descriptions and analyses of violence mediating the social field and fracturing it through paralyzing fear and anxiety; the colonization of bodies and pleasures; and the nuanced discussion of how state violence, surveillance, and disposability connect. Big ideas explained using a fresh, straightforward voice." —Adrian Parr, author of *The Wrath of Capital: Neoliberalism and Climate Change Politics*

DISPOSABLE FUTURES

THE SEDUCTION OF VIOLENCE IN THE AGE OF SPECTACLE

BRAD EVANS AND HENRY A. GIROUX

Open Media Series | City Lights Books

Open Media Series Editor: Greg Ruggiero

Front cover art: Isaac Cordal

Library of Congress Cataloging-in-Publication Data

Evans, Brad, 1968-
 Disposable futures : the seduction of violence in the age of spectacle / Brad
Evans and Henry A. Giroux.
     pages cm. — (City lights open media)
 Includes bibliographical references and index.
 ISBN 978-0-87286-658-4 (paperback)
 ISBN 978-0-87286-659-1 (e-book)
 1. Violence. 2. Violence—Political aspects. I. Giroux, Henry A. II. Title.

HM886.E93 2015
303.6—dc23

                          2015004112

City Lights Books
Open Media Series
www.citylights.com

CONTENTS

For Tony Penna, my mentor and lost friend.

HENRY GIROUX

For Amelie, my beautiful little girl

BRAD EVANS

THE DROWNING

Writing one of the most important personal testimonies on the extreme horrors of the twentieth centry, Primo Levi observes: "Logic and morality made it impossible to accept an illogical and immoral reality; they engendered a rejection of reality which as a rule led the cultivated man rapidly to despair." Indeed, the tragedy of ideological fascism for Levi is both the forced complicity of victims into systems of brutal slaughter, and the seductions of violence made desirable by those interned to render them accomplices in their own destruction. As he further states, "the harsher the oppression, the more widespread among the oppressed is the willingness, with all its infinite nuances and motivations, to collaborate: terror, ideological seduction, servile imitation of the victor, myopic desire for any power whatsoever." Central to Levi's analysis here is the way in which the spectacle of violence becomes a substitute for human empowerment—a last refuge if you will—for those who are already condemned by the system.

Levi exposes us to the depths of human depravity and the dehumanization of our worldly fellows. He also warns us about the dangers of reducing the human condition to questions of pure survival, such that a truly dystopian condition accentuates the logic of violence by seducing the oppressed to desire their own oppression or to imagine a world in which the only condition of agency is survival. Eventually, as Levi points out, the spectacle of violence becomes so ingrained that everybody is infected, to the extent that clear lines concerning morality, ethics, and political affinities blur into what he termed "the gray zone." If the system strips some lives of all sense of humanity and dignity—the killing of the subject while the person is still alive—so they come to embody what he named "the drowned," those who remain are forever burdened by the guilt of surviving, the shame of being "saved" from a wretchedness that destroys the very notion of humanity.

Levi's notion of disposability was rooted in a brutalism in which genocide became a policy and the slaughter of millions the means to an end. What Levi couldn't have foreseen given the extreme dystopian historical circumstances of his time, however, was that disposability or the notion of intolerable violence and suffering in the twenty-first century would be recast by the very regimes that claimed to defeat ideological fascism. We are not in any way suggesting a uniform history here. The spectacle of violence is neither a universal nor a transcendental force haunting social relations. It emerges in different forms under distinct social formations, and signals in different ways how cultural politics works necessarily as a pedagogical force. The spectacle of violence takes on a kind of doubling, both in the production of subjects willing to serve the political and economic power represented by the spectacle and increasingly in the production of political and economic power willing to serve the spectacle itself. In this instance, the spectacle of violence exceeds its own pedagogical aims by bypassing even the minimalist democratic gesture of gaining consent from the subjects whose interests are supposed to be served by state power.

It was against twentieth-century forms of human disposability that we began to appreciate the political potency of the arts as a mode of resistance, as dystopian literatures, cinema, music, and poetry, along with the visual and performing arts, challenged conventional ways of interpreting catastrophe. We only need to be reminded here of George Orwell's *Animal Farm*, Alain Resnais's *Hiroshima Mon Amour*, Bretolt Brecht's *The In-*

terrogation of the Good, Max Ernst's *Europe After the Rain*, and Gorecki's *Symphony No. 3* to reveal the political value of more poetic interventions and creative responses to conditions we elect to term "the intolerable." Indeed, if the reduction of life to some scientific variable, capable of being manipulated and prodded into action as if it were some expendable lab rat, became the hallmark of violence in the name of progress, it was precisely the strategic confluence between the arts and politics that enabled us to challenge the dominant paradigms of twentieth-century thought. Hence, in theory at least, the idea that we needed to connect with the world in a more cultured and meaningful way appeared to be on the side of the practice of freedom and breathed new life into politics.

And yet, despite the horrors of the Century of Violence, our ways of thinking about politics not only have remained tied to the types of scientific reductions that history warns to be integral to the dehumanization of the subject, but such thinking has also made it difficult to define the very conditions that make a new politics possible. At the same time accelerating evolution of digital communications radicalizes the very contours of the human condition such that we are now truly "image conscious," so too is life increasingly defined and altered by the visual gaze and a screen culture whose omniscient presence offers new spaces for thinking dangerously. This hasn't led, however, to the harnessing of the power of imagination when dealing with the most pressing political issues. With neoliberal power having entered into the global space of flows while our politics remains wedded to out dated ways of thinking and acting, even the leaders of the strongest nations now preach the inevitability of catastrophe, forcing us to partake in a world they declare to be "insecure by design."

Isaac Cordal's *Follow the Leaders*, which appears on the cover of this book, captures this horrifying predicament of our contemporary neoliberal state of decline. While Cordal's work is commonly interpreted as providing commentary on the failures of our political leaders to prevent climate change, we prefer to connect it more broadly to the normalization of dystopian narratives in a way that forces us to address the fundamental questions of memory, political agency, responsibility, and bearing witness to the coming catastrophes that seemingly offer no possibility for escape. Indeed, while the logics of contemporary violence are undoubtedly different from those witnessed by Levi in the extermination camps of Nazi Germany, Cordal's work nevertheless points to emergence of a new kind of terror haunting possibilities of a radical democracy, threatening to drown us all beneath the contaminated waters of a system that pays little regard to the human condition. To quote the contemporary artist Gottfried Helnwein:

> Mussolini once said: "Fascism should rightly be called Corporatism, as it is the merger of corporate and government power." Well, look around—does it look like there is a growing influence of bankers and big corporations on our governments and our lives? The new Fascists will not come as grim-looking brutes in daemonic black uniforms and boots, they will wear slick suits and ties, and they will be smiling.[1]

With this in mind, our decision to write this book was driven by a fundamental need to rethink the concept of the political itself. Just as neoliberalism has made a bonfire of the sovereign principle of the social contract, so too has it exhausted its claims to progress and reduced politics to a blind science in ways that eviscerate those irreducible qualities that distinguish humans from other predatory animals—namely love, cooperation, community, solidarity, creative wonderment, and the drive to imagine and explore more just and egalitarian worlds than the one we have created for ourselves. Neoliberalism is violence against the cultural conditions and civic agency that make democracy possible. Its relentless mechanisms of privatization, commodification, deregulation, and militarization cannot acknowledge or tolerate a formative culture and social order in which non-market values as solidarity, civic education, community building, equality, and justice are prioritized.

This is a problem we unfortunately find evident in dominating strands of leftist thought which continue to try to resurrect the language, dogmatism, and scientific idealism of yesteryear. Rather than being mined for its insights and lessons for the present, history has become frozen for too many on the left for whom crippling orthodoxies and time-capsuled ideologies serve to disable rather than enable both the radical imagination and an emancipatory politics. There can be no twentieth-century solu¬tions to twenty-first-century problems, what is needed is a new radical imagination that is able to mobilize alternative forms of social agency. It is therefore hoped that the book will both serve as a warning against the already present production of our disposable futures, and provide a modest contribution to the much needed conversation for more radically poetic and politically liberating alternatives.

ONE

CULTURES OF CRUELTY

Critique of Violence

Imagine a world where spectacles of violence have become so ubiquitous that it is no longer possible to identify any clear civic, social, or ethical qualities in the enforced social order. Imagine a world where those who live on the margins of such a social order are condemned for their plight, while those who control the political processes prosper from those very policies that bring about social abandonment and human destruction. Imagine a world where the technological promise of human connectivity is supplanted by forms of surveillance that encourage citizens to actively participate in their own inescapable oppression. Imagine a world that proclaims an end to the brutality of colonialism, all the while continuing to consciously vilify, target, incarcerate, and kill those of a different color. Imagine a world where the forces of militarism have become so ingrained that they are inseparable from the daily functioning of civic life. Imagine a world where the institutions tasked with producing the most brilliant and publicly engaged minds are put to the service of an uncompromising war machine. And imagine a world that has lost all faith in its ability to envisage—let alone create—better futures, condemning its citizens instead to a desolate terrain of inevitable catastrophe. The great tragedy of the current historical moment is that we can imagine this world all too easily, for it is the picture of the world that dominates the realities of our present condition. It is a world most people experience on a daily basis—a world that has become normalized and for which there is no immediate alternative—a world we understand as neoliberalism.

Neoliberal power is unmediated in its effects on people as it operates throughout the global space of unregulated flows. Whereas in an earlier industrial period capital was largely rooted and peoples migrated, for the most part today capital flows while peoples are contained. What becomes of sovereignty in this economically driven environment is a military and policing protectorate put to the service of global capital in ways that work by condemning the already condemned. At the same time, neoliberal ideology, policies, and modes of governing are normalized as if there is no outside or alternative to capitalism. As corporate power replaces political sovereignty, politics becomes an extension of war and all public spaces are transformed into battle zones. Not only are all vestiges of the social contract, the safety net, and institutions of democracy under siege, but so too are all public spheres that support non-market values such as trust, critical dialogue, and solidarity. How else to explain Heartland Institute President Joseph Best denouncing public schools as "socialist regimes." Paul Buchheit is right in arguing that "privatizers believe that any form of working together as a community is anti-American. To them, individual achievement is all that matters. They're now applying their winner-take-all profit motive to our children." They are also punishing those individuals, groups, and institutions that refuse the individualized and cut throat values of a market-driven casino capitalism.

At the same time, under the interlocking regimes of neoliberal power, violence appears so arbitrary and thoughtless that it lacks the need for any justification, let alone claims to justice and accountability. It is truly as limitless as it appears banal. All that matters instead is to re-create the very conditions to further and deepen the crises of neoliberal rule. Violence, with its ever-present economy of uncertainty, fear, and terror, is no longer merely a side effect of police brutality, war, or criminal behavior; it has become fundamental to neoliberalism as a particularly savage facet of capitalism. And in doing so it has turned out to be central to legitimating those social relations in which the political and pedagogical are redefined in order to undercut possibilities for authentic democracy. Under such circumstances, the social becomes retrograde, emptied of any democratic values, and organized around a culture of shared anxieties rather than shared responsibilities. The contemporary world, then—the world of neoliberalism—creates the most monstrous of illusions, one that functions by hiding things in plain sight. We see this most troublingly played out as its simulated spectacles of destruction are scripted in such a way as to support the narrative that violence itself is enjoying a veritable decline as a result of liberal influence and pacification. Howard Zinn understood this perversion better than most:

> I start from the supposition that the world is topsy-turvy, that things are all wrong, that the wrong people are in jail and the wrong people are out of jail, that the wrong people are in power and the wrong people are out of power, that the wealth is distributed in this country and the world in such a way as not simply to require small reform but to require a drastic reallocation of wealth. I start from the supposition that we don't have to say too much about this because all we have to do is think about the state of the world today and realize that things are all upside down.[1]

There is no greater task today than to develop a critique of violence adequate to our deeply unjust, inequitable, and violent times. Only then might we grasp the magnitude and depths of suffering endured on a daily basis by many of the world's citizens. Only then might we move beyond the conceit of a neoliberal project, which has normalized violence such that its worst manifestations become part of our cultural "pastimes." And only then might we reignite a radical imagination that is capable of diagnosing the violence of the present in such a manner that we have the confidence to rethink the meaning of global citizenship in the twenty-first century.

Following on from the enduring legacy and inspiration of Zinn and other cautionary voices of political concern such as Paulo Freire, our critique begins from the supposition that mass violence today must be understood by comprehending the ways in which systemic cruelty is transformed into questions of individual pathology. What is more, with the burden of guilt placed on the shoulders of the already condemned, those whose lives are rendered disposable, we must question more rigorously the imaginaries of violence, which instigate a forced partaking in a system that encourages the subjugated to embrace their oppression as though it were their liberation. Nowhere is this more apparent today than in the doctrine of "resilience" which, as critiqued elsewhere, forces us to accept our vulnerabilities without providing us with the tools for genuine transformation of those systematic processes that render us insecure in the first place.[2] Neoliberalism's culture of violence is reinforced by what Zsuza Ferge calls the "individualization of the social,"[3] in which all traces of the broader structural forces producing a range of social problems such as widening inequality and mass poverty disappear. Under the regime of neoliberalism, individual responsibility becomes the only politics that matters and serves to blame those who are susceptible to larger systemic forces. Even though such problems are not of their own making, neoliberalism's discourse insists that the fate of the vulnerable is a product of personal issues ranging from weak character to bad choices or simply moral deficiencies. This makes it easier for its advocates to argue that "poverty is a deserved condition."[4]

Systematic violence has never been "exceptional" in the history of capitalistic development. How might we explain David Harvey's apt description of capitalist expansion as "accumulation by dispossession,"[5] if the rise of capitalism did not signal the advent of a truly predatory social formation? Indeed, even the contemporary advocates of neoliberal markets recognize that their notion of a "just world" depends on coercion and violence as a way to enforce capitalism's uneven distribution of wealth and impoverishment. As the Oxford economic historian Avner Offer explained to Chris Hedges, "those who suffer deserve to suffer."[6] The neoliberal model is, after all, "a warrant for inflicting pain."[7] The regime of neoliberalism is precisely organized for the production of violence. Such violence is more than symbolic. Instead of waging a war on poverty it wages a war on the poor—and does so removed from any concern for social costs or ethical violations. Such a brutal diagnosis argues in favor of a neoliberal model despite its perverse outcomes: "It is perhaps symptomatic that the USA, a society that elevates freedom to the highest position among its values, is also the one that has one of the very largest penal systems in the world relative to its population. It also inflicts violence all over the world. It tolerates a great deal of gun violence, and a health service that excludes large numbers of people."[8] Its effects in the United States are evident in the incarceration of more than 2.3 million people, mostly people of color. Not only are 77 percent of all inmates people of color, but, as Michelle Alexander has pointed out, as of 2012 "more African-American men were disenfranchised (due to felon disenfranchisement laws) than in 1870, the year the Fifteenth Amendment was ratified, prohibiting laws that explicitly deny the right to vote on the basis of race."[9] The necropolitics of neoliberal policies is evident in the unnecessary deaths of up to 17,000 more Americans each year because partisan ideologues opted out of the expansion of the Medicare program offered by the Obama administration.[10] Across the globe, violence creeps into almost all of the commanding institutions of public life, extending from public schools to health care apparatuses. Uruguayan author Eduardo Galeano knew the impacts of neoliberalism's theater of cruelty better than most: "Our defeat was always implicit in the victory of others; our wealth has always generated our poverty by nourishing the prosperity of others—the empires and their native overseers. In the colonial and neocolonial alchemy, gold changes into scrap metal and food into poison."[11]

Zygmunt Bauman has taken this further by showing us how the most appalling acts of mass slaughter have been perfectly in keeping with the modern compulsion to destroy lives for more progressive times to come.[12] Acts of non-violence, in fact, are the exceptional moments of our more recent history. They also confirm Hannah Arendt's insistence that power and violence are *qualitatively* different.[13] There is no doubt something truly powerful, truly exceptional, to the examples set by Martin Luther King Jr., Rosa Parks, Mahatma Gandhi, and indigenous movements such as the Zapatistas of Mexico, whose choice of non-violence as an insurgent strategy reveals more fully the violence of oppressive contemporary regimes. Violence easily deals with violence on its own terms. Carlos Marighella was wrong to suggest otherwise.[14] What violence, however, cannot deal with, except by issuing more violence, remains the power of a dignified response and movements of collective resistance by those who refuse to get caught up in a cycle of cruelty that corrupts every good intention. Frantz Fanon was most clear in this respect.[15] Who are the "wretched," after all, if not those who fail to see that their recourse to violence only produces a mirror image of that which was once deemed intolerable?

Our history—the history of our present—is a history of violence. Beneath the surface of every semblance of peace, it is possible to identify all too easily the scars of sacrifice and the bloodshed of victims whose only error was often to be born in a cruel age. There are many ways in which we could try to make sense of this burden of sacrificial history. Why do so many continue to die for the sake of the living? Why do we continue to protect inhuman conditions through the endless wars fought in the name of humanity? Why is killing so often presented as necessary? How is it that the police in the United States can kill blacks at a rate twenty-one times higher than whites and not only act with impunity but respond to protests by the larger public almost exclusively with massive militarized responses, as if the use of violence is the only legitimate form of mediation to any problem that emerges in the larger society? While all these questions are important, it is precisely the spectacle that most perturbs us here. For it is through the spectacle of violence that we begin to uncover the abilities to strip life of any political, ethical, and human claim. Violence seeks to curate who and what is human even though the physical body might still be in existence. When violence becomes normalized and decentered, the disposability of entire populations becomes integral to the functioning, the profiteering, and the entrenchment of the prevailing rationalities of the dominant culture. Such violence, in other words, offers the most potent diagnosis of any political project by revealing what is deemed culturally acceptable and socially normalized.

There is an important point to stress here regarding the logics of brutality. Violence is easily condemned when it appears exceptional. This also unfortunately precludes more searching and uncomfortable questions. Normalized violence, by contrast, represents a more formidable challenge, requiring a more sophisticated and learned response. Exposing more fully how these normalized cultures of cruelty shape the historic moment is the main purpose of this work, as it is integral to the critical imagination and those forms of political agency necessary for successfully living in a nonviolent and civilian future.

Our motivation for writing this book is driven by a commitment to the value of critical pedagogy in countering mechanisms of dehumanization and domination at play in neoliberal societies and beyond. We have no time whatsoever for those who reason that violence may be studied in an "objective" or "rational" way. There are no neutral pedagogies indifferent to matters of politics, power, and ideology. Pedagogy is, in part, always about both struggle and vision—struggles over identities, modes of agency, values, desires, and visions of the possible. Not only does the apologetics of neutrality lead to the most remiss intellectualism when the personal experience of violence is reduced to emotionless inquiry, but it also announces complicity in the rationalizations of violence that depend upon the degradation of those qualities that constitute what is essential to the human condition. Thus, education is by definition a form of political intervention. It is always disentangling itself from particular regimes of power that attempt to authenticate and disqualify certain ways of perceiving and thinking about the world. The larger issue is that not only is education central to politics, but the educative nature of politics begins with the assumption that how people think, critically engage the world, and are self-reflective about the shaping of their own experiences and relations to others marks the beginning of a viable and oppositional politics.

We dare to perceive and think differently from both neoliberal rule and the increasingly stagnant and redundant left, which does little to counter it. The world that we inhabit is systematically oppressive and tolerates the most banal and ritualistic forms of violence. It educates us of the need for warfare; it prizes, above all, the values of militarism and its conceptual apparatus of "civic soldierology." It sanctions and openly celebrates killings as if they are necessary to prove our civilization's credentials. It takes pride, if not pleasure, in punishing peoples of distinct racial and class profiles, all in the name of better securing society. It promotes those within that order with characteristics that in other situations would be both criminalized and deemed pathological.[16] And it invests significantly in all manner of cultural productions so that we develop a taste for violence, and even learn to appreciate aesthetics of violence, as the normal and necessary price of being entertained.

This book inevitably draws upon a number of critical visionaries whose fight for dignity cannot be divorced from their intellectual concerns. The spirit of the late Paulo Freire in particular is impressed upon each of these pages.[17] His critical pedagogy was unashamedly tasked with liberating both the oppressed and their oppressors from the self-perpetuating dynamics of subjugation. Freire's prose echoed the humanizing call for a more just, literate, and tolerant world. He remains a strong influence in the field of education and in other areas of practice that require thinking about the possibility of an ethics of difference that resists violence in all its forms.

The power and forcefulness of Freire's works are to be found in the tensions, conflicts, poetry, and politics that make it a project for thinking about (non)violence meaningfully. Siding with the disempowered of history—those at the raw ends of tyranny—Freire's work calls for a more poetic image of thought that is a way of reclaiming power by reimagining the space and practice of cultural and political resistance. His work thus represents a textual borderland where poetry slips into liberation politics, and solidarity becomes a song for the present begun in the past while waiting to be heard in the future. Freire, no less trenchant in his critique of illegitimate rule, refuses to dwell in hopelessness. His resistance is empowering because it is infused with a fearless belief in people's abilities and finds reasons to rejoice in the transformative possibilities of living:

> The more radical the person is, the more fully he or she enters into reality so that, knowing it better, he or she can transform it. This individual is not afraid to confront, to listen, to see the world unveiled. This person is not afraid to meet the people or to enter into

a dialogue with them. This person does not consider himself or herself the proprietor of history or of all people, or the liberator of the oppressed; but he or she does commit himself or herself, within history, to fight at their side.[18]

Freire is not only our source of inspiration. Nearly a century ago Walter Benjamin responded to the tyranny of his times by writing his famous "Critique of Violence."[19] Ours is a different age. And yet the need for a critique adequate to our times is as pressing as ever. We are not lacking in knowledge of our own oppression. Let's be sure of that. Oppressive power reveals enough of its violent traces for even a casual cartographer to expose its deceptions or else retreat into conspiracy. What we do lack is a rigorous critique of the historical moment and its varied modes of imaginative resistance. Such modes of artistic imagination are as important as contemporary sources of oppression are in mediating suffering in the service of established contemporary power. This requires a critique of violence that once again encourages us to think beyond its necessity, so as to make clear that in a world in which violence is normalized, it once again becomes possible to imagine the unimaginable, particularly the notion that collective resistance not only is possible but can transform the world with confidence.

Hence, while authors like Steven Pinker cloud our perception by claiming the current era is the least violent era in human history, relying upon crude per capita human death rates etc.,[20] it takes only a slightly different angle of vision to see the current social order's full range of preventable violence: impoverishment, financial predation, malnutrition, mass incarceration, and rapidly accelerating deforestation, ecological degradation, and irreversible biocide. Pinker would do well to acknowledge that political violence is poorly understood if it simply refers to a failure of liberal modernity. Political violence cannot be reduced to such a crude and reductionist metric. Indeed, conventional demarcations between times of war and times of peace, zones of security and zones of crises, friends and enemies, have long since evaporated. We live in complex and radically interconnected societies, whose social morphology has radically altered our sense of the world such that we are taught to accept insecurity as the natural order of things.[21] This is fully in keeping with the proliferation of media output, factual and fictional, that bombards us continuously with images of violence and catastrophe for subtle political gain. Indeed, what is new about the current historical conjuncture is not only a commodified popular culture that trades in extreme violence, greed, and narcissism as a source of entertainment, but the emergence of a predatory society in which the suffering and death of others becomes a reason to rejoice rather than mourn. Extreme violence has become not only a commodified spectacle, but one of the few popular resources available through which people can bump up their pleasure quotient.

Our critique begins from the realization that violence has become ubiquitous, "settling like some all-enveloping excremental mist . . . that has permeated every nook of any institution or being that has real influence on the way we live now."[22] We cannot escape its spectre. Its presence is everywhere. It is hardwired into the fabric of our digital DNA. Capitalism in fact has always thrived on its consumption. There is, after all, no profit in peace. We are not calling here for the censoring of all representations of violence as if we could retreat into some sheltered protectorate. That would be foolish and intellectually dangerous. Our claim is both that the violence we are exposed to is heavily mediated, and that as such we are witness to various spectacles that serve a distinct political function, especially as they either work to demonize political resistance or simply extract from its occurrence (fictional and actual) any sense of political context and critical insight. Moving beyond the spectacle by making visible the reality of violence in all of its modes is both necessary and politically important. What we need then is an ethical approach to the problem of violence such that its occurrence is intolerable to witness.

Exposing violence is not the same as being exposed to it, though the former too often comes as a result of the latter. The corrupting and punishing forms taken by violence today must be addressed by all people as both the most important element of power and the most vital of forces shaping social relationships under the predatory formation of neoliberalism. Violence is both symbolic and material in its effects and its assaults on all social relations, whereas the mediation of violence coupled with its aesthetic regimes of suffering is a form of violence that takes as its object both memory and thought. It purges the historical record, denying access to the history of a more dignified present, purposefully destroying the ability to connect forms of struggle across the ages. Memory as such is fundamental to any ethics of responsibility. Our critique of violence begins, then, as an ethical imperative. It demands a rigorous questioning of the normalized culture of violence in which we are now immersed. It looks to the past so that we may understand the violence of our present. It looks to the ways that ideas about the future shape the present such that we learn to accept a world that is deemed to be violent by design. This requires a proper critical reading of the way violence is mediated in our contemporary moment; how skewed power relations and propagators of violence are absolved of any wider blame in a pedagogical and political game that permits only winners and losers; how any act of injustice is made permissible in a world that enshrines systemic cruelty.

The Dystopian Imagination
The twentieth century is often termed the "Century of Violence." And rightly so, given the widespread devastation of an entire continent during the two World Wars; the continued

plunder and suppression of former colonial enclaves; the re-birth of extermination camps in the progressive heart of a modern Europe; the appalling experiments in human barbarism that incinerated Hiroshima and Nagasaki; the torture and symbolic acts of disappearance so widespread in Latin America; the passivity in the face of ongoing acts of genocide; the wars and violence carried out in the name of some deceitful humanitarian principle. This legacy of violence makes it difficult to assess this history without developing profound suspicions about the nature of the human condition and its capacity for evil. One of the particular novelties of this period was the emergence of dystopia literatures and compelling works of art that proved integral to the lasting critique of totalitarian regimes. Indeed, some of the most appealing prose of the times was put forward not by recognized political theorists or radical philosophers, but by the likes of Yevgeny Zamyatin, H. G. Wells, George Orwell, and Aldous Huxley, amongst others, who managed to reveal with incisive flair and public appeal the violence so often hidden beneath the utopian promise of technologically driven progress.[23] Dystopia in these discourses embodied a warning and a hope that humankind would address and reverse the dark authoritarian practices that descended on the twentieth century like a thick, choking fog.

Hannah Arendt understood how the authoritarian violence of the twentieth century needed a broader frame of reference.[24] The harrowing experimental camps of the colonies would all too quickly blow back into the metropolitan homelands as gulags, death camps, and torture chambers become exportable elements in the production of theaters of cruelty. The utopian promise of the Enlightenment thus contained within it the violence and brutalities embedded in the logic of instrumental rationality and the unchecked appeal to progress and ideological purity, all of which was later rehearsed within the most terrifying fictions and rewritten with the same devastating effect for those expendable millions that made up a veritable continent of suffering we could rightly map as the globally dispossessed.

We live, however, in a different political moment. The state is no longer the center of politics. Neoliberalism has made a bonfire of the sovereign principles embodied in the social contract. Nor can we simply diagnose twenty-first-century forms of oppression and exploitation by relying on well-rehearsed orthodoxies of our recent past. With power and its modalities of violence having entered into the global space of flows—detached from the controlling political interests of the nation-state utilizing technologies far beyond those imagined in the most exaggerating of twentieth-century fictions—the dystopian theorists of yesteryear prove to be of limited use.[25] The virtues of political affirmation and confidence appear increasingly to have fallen prey to formations of global capitalism and its engulfing webs of precarity that have reduced human life to the task of merely being able to survive. Individual and collective agencies are not only under siege to a degree unparalleled at any other time in history, but have become depoliticized, overcome by a culture of anxiety, in-security, commodification, and privatization.

More specifically, under neoliberal rule the vast majority are forced to live a barely sustainable precariousness and to accept that our contemporary society is naturally precarious. That the future is a terrain of endemic and unavoidable catastrophe is taken as given in most policy circles. Dystopia, in other words, is no longer the realm of scientific fiction—as suggested, for instance, by increasingly urgent recent climate reports warning that the integrity of the planet's diversity-sustaining biosphere is collapsing. It is the dominant imaginary for neoliberal governance and its narcissistic reasoning.

If Theodor Adorno was right to argue that the apocalypse already occurred with the realization of the Holocaust and the experience of World War II, what has taken its place is a discourse signaling the normalization of a catastrophic imagination that offers few means for possible escape.[26] Despite their relation to "end of times narratives," as Jacob Taubes once noted,[27] there is perhaps something different at work here between the pre-modern apocalyptic movements and the shift toward catastrophic reasoning that has come to define the contemporary moment. For all their nihilism and monotheistic servitude, at least the apocalyptic movements actively imagine a better world than the one they are in. Theirs was and is open to the idea of a different time-to-come. Under neoliberalism, imagining a better future is limited entirely to imagining the privatization of the entire world or, even worse, imagining simply how to survive.

It is within this historical conjuncture and the current savagery of various regimes of neoliberal capitalism that we conceived of the need to develop a critical paradigm that interrogates and resists the intensification of the *politics of disposability*—the ways in which people, families, and communities are not only increasingly considered excess to be discarded, but also alienated from the millions of similarly oppressed others so as to prevent them from developing the solidarity necessary to successfully challenge the wider political dynamics and circumstances at play against them.[28] Such a politics, we argue, normalizes disposability in such a way as to place the burden of social ills on the shoulders of the victims.

Dystopian politics has become mainstream politics as the practice of disposability has intensified, and more and more communities are now considered excess, consigned to "zones of social abandonment,"[29] surveillance, and incarceration. The expansive politics of disposability can be seen in the rising numbers of homeless, the growing army of debt-ridden students whose prospects remain bleak, those lacking basic necessities amid widening income disparities, the surveillance of immigrants, the school-to-prison pipeline, and the widespread destruction of the middle class by new forms of debt servitude.[30] Citizens, as Gilles Deleuze foresaw,[31] are now reduced to data, consumers, and commodities and as such inhabit identities in which they increasingly become unknowables, with no human or civic rights and with no one accountable for their condition.

There is, however, more at stake here than the contemporary plight of those millions forced to live in intolerable conditions. What we will argue throughout this book is that contemporary forms of disposability are so abhorrent precisely because they now shape *disposable futures*. The future now appears to us as a terrain of endemic catastrophe and disorder from which there is no clear escape except to continue to show allegiance to those predatory formations that put us there in the first place. Devoid of any alternative image of the world, we are requested merely to see the world as predestined and catastrophically fated. Frederic Jameson's claim, then, that it is easier to "imagine the end of the world than it is the end of capitalism"[32] is more than a reflection on the poverty of contemporary imaginations. It is revealing of the nihilism of our times which forces us to accept that the only world conceivable is the one we are currently forced to endure. A world that is brutally reproduced and forces us all to consume its spectacles of violence, and demands we accept that all things are ultimately built to be vulnerable. In this suffocating climate, we are indoctrinated to imagine that the best we can hope for is to be connected to some fragile and precarious life-support system—the neoliberal grid of credit, precarious insurance, and privilege—that may be withdrawn from us at any moment.

Political affirmation is increasingly dissolved into pervasive nihilism as our politics is increasingly reduced to the quest for mere survival. For if there is a clear lesson, as New Yorkers now testify better than most, to living in these times, it is precisely that the lights can go out at any given moment, without any lasting concern for social responsibility. This is simply the natural order of things (so we are told), and we need to adapt our thinking accordingly.

Little wonder that we have seen a revival in these times of all sorts of monstrous fictions. As Jane and Lewis Gordon explain, "Monsters of disaster are special kinds of divine warning. They are harbingers of things we do not want to face, of catastrophes, and we fear they will bring such events upon us by coming to us."[33] Only a decade or so ago, citizens feared the wrath of robots, terminators, and cyborgs who wanted to destroy us—the legacy of a highly rationalized, technocratic culture that eludes human regulation, even comprehension. Now, those who are not part of a technocratic elite appear helpless and adrift, caught in the grip of a society that denies them any alternative sense of agency or hope. This raises some important questions on the advent of monstrosity, not least the fascination in popular culture today with the figure of the zombie, which has its own distinct politics.

The zombie genre can be traced to earlier critiques of capitalism, with the undead in particular appearing at a time when the shopping mall started to become a defining symbol of modernity. Zombies here would become the embodiment of a political form, one that had lost all sense of the past and had no future to speak of. The only performance it knew was the desire for violence, as it was suspended in a state of purgatory that offered no means of escape. To become a zombie was to be devoid of any political, ethical, and social claim or responsibility (including the capacity to show compassion and love) other than the eventual completion of the nihilistic project.[34]

The marketing of this metaphorical figure in today's popular culture is most revealing. It speaks to both the nihilistic conditions in which we live, along with the deadly violence of neoliberal regimes of power and the modes of political subjectivity it seeks to authenticate/destroy. It also speaks to a future in which survival fully colonizes the meaning of life, a future that both anticipates and consents to the possibility of extinction. As Keir Milburn and David Harvie have noted:

> Neoliberalism no longer "makes sense," but its logic keeps stumbling on, without conscious direction, like a zombie: ugly, persistent and dangerous. Such is the "unlife" of a zombie, a body stripped of its goals, unable to adjust itself to the future, unable to make plans. It can only act habitually as it pursues a monomaniacal hunger. Unless there is a dramatic recomposition of society, we face the prospect of decades of drift as the crises we face—economic, social, environmental—remain unresolved. But where will that recomposition come from when we are living in the world of zombie-liberalism?[35]

One of the most remarkable recent examples of this genre that offers a truly potent exposition of contemporary nihilism is Marc Forster's *World War Z*. While the source of the outbreak remains somewhat elusive in the movie, from the outset Forster situates the problem in connection with contemporary concerns of the biosphere and the all too real mutation of viruses capable of destroying a world with little care or responsibility for its social habitat. The movie further amplifies the relevance of this genre for exposing the futility of nation-states, as societies quickly learn that the media are the only message, while emphasizing the biopolitical (life-centric) dimensions to power wherein it is widely accepted today that anybody and anything can become the source of contamination. The movie portrays a world in which nobody is safe and no location might provide sanctuary. Indeed, while the burning of Manhattan offers a provocative screening of potential devastation brought about by widespread human abandonment, it is the zombies' breach of the walls of Jerusalem that will no doubt unsettle many (for obvious reasons).

However, instead of following the conventional deconstruction of the zombie here as revealing of the death of subjectivities brought about by commodification, on this occasion there is more to be gained by analyzing the survivors. *World War Z* does not allow the viewer to be under any illusions given its message that the best that can be imagined is *pure survival*. Indeed, the only way to survive is by engaging in a form of self-harm by using a lethal microbe as a form of "camouflage" so that the health of the body no longer registers, hence the body is no longer a target for the undead. It is further revealing that the eventual fate of the survivors is in no way certain, as the final scenes tell that this is merely the start of a perpetual state of violence that allows for some strategic gains, but remains ultimately a state infested with the decay of a political and social order that might never recover its humanness. The movie as such is perhaps less meditation on the already dead than contemplation of the fate of those who are hoping to survive the ubiquitous war. For they are also denied the possibility of another world, forced to partake instead in a world of personal risk and deadly infection that continually puts into question their destiny as political subjects who are able to transform the world for the better. This is political nihilism taken to the *nth* degree: the most violent of conditions that renders the will to nothingness the start and ending for all collective actions and viable notions of human togetherness.

Such a vision of the world, mass marketed as entertainment, is actually far more disturbing than the dystopian fables of the twentieth century. Our condition denies us the possibility of better times to come as the imagined and the real collapse in such a way that we are condemned to already be living amongst the ruins of the future. All we can seemingly imagine is a world filled with unavoidable catastrophes, the source of which, we are told, remains beyond our grasp, thereby denying us any possibility for genuine systemic transformation in the order of things. How do we explain the current fetish for the doctrine of resilience if not through the need to adapt to the inevitability of catastrophe, and to simply partake in a world that is deemed to be "insecure by design"?[36] Such adaptation both forces us to accept narratives of vulnerability as the authentic basis of political subjectivity, regardless of the oppressive conditions that produce vulnerable subjects, and neutralizes all meaningful qualitative differences in class, race, and gender.

The Seductions of Violence

Wilhelm Reich profoundly altered our understanding of oppression by drawing attention to its *mass psychology*.[37] Focusing on the nature of twentieth-century fascism, he explained how predatory political and economic formations promote the disposability of entire populations as they indoctrinate the disadvantaged to desire what is patently oppressive. Reich showed how micro-specific questions of agency were intimately bound to imaginaries of threat and survivability such that the masses end up willfully accepting a suffocating and depoliticizing embrace. Notions of endangerment thus operate here affectively by appealing to concerns of the everyday.[38] As Gilles Deleuze and Félix Guattari would explain, "Reich is at his profoundest as a thinker when he refuses to accept ignorance or illusion on part of the masses as an explanation of fascism, and demands an explanation that will take their desires into account, an explanation formulated in terms of desire: no, the masses were not innocent dupes; at a certain point, under certain conditions, they *wanted* fascism, and it is this perversion of desire of the masses that needs to be accounted for."[39] Hence, as Reich understood, it is misguided to simply blame a handful of individuals for the "abuse of power" and their privilege. Rather than recoil in horror or exempt ourselves from deeper reflection, we must ask more searching questions about the normalization of violence and how it relates to the prevailing rationalities of the times. And we must do so while reflecting upon on our own shameful compromises, acknowledging the ways we are all being openly recruited into everyday forms of passivity, inactivism, subjugation, intolerance, and a denial of our humanity. Violence under such conditions becomes central to understanding a politics of desire and the production of subjectivities in the interest of their own oppression, but also how that politics functions as part of a struggle over agency itself.

It is impossible to comprehend the mass psychology of violence in the contemporary period without recognizing the centrality of commercial media that underpins its seductive potency.[40] No longer peripheral to public life, constantly evolving, increasing mobile media technologies such as smart phones, tablets, and wearable devices have enacted a structural transformation of everyday life by fusing sophisticated networking technologies with a ubiquitous screen culture, while simultaneously expanding the range of cultural producers and recipients of information and images.[41] The accelerating evolution of personal media technologies enables modes of spectatorship that seem to resist bundling users into a monolithic mass. Such technologies deploy unheard-of powers in the shaping of time, space, knowledge, values, identities, and social relations. They not only transform the relationships between the specificity of an event and its public display by making events accessible to a global audience, they also usher in an era of increasing awareness—the age of the spectacle—in which screen culture and visual politics *create* spectacular events just as much as they record them.[42] Given that screen culture now dominates much of everyday life in privileged populations across the globe, the "audio-visual mode has become our primary way of coming in contact with the world and at the same time being detached (safe) from it."[43]

Individuals' capacity to create and globally distribute imagery, first-person accounts, and live video streams, however, are continually transforming relationships between politics, spectacular violence, and possibilities for community resistance to oppression, as has been the case in Ferguson, Missouri.

While individual and community access to state, national, and global audiences does open new vistas for organizing resistance, the same technology is also used by authorities to increase surveillance, and for employers to keep employees working all the time. As Brian Massumi has argued, such technology all too often can increase social control and act as "a workstation in the mass production line of fear."[44]

While the association between mid-century fascism and aesthetics, and by implication its fetishistic spectacles, has been the subject of sustained critical analysis, the most promising work on the politics of the spectacle has been organized around its relationship with neoliberalism. Not, of course, to buy into the conceit here that fascism has been somehow defeated by neoliberal "conquerors," or for that matter that neoliberalism is immune to fascistic ways of manipulating desires for political ends. Fascism remains as diverse as power. Indeed, as we shall explain, while philosophers and cultural critics have recognized in a prescient fashion the emergence of a new era of the spectacle under neoliberalism, and how such spectacles have wielded the potential to utterly transform the social order, what is particularly novel about the historical conjuncture in which we live is the ability to secure mass consent by shattering the familiar demarcations between inside/outside, friend/enemy, private/public, times of war/peace, that hallmark of ideological fascism in the twentieth century.

In our contemporary moment, we owe it to thinkers such as Guy Debord, Gilles Deleuze, Susan Sontag, Jean Baudrillard, François Debrix, and Douglas Kellner, among others, who have greatly extended our knowledge of how the spectacle has become a dominant mode of indoctrination that reinforces the foreclosure of civic agency once available to individuals and communities within capitalistic regimes of power. They have raised crucial questions about how the concepts and practices associated with the spectacle can lead to genuine civic advances and defiant acts of radical imagination, the very thought of which are increasingly considered with alarm by authorities who treat such non-market values as insurrectional, and see public displays of disobedience as gateways to crime and terrorism. That national anti-terrorism resources were marshalled to assist the surveillance and repression of the Occupy movement, leading to more than 7,000 arrests, is evidence of just how threatened the neoliberal order feels, and how drastically it reacts when sectors of society begins behaving off-message from the privatized grid of finance that dominates all aspects of society, culture, politics, and law.

Guy Debord's pioneering work in *The Society of the Spectacle*[45] provides a number of important theoretical insights for critically understanding the transformation of the spectacle and its role today. According to Debord, the spectacle that has emerged represents a new form of social control that is quite different from, but contains the political traces of, earlier forms of spectacle that were instrumental to fascism. Debord views the spectacle as a product of the market and a new form of cultural politics. He argues that the spectacle represents a "new stage in the accumulation of capital [in which] more and more facets of human activity and elements of everyday life were being brought under the control of the market."[46] The spectacle, in other words, is no longer put to use for the creation of a mythical unity of superior beings. It now operates for its own purpose—complete commercialization, commodification, and marketization. Indeed, in its willful manipulation of desires through the sophisticated deployment of mechanisms that prompt people to tolerate conditions that ordinarily would appear politically oppressive, the spectacle is in fact, a predatory strategy and politically fascistic. Such mechanisms resonate with Reich's concerns about the ability to manipulate large sectors of society by inducing a form of mass psychosis of consent that manipulates reasoning and conscience and thus normalizes the most abhorrent form of subjugation and violence.

Under late capitalism, the spectacle has been reforged in the crucible of mass consumption and the mass media, producing new modes for power to advantage itself through the domination of everyday life. Although the spectacle is often viewed by the public as mere entertainment, disconnected from power and politics, Debord insists that "the spectacle is the self-portrait of power in the age of power's totalitarian rule over the conditions of existence."[47] For Debord, new technological developments in communications now establish the mode of information as a category as important for reproducing social life as labor had been for Marx. Moreover, for Debord, the society of the spectacle is not a discrete element of social existence; it has become a constituting activity that refigures the very nature of common sense and social relations.

According to Debord, the "whole of life [now] presents itself as an immense accumulation of spectacles. All that was once directly lived has become mere representation."[48] The educational force of the culture, whether it be "news or propaganda, advertising or the actual consumption of entertainment" has been transformed into a spectacle, which "epitomizes the prevailing model of social life."[49] Debord rightly recognizes that the dynamics of domination under late capitalism can no longer be explained exclusively within the primacy of the economic sphere and its exploitative mode and relations of production. Rejecting conventional Marxist notions of social reproduction, Debord follows the lead of Antonio Gramsci, the Frankfurt School, and other neo-Marxist theorists arguing that domination is secured increasingly through "a social relationship between people that is mediated by images,"[50] and that capitalism has successfully employed an image industry to transform commodities into appearances and history into staged events. Under such circumstances, the "society of the spectacle" "proclaims the predominance of appearances and asserts that all human life, which is to say all social life, is mere appearance."[51] The degree to which society permits visual mediation—screen culture—to become its primary mode of education, self-understanding, and socializing is the degree to which it opens the door for spectacle to dominate as a depoliticizing substitute for unmediated social formations, thinking, and creativity. Thus, according to Debord, "any critique capable of apprehending the spectacle's essential character must expose it as a visible negation of life—and as a negation of life *that has invented a visual form for itself.*"

In Debord's theory, media have become the quintessential tool of contemporary capitalism, and consumerism is its legitimating ideology. Or, to cite Debord's famous quip, "the spectacle is capital accumulated to the point where it becomes image."[52] What is crucial about Debord's theory is that it connects the state's investment in social reproduction to its commitment to, "and control of, the field of images—the alternative world conjured up by the new battery of 'perpetual emotion machines' of which TV was the dim pioneer and which now beckons the citizen every waking minute."[53] Not only is the world of images a structural necessity for capitalism, it affirms the primacy of the pedagogical as a crucial element of the political. It enforces "the submission of more and more facets of human sociability—areas of everyday life, forms of recreation, patterns of speech, idioms of local solidarity . . . to the deadly solicitation (the lifeless bright sameness) of the market."[54]

By exposing how the spectacle colonizes everyday life, Debord shows how power operates through a merger of state and corporate forces that seek both to control the media through which society experiences itself and to completely depoliticize and redefine the agency of citizenry in terms of prefabricated choices of consumerism and the status of ownership. Under contemporary capitalism, state-sanctioned violence makes its mark through the prisons, courts, police surveillance, and other criminalizing forces; it also wages a form of symbolic warfare mediated by a regime of consumer-based images and staged events that narrow individual and social agency to the dictates of the marketplace, reducing the capacity for human aspirations and desires to needs embodied in the appearance of the commodity. In Debord's terms, "the spectacle is the bad dream of modern society in chains, expressing nothing more than its wish for sleep."[55]

Contemporary culture has long become a society organized around a vast array of commodities, various image-making technologies used to promote them, and numerous sites from which to circulate them that leaves no spaces for contemplating that other worlds are possible. For Debord, our "society of the spectacle" is a form of soft violence that perpetually cultures the conformity, inactivism, and passivity necessary to repress critical engagement and resistance by relentlessly privatizing, marginalizing, or openly criminalizing educational and liberatory forces.

Debord's notion of the spectacle makes a significant contribution in mapping a new form of social control associated with the accumulation of capital. He makes clear that the whole industry of leisure, consumption, entertainment, advertising, fantasy, and other pedagogical apparatuses of media culture has become a crucial element of life, and thus a primary condition of politics. Debord does not argue that commodities were the source of domination. As Eugene L. Arva points out, Debord insists that "the system of mediation by representation (the world of the spectacle, if you wish) has come to bear more relevance than commodities themselves."[56] Participation in commodity culture and its symbolic networks, rather than simple ownership of commodities, has become an essential feature of social status and belonging. Debord thus furthers our understanding that domination has to be analyzed as part of a politics of consent in which all aspects of social life are increasingly shaped by the communication technologies under the control of corporate forces.

Although Debord has been accused of overestimating the all-encompassing power of the spectacle, media, and other control mechanisms of late capitalism ("a permanent opium war"),[57] he never harbors the often politically crippling pessimism of the Frankfurt School. His *Society of the Spectacle* "reads, rather, as a warning against the paralysis of the senses, the lethargy of the mind, and the political inertia with which a primarily visually determined, visually accessible, and most visually livable reality threatens" any viable notion of the autonomous subject.[58] He militates against the dystopian notion of the totally administered society and begins advancing forms of political rupture and cultural insurgency that connect individual and collective agency to historical critique and creative social transformation. For Debord, the struggle for collective freedom was impossible without self-emancipation.

Yet the enormous analytic challenge facing Debord reveals itself in precisely that which, in a globalizing post-9/11 world, his theory cannot sufficiently explain. As Lutz Koepnick points out, we now live in a culture "characterized by hybrid multimedia aggregates and diversified strategies of consumption."[59] Within this new era, technology and media merge, resulting in a massive cultural reorganization involving the production, distribution, and consumption of information and images. Not only has the old model of a monolithic system of media control and cultural reproduction been undermined by Internet-driven media and technologies, but entirely new configurations of communication relations have emerged and continue to evolve. Although dependent on corporate infrastructure and software and wide open to state surveillance and tracking, the production and dissemination of content have become radically more accessible to massive non-market sectors of society—the public—with enormous consequences on business, law enforcement, politics, education, and culture.[60] At the same time, Internet-driven media are shaping new types of individual agency and social formations that are actively co-evolving with the unprecedented speed, immediacy, and global reach of increasingly accessible personal communication technology.

Past assumptions about time and space being homogeneous and fixed are no longer applicable. Digital networks have stretched and compressed the relationships among time, space, and place. Technology is constantly accelerating the speed with which we can publish information, disseminate images, and communicate with large networks of people around the planet. Just as new forms of social media and cultural representation make possible highly individualized modes of symbolic expression, the undiversified masses have given way to a diverse globalized public far removed from the homogeneous community of viewers and producers that was characteristic of the older broadcasting age of media.

Of course, we are not suggesting here that new media and technological developments have ushered in structural changes amounting to a more democratic society. This perspective is as inaccurate as it is overly romantic, especially in light of the way in which the Internet and social media are exploited for government surveillance and corporate data collection and marketing. At the same time, any analysis of the reconfiguration of public culture by neoliberal forces must take into account the unprecedented effects of evolving media technologies—including the speed, distances, rhythms of information and communication, real-time images, and differential modes of control associated with consumption. Stuart Hall understood this better than most:

> Neoliberalism's victory has depended on the boldness and ambition of global capital, on its confidence that it can now govern not just the economy but the whole of social life. On the back of a revamped liberal political

and economic theory, its champions have constructed a vision and a new common sense that have permeated society. Market forces have begun to model institutional life and press deeply into our private lives, as well as dominating political discourse. They have shaped a popular culture that extols celebrity and success and promotes values of private gain and possessive individualism. They have thoroughly undermined the redistributive egalitarian consensus that underpinned the welfare state, with painful consequences for socially vulnerable groups such as women, old people, the young and ethnic minorities.[61]

Mark Poster suggests that as communication technologies today surpass the first media era in which "a small number of producers" in control of "film, radio, and television sent information to a larger number of consumers, an entirely new configuration of communication relations has emerged."[62] The second age of media, which Poster argues has developed in the last few decades, not only generates new modes of appropriation and production, but also radicalizes the conditions for creating critical forms of social agency and resistance. This has resulted in calls for more democratic and ethical use of knowledge, information, and images. New modes of communication, organizing, disruption, and resistance based on wireless technologies are on full display in the spontaneous emergence of social movements like Occupy, the global impact of whistle-blowers like Edward Snowden, the advance of citizens holding corporate and government powers more accountable through online reporting, and the sudden street protests that can unexpectedly erupt when a smart phone video circulates documenting state violence against civilians, as is increasingly the case of police brutality and killings of unarmed civilians in communities of color.[63]

As Stanley Aronowitz points out: "The excluded can use

image-making as a weapon for laying hold and grasping cultural apparatuses . . . Placing old forms in new frameworks changes their significance."[64] In analyzing the opposition to the U.S. occupation of Iraq, for example, James Castonguay underscores the subversive potential of these new modes of agency. He writes: "Newer media of the Internet and the Web not only have afforded mainstream media such as WB and CNN new modes of representation but have also provided new opportunities for the expression of dissent, new avenues of distribution for audio and video, and alternative representations of war unavailable during previous major U.S. conflicts."[65] Multiple identities, values, desires, and knowledge are now formed through globally accessible imagery, offering up new modes of agency and possibilities for critique, resistance, and networking. While arguments suggesting that technologies such as the Internet constitute a new democratic public sphere may be vastly optimistic, the emerging media have not entirely defaulted on their potential both to multiply sites of cultural production and to offer "resources for challenging the state's coordination of mass culture."[66]

While we are no closer to the revolutionary liberation of everyday life that he imagined is both possible and necessary, Debord did not anticipate either the evolution of media along its current trajectories, with its multiple producers, distributors, and access, or the degree to which the forces of militarization would dominate all aspects of society, especially in the United States, where obsession with law enforcement, surveillance, and repression of dissent has at least equaled cultural emphasis on commercialization from 9/11 forward.[67] The economic, political, and social safeguards of a past era, however limited, along with traditional spatial and temporal coordinates of experience, have been blown apart in the "second media age," as the spectacularization of anxiety and fear and the increasing militarization of everyday life have become the principal cultural experiences shaping identities, values, and social relations.[68] Debrix's incisive commentary on the production of emergency cultures captures the mood of this shift perfectly:

> A generalized, illogical, and often unspecified sense of panic is facilitated in this postmodern environment where all scenarios can [be] and often are played out. This generalized panic is no longer akin to the centralized fear which emanates from the power of the sovereign in the modern era. Rather, it is an evanescent sentiment that anything can happen anywhere to anybody at any time. This postmodern fear is not capable of yielding logical, reasonable outcomes. All it does instead is accelerate the spiralling vortex of media-produced information. All it does is give way to emergencies (which will only last until the next panic is unleashed). This panic, I believe, is the paroxysmic achievement of media power.[69]

Building on Debord's pioneering critique, a number of theorists have developed a better understanding of how the spectacle itself has changed, particularly in light of the emergence of new mass and image-based media technologies.[70] Douglas Kellner, in particular, has written extensively on the notion of the spectacle and concludes, in agreement with Debord, that the spectacle of late capitalism has essentially taken over the social order.[71] Building on these important interventions, what concerns us today are the ways in which mainstream media and popular culture typically sensationalize violence (from the large-scale catastrophe to individual assault) in a way that drains from such events any viable ethical and political substance. It is precisely the alienating cultural, social, and political climate achieved through spectacle that normalizes violence, terror, and insecurity, while editing out the human realities of suffering in order to cauterize social conscience and incapacitate political responses that are in any way off-message from the ever-narrowing grid of tolerable responses to authority and its enforcement. This understanding of the problematic allows us to propose the following critical definition that will inform the rest of the book:

> *The spectacle of violence represents more than the public enactment and witnessing of human violation. It points to a highly mediated regime of suffering and misery, which brings together the discursive and the aesthetic such that the performative nature of the imagery functions in a politically contrived way. In the process of occluding and depoliticizing complex narratives of any given situation, it assaults our senses in order to hide things in plain sight. The spectacle works by turning human suffering into a spectacle, framing and editing the realities of violence, and in doing so renders some lives meaningful while dismissing others as disposable. It operates through a hidden structure of politics that colonizes the imagination, denies critical engagement, and preemptively represses alternative narratives. The spectacle harvests and sells our attention, while denying us the ability for properly engaged political reflection. It engages agency as a pedagogical practice in order to destroy its capacity for self-determination, autonomy, and self-reflection. It works precisely at the level of subjectivity by manipulating our desires such that we become cultured to consume and enjoy productions of violence, becoming entertained by the ways in which it is packaged, which divorce domination and suffering from ethical considerations, historical understanding and political contextualization. The spectacle immerses us, encouraging us to experience violence as pleasure such that we become positively invested in its occurrence, while attempting to render us incapable of either challenging the actual atrocities being perpetrated by the same system or steering our collective future in a different direction.*

We must do more than concentrate on how the spectacle works to culture disillusionment, domination, and depoliticization. There is a need to specifically recognize the question of agency in ways that force us to look at the more uncomfortable issues of human desire and our own shameful compromises and complicity with the system. What is more, we must also be concerned with the internal contradictions that characterize spectacles, how to identify and sustain oppositional moments, and how to develop successful strategies for creative resistance and rethinking what the political might actually mean for us going forward.

All networks of power retain a capacity for resistance. Without this counter-force to domination, as Michel Foucault understood all too well, there would be no power relationship. Power by definition is relational, and thus is constituted by the capacity to resist. It is never totalizing. Having said this, we cannot stress enough how the intersection of violence, subjugation, and the media has produced yet another complicated twist in the drama of the spectacle—one that offers a distinctively different set of political registers for grasping its effects on both the contemporary and future shape of media and the broader global public sphere. Interrogating the spectacle of violence in our dystopian times demands a new pedagogical awareness that must open new lines of thinking that gesture *beyond* its normalization.

Voyeurs of Suffering

Spectacles of violence are powerful modes of public pedagogy that function, in part, to fragment and alienate an active and engaged citizenry, transforming it into a passive audience. Who is targeted tells us a great deal about the strategic ambitions and rational underpinnings of the violence. Contemporary neoliberal societies deal with spectacles of violence in a particularly novel way. Unlike previous totalitarian systems that relied upon the terror of secrecy, modern neoliberal societies bring most things into the open. They continually expose us to that which threatens the fabric of the everyday. Even the violent excesses of neoliberal societies—which past generations would surely have viewed as pathologically deranged—are all too easily repackaged for acceptable public consumption. While serial murder, excessive torture, cruel and unusual punishment, secret detentions, and the violation of civil liberties are deeply ingrained in the history of Western imperial domination, in the contemporary moment they no longer elicit condemnation, disgust, and shame. Rather, they have become normalized—celebrated even—in both popular culture and state policy. A lack of public outcry in response to both reports of government torture and its legimation by high-ranking government officials such as former vice president Dick Cheney are surely linked to an explosion of coldblooded portrayals of torture in the mainstream media, extending from the documentaries and news that provide graphic detail of the activities of serial killers to more highbrow fare such the highly acclaimed television drama *24*, or the Hollywood film *Zero Dark Thirty*, with their depictions of utterly unscrupulous characters as admirable, almost heroic, figures. Whereas popular representations of torture prior to 2001 were typically presented as acts of atrocity, the post-9/11 climate has accepted such representations as common fare, even those depictions of blatant human rights violations designed to elicit the audience's respect. Today's screen culture thus contains within it "an echo of the pornographic in maximizing the pleasure of violence."[72]

Consider in this context the justification offered by director Kathryn Bigelow for the depiction of torture in her film *Zero Dark Thirty*: "Those of us who work in the arts know that depiction is not endorsement. If it was, no artist would be able to paint inhumane practices, no author could write about them, and no filmmaker could delve into the thorny subjects of our time."[73] There is no doubt some truth to what Bigelow points out here. It is incumbent upon the arts to waken us out of our dogmatic slumber. If art has any purpose, surely it is to disrupt what we take for granted, and thereby dignify voices and affirm differences that are customarily dismissed. Art in this regard is not simply communication. It is inseparable from the fight for the articulation of new sensibilities that by their very nature reveal and challenge the violence of the contemporary moment. Or else it merely becomes product or the worst type of sentimentality. What Bigelow's statement fails to grasp, though, is the manner in which her movies (including *The Hurt Locker*) actively celebrate the militarization of entertainment while lacking any critical edge whatsoever in terms of their representations or a broader narrative. Not only does she fail to offer any meaningful rupture of mainstream representational narratives that continue to normalize the use of torture and indefinite detention, but she becomes complicit in her rendering of such atrocities as legal, useful, and necessary acts "of our time." While she depicts violence as ubiquitous and inevitable, it is surely the absences in her films that define their overarching messages. Indeed, in *The Hurt Locker*, the voices of disposable "Arabs" are almost fully written out of the movie's dialogue, while those who are killed in action (including the British mercenaries) are shown as having more rational and compassionate qualities. Also written out of her script is the fact that torture often does not even work in securing vital information. More often than not, it prompts its victim to say anything in order to get the torture to cease. Not only does the film make the false claim that the use of torture on the part of the CIA led to Bin Laden's killing, it also, as Naomi Wolf points out, "makes heroes and heroines out of people who committed violent crimes against other people based on their race—something that has historical precedent."[74] A desire for violence, it seems, is the surest guarantee of survivability throughout Bigelow's movie scores.

A case against artistic neutrality is likewise stressed by Slavoj Žižek: "Imagine a documentary that depicts the Holocaust in a cool, disinterested way as a big industrial-logistical operation, focusing on the technical problems involved (transport, disposal of bodies, preventing panic among the prisoners to be gassed). Such a film would either embody a deeply immoral fascination with its topic, or it would count on the obscene neutrality of its style to engender dismay and horror in spectators."[75] Hence, for Žižek, Bigelow's claim to political neutrality is not only absurd in light of the subject matter, which is by nature deeply political, it is a mockery of the art of cinema, which cannot be divorced from the political content it consciously chooses to screen:

> One doesn't need to be a moralist, or naïve about the urgencies of fighting terrorist attacks, to think that torturing a human being is in itself something so profoundly shattering that to depict its neutrality—that is, to neutralize or sanitize this shattering dimension—is already a kind of endorsement. . . . This is normalization at its purest and most efficient—there is a little unease, but it is more about the hurt sensitivity than about ethics, and the job has to be done.[76]

Indeed, it would appear that the spectacle of violence now mimics a new kind of—to quote Susan Sontag—"fascinating fascism" that overtly politicizes representations of violence and discredits critically engaged aesthetics.[77] Torturing people is now a mainstay of what might be called the "carnival of cruelty" designed to entertain and exhilarate on the screen, while in real life torture is militantly sanctioned as a security necessity. At the same time, mainstream entertainment programming is flooded with endless representations of individuals, government officials, and the police operating outside of the law as a legitimate way to seek revenge, implement vigilante justice, and rewrite the rationales for human rights and domestic law. Television programs such as *Dexter* and *Game of Thrones*, as well as a spate of blockbuster Hollywood films such as *Oldboy*, have provided a spectacle of violence unchecked by ethical considerations. Any action, no matter how cruel, is justified by the pursuit of ends that claim to provide greater security and often result in a retrenchment of uncontested power. In the actions of the surveillance state and its turn toward vigilante violence, we see these entertainment narratives writ large. This invariably has political and ethical implications for our societies, especially when the use of force and disregard for democratic accountability become familiar but comfortable entertainment themes—ones we can easily connect to. It is clear that the line between fiction and material reality, along with any distinction between the cultural sphere and the traditional sphere of politics and governance, has blurred to the point where it is now difficult to determine one from the other. If this perspectival and moral confusion has become character-istic of our daily experiences, it is likewise the case that forms of violence and violations of civil rights that should be routinely critiqued as unacceptable are now lauded as necessary and ef-fective tactics in the maintenance of power, so rarely are they subjected to critical interrogation.

It is not merely traditional film and broadcast media that nor-malize a culture of cruelty and the inevitability of the contempo-rary crises of chronic social disparities and political domination. As already indicated, people are increasingly socializing—and publishing—through ever-evolving Internet-centered technolo-gies. At the cutting edge of this is Google's remarkable "Earth" platform. Acquired in 2004, it maps the Earth by the superim-position of images obtained by satellite imagery, aerial photog-raphy, and GIS 3-D modeling. Many people no doubt begin their use of this site by walking down various streets where they may have previously lived, harmlessly reminiscing about their childhood. They may even dwell on the corners of the streets where various misdemeanors of youth took place. Google Earth, however, has a more sinister dimension that reworks the voyeuristic terrain. Increasingly, media stories and news articles about high crime–rate areas are using various stills from the site as a safe and effective way to produce visual images. Camden, New Jersey—tragically anointed "most dangerous place in the United States"—frequently suffers from such digital representations. Camden is often described as a "no-go" area, not only for strangers and outsiders but also for the local police force, which is increasingly suffering casualties and deaths. And yet through Google Earth, we are continually reminded that it is possible to walk these dangerous streets. It is possible to venture down the back alleys. It is possible to view the boarded-up houses. It is possible to really see the impoverishment and abandonment. And it is possible to glide past groups of young men on the street corners—precisely those whom we are taught to fear. Except that in this corporate-owned space we can walk through the worst of Camden's blight while remaining invisible. With the faces of those who live there edited out by Google, they are stripped of political agency and relegated to voicelessness in a medium that offers them up as much for data for as entertainment. Through the corporate gaze of the Internet we engage in reality touring of the most voyeuristic and ethically compromised kind. Such a window into the structural violence experienced by others is justified in terms of technological progress, but reflects a disturbing culture of cruelty that reinforces that the misery of others can be packaged and presented as fodder for an oppressive consumer gaze long trained to spectate uncritically, and then move on to something else.

All this has contributed to the veritable glut of images of suffering that is having disastrous effects on its real occurrences. The sheer ubiquity of violence as a consciously produced and mediated spectacle has contributed to a closure of conscience, compassion, and sensitivity to otherness. Nowhere is this more apparent than in the commercialization of new video game systems that openly market violence as a form of fun. Nick Robinson observes that "games have been important in embedding support for militarization through the operation of the so-called 'military–entertainment complex,' which has seen close collaboration between the military and videogames industry, the widespread development of military games, and the spread of the military into the production of commercial games."[78] Such interactivity, which eradicates the lines between "virtual" and "realities" continues to infuse everyday life with a militaristic experience in ways that are deeply troubling. As war photographer Ashley Gilbertson notes regarding the request to "embed himself" in the recently released PS4 game *The Last of Us Re-mastered*, a post-civilizational drama that allows the user to "freeze the game and lets players shoot, edit, and share photographs of their achievements":

> None of the game's characters show distress, and that to me was bizarre—it's a post-apocalyptic scenario, with a few remaining humans fighting for the survival of their race! To be successful, a player must be the perpetrator of extreme, and highly graphic, violence. I'm interested in a more emotionally engaged type of photography, where the human reaction to a scene is what brings a story to life. That was tough inside this game. Occasionally the characters show anger, though generally they're nonchalant about the situation they've found themselves in. In the end, their emotions mimicked that of the zombies they were killing. By the time I finished this assignment, watching the carnage had become easier. Yet I left the experience with a sense that familiarizing and desensitizing ourselves to violence like this can turn us into zombies. Our lack of empathy and unwillingness to engage with those involved in tragedy stems from our comfort with the trauma those people are experiencing.[79]

Violence as a subject is seldom broached with ethical care or duty of thought in terms of its political or cultural merit. Little wonder that people evidence a certain desensitization, as it appears almost impossible to differentiate between the various forms of violence-laden entertainment, most of which is stripped of all meaningful content for the purpose of sales and marketing. Driven by a corporate agenda whose only guiding principle is the commodification and privatization of everything, daily spectacles of violence are now tolerated more than any due care for the subject, as the power of finance dictates a political agenda that profits from their stripped-down, media-packaged productions. Let's be clear here: there is no such thing as a cultural "pastime" that would allow us to separate or parcel aspects of our existence into neatly marked boxes for intellectual consideration. Every cultural production impacts the attitudes and ideas of its viewing audience, even if only to promote indifference and the numbing of critical thought. How we reintroduce the political into these cultural regimes is therefore of the gravest importance, for it is integral to the experience of everyday life as socially aware citizens aspiring toward a better collective future.

The Ethical Subject of Violence

Jacques Rancière provides an important intervention into the politics of aesthetics by asking how we might move toward a more emancipated conception of the spectator. Or, to put it in more pedagogical terms, how might we give the subject of violence the proper ethical consideration it deserves? For his part, Rancière takes direct aim at the theatrical nature of the spectacle. Such theater, Rancière notes, is politically debilitating, as it strips the audience of any chance to partake in the world on display; for while there is no theater without spectators, our gaze constitutes a "looking without knowing," in that the order of the appearance is simply taken as given and not opened up to critical interrogation. "He or she who looks at the spectacle," Rancière explains, "remains motionless on his or her seat, without any power of intervention." This passivity implies that the spectator is doubly debilitated, separated from the ability to know the conditions of the performance as well as from the ability to act in order to change the performance itself. It therefore forbids us from acting with any degree of knowledge. Passivity works by rendering the audience catatonic and incapable of grasping the magnitude of what just happened. Such passivity thus denies us the ability to act, except in ways that are coded into and prompted by the program. What therefore is required is the creation of counter-cultures that don't simply retreat into some pacifistic purity avoiding violence altogether, but engage the subject of violence with the ethical care and consideration its representation and diagnosis demand.

We might begin by arguing that there is no such thing as an impartial bystander to traumas of violence. Doing nothing or remaining indifferent while witnessing the perpetration of violence is taking a position, even if we neither intervene nor walk away. And yet, on occasions, the trauma can immobilize us. Silence in this context can often bespeak terror in the moment that one is faced with aggression. Such silence sometimes speaks louder than our words as language fails us. How many of us were utterly speechless and immobilized as we witnessed those planes fly into the Twin Towers that fateful autumn morning in 2001? How many suffer in silence, too afraid of the consequences to speak out against the injustices they and others face on a daily basis? And how many simply prefer to walk on by instead of confronting the realities of the slow structural violence we often encounter on our city streets? Such silences often reveal the real horror and difficulties of bearing witness and the complexities of our responses. As Berel Lang has noted with respect to horrors witnessed during the Holocaust of World War II, "silence arguably remains a criterion for all discourse, a constant if phantom presence that stipulates that whatever is written ought to be justifiable as more probative, more incisive, more *revealing*, than its absence or, more cruelly, its erasure."[80] Primo Levi understood the ethical stakes better than anyone. As he once wrote on his experience of surviving the unspeakable horrors of Auschwitz, "Even in this place one can survive, and therefore one must want to survive, to tell the story, to bear witness; and that to survive we must force ourselves to save at least the skeleton, the scaffolding, the form of civilization. We are slaves, deprived of every right, exposed to every insult, condemned to certain death, but we still possess one power, and we must defend it with all our strength for it is the last—the power to refuse our consent."[81]

When dealing with the vexing ethical dimensions of what it means to witness aggression today, it is worth bearing in mind that there is no such thing as a "random act" of political violence. A defining characteristic of such violence is its public display—the spectacle of its occurrence that through its very performance makes a metaphysical claim such that the individual act relates to a broader historical narrative. Being a witness as such means that we need to understand more fully how the justification of violence is presented as a matter of rational choice and the broader historical narrative in which this reasoning must be situated. Violence is never unitary. There is always a process.

The images produced from the victimization and the trauma it fosters resonate far beyond the initial acts perpetrated. The spectacle of violence is therefore more than a mere after-effect of the original act of violation. Violence continues to occur in the imagination of the victims who have been removed from "the realm of moral subjects."[82] It haunts the victim, forcing conformity to its modes of suffocation and despair. What is more, the cycle continues through the imposition of uncontroversial claims that sanction violence as retribution. This unending process offers no way out of the dialectical tragedy. Indeed, as Fanon understood, the dialectic arrangement is absolutely integral to the normalization of the violence and perpetuates the (non)value of the lives that are all too easily forgotten as the detritus and excess of such violence. So how might we emancipate ourselves from the daily spectacles of violence we are forced to endure so that we don't shamefully compromise with the oppressive forms of power?

Theodor Adorno once infamously stated that "to write poetry after Auschwitz is barbaric." While some have read this to mean that the poetics of art have nothing to offer in response to catastrophe, we maintain that a different interpretation of Adorno is required. Art must be examined, not destroyed or shunned, and its critical/ethical potential restored by those who refuse to limit art's purpose to mere aesthetic pleasure or entertainment. Hence, while we are troubled somewhat by Adorno's positions on the political potential of art, we argue that contained within his critique is the call to constructively produce a new radical imagination that could serve as a bridge to inform the ethical imagination and layers of suffering, a bridge that, contra Adorno, recognizes the role of affect and art in supporting the ethical intellect. Under such circumstances, art has the capacity to reveal the ethical grammar of suffering and create a multiplicity of ruptures that opens up new political spaces between our spectacularized present and a different future. In this regard, instead of condemning poetry or suggesting that all representations of violence are complicit in its banalization and the numbing of the human response, we wish to highlight more the ethical problem of representation providing a meaningful cultural critique of a political atrocity. In other words, how might we respond with ethical care and dignity once these exact principles are denied?

As Adorno himself later qualified, unimaginable "suffering . . . also demands the continued existence of the very art it forbids."[83] Indeed, as he further wrote: "When even genocide becomes cultural property in committed literature, it becomes easier to continue complying with the culture that gave rise to the murder."[84] So it is not a question as to whether violent atrocities are unrepresentable or unspeakable. What is at stake is precisely how one responds, by rethinking the art of political engagement. Adorno's call then, as we choose to hear it, is both to take seriously the ethical subject of violence, to bear witness to that which appears "intolerable," not only to human suffering but also to the power of critique in transforming the modes of subjectivities that violence produces. This is as much a pedagogical as a political call for a new "imagination"—one that declares an open conflict with violence in all its forms, such that nonviolence becomes a real and lived possibility. At stake here is a call to make visible those subjectivities that are both discarded and unrecognized while contesting those zones of abandonment that accelerate the domestic machinery of human disposability. Spectacles of violence thrive on the "accelerated death of the unwanted" and must be addressed through the educative nature of politics, a politics that makes subjectivity the material force of collective resistance and provides the disposable with a chance both to be heard and to transform their symbolic relation to the world into action.[85] It might seem impossible for us today to break away from the daily spectacles of violence that serve to reinforce the catastrophic political imaginary of our times. Such a sense of impossibility makes the task all the more urgent and necessary.

TWO

THE POLITICS OF DISPOSABILITY

On Human Disposal

Contemporary neoliberal societies are increasingly defined by their waste. Their productive outputs are complemented by what Zygmunt Bauman identifies as "waste management" for a social order that has been cultured to obey the planned obsolescence of everything, including people and communities. In a social fabric disordered by market-driven imperatives in which politics is beholden to money and removed from any sense of civic and ethical considerations, there is a strong tendency to view the vast majority of society as dead weight, disposable just like anything that gets hauled off and dumped in a landfill.[1] These others removed from ethical calculations and the grammar of suffering are rendered both obsolete and overwhelmed by machineries of social death, to the point where they become unknowable. Bauman's work is significant here, for not only does he show how the categories of waste are integral to the logics of modernist systems, but in doing so he also asks us to consider the human stakes. As he writes, we live in "liquid" times characterized by a "civilization of excess, redundancy, waste, and waste disposal."[2] Rather than seeing waste as politically useless, Bauman affirms that the production of wasted lives shores up the productivity of the whole system, as the very idea of progress requires the setting aside of those who don't or are unable to perform in a way that would appear meaningful. Criminalization, for example, performs a vital task by providing scapegoats for the various types of race- and class-based insecurities; such scapegoats offer an "easy target for unloading anxieties prompted by the widespread fears of social redundancy."[3] These "others" are integral to fear-based societies and the carceral industries of violence and punishment that profit immensely from their management.

Bauman's work continually forces us to consider how the production of "wasted lives" at a systemic level is entirely fitting in the logics of modern societies as they retain their *order-making* and *progressive* orientations. Modernity, in fact, is yet another chapter in the story of the production of "disposable humans," or what he terms elsewhere "collateral damage,"[4] which designates both the intentional and arbitrary logic of inequality and exclusion of human societies. Indeed, for Bauman, order-building functions largely to designate those lives that simply don't belong to the privileged social order as a result of their perceived identities and attributes; moreover, the incessant drive to progress justifies a form of societal assay that allows for the casting aside of people who are registered as such on account of their own failure to have resources worth extracting. As in all other sectors of neoliberal control, public and environmental concerns are perpetually compromised and deferred by the fiscal imperatives of private gain. Significantly, for Bauman, it is the continued production of wasted lives that defines all modern projects regardless of their ideological emblem. In a world where ideas of technological progress continue to provide the benchmark for determining human progress, the task of targeting entire communities for disposal has itself become not only an easier job than ever, but also an increasingly privatized industry alongside so much else in neoliberal societies. Angela Y. Davis and many others have a term for it: the prison-industrial complex.

Some dispute Bauman's work for being overly deterministic in terms of the logics of modernity, while also being troubled by the labeling of human subjects as waste.[5] Such claims regarding the over-determining nature of power are, however, often cited by those who remain uncomfortable with its interrogation in ways that allow us to focus on the real perniciousness of its effects—especially the forms of depoliticization and violence supported by a range of frameworks from the cosmopolitan to the more ideologically fundamentalist. Our reading of Bauman, as of Foucault before him, understands that a critique of power is a theoretical and political necessity, since it is committed to exposing and challenging the normalization of subjugation in all its forms. Confronting this bleak and often disavowed reality unsettles the normalized conditions of our lives in such a way that we can begin to grasp the operations of power evident in the increasing use of violence by the state as it divests from social welfare in favor of corporate welfare and embraces its role as an increasingly oppressive state funded by, beholden to, and in the service of a small financial elite.

In terms of Bauman's critics, while some might be uncomfortable with discussing people in terms of "waste," nowhere in Bauman's work does he suggest that people, families, communities belong on the scrapheaps of history. His deployment of the term "wasted lives" is a both a provocative intervention and a precise meditation on the scripting of human life by exploitative regimes of contemporary power. It is also a rallying cry both to expand the notion of critique and to recognize the urgency of rethinking politics beyond a neoliberal framework.

We do nevertheless depart from Bauman's analysis in two ways. First, despite Bauman's attentive detail to systems of oppression and the production of subjectivities that have no meaningful place within the order of societies, we are somewhat troubled by the discourse of "waste" insofar as it can be read as the *arbitrary* outcome of all modern societies. Neoliberalism is never arbitrary in its logic or complex design. It is a political project whose predatory formations take over all life systems, even if to cast aside, contain, or render them a continual source of suspicion and endangerment. Indeed, implied within the discourse of waste is a further arbitrary theory of subjectivity wherein the collateral casualties of the neoliberal wasteland might be deemed simply wasted potential. Our concern then is that the possibility for seeing the production of wasted lives in arbitrary terms might be complicit in absolving regimes of power of intentionality. We prefer instead a discourse of *disposability*. It centers our attention more on the verb *to dispose*, thereby moving us beyond the unavoidable production of excess waste to take into account the activity (who and what is being disposed of), the experience (the subjective stakes), and the state of relations (the machinery of disposability) that permit particular forms of wastefulness. In this regard, disposability conveys the violence of human expulsions as it concentrates on the *active production* of wastefulness, thereby requiring us to take seriously the truly predatory political and economic nature of neoliberalism. Similarly, we recognize the pedagogical nature of neoliberal wastefulness in that it suggests not only the power to dispose economically and politically of those considered excess but also to create those affective and ideological spaces in which the logic of control rooted in economic and governing institutions, is rooted as well in the construction of subjectivity itself.

Second, while we remain admirers of Bauman's critique of modernity and the ways in which claims to progress have led to the evisceration of the human, our contention is that neoliberalism today has openly abandoned this claim as it increasingly pitches a dystopian vision of the future. Again, we might point to the doctrine of resilience here, which not only forces us to partake in a world that is presented as fundamentally insecure, but denies us the possibility of even conceiving that there is a world beyond unending catastrophe. Even the most stalwart neoliberal economist now asks that we accept a more austere and tempered imaginary, relegating the dream of unending growth and unlimited human potential to a bygone era. Indeed, if wars and local crises overseas continue to be used as an opportunity for intervention and imposing neoliberal regimes of political rule, back home the neoliberal appropriation of disaster and general insecurities has profoundly shifted the logic of capital such that *regression* (as crudely presented to be the underside of modernity by political economists since its inception) is the dominant maxim for political rule. Hence, if questions of "sustainability" once emerged in the zones of impoverishment as a way to temper local claims for empowerment, contemporary neoliberalism thrives upon the fact that we are all "going South"! It demands socialism (in terms of state investment as per bailouts and protection as per ongoing militarization of the poor for the rich), while promoting austerity and tempered visions of growth for the rest of us. From terror to weather and everything in between, capital exploitation has industrialized the potential for catastrophe and the profitability of disaster management.[6] Under neoliberal regimes, the discourse of critique and catastrophe decreasingly gives rise to collective resistance and struggle but increasingly fosters obedience and despair, as neoliberal's death-march is naturalized and frozen as a moment in history that cannot be changed, only endured.

The Machinery of Disposability

Under the regime of neoliberalism, especially in the United States, war has become an extension of politics as almost all spheres of society have been transformed into a combat zone or in some cases a killing zone. One only has to look at Ferguson, Missouri, or the killing of Eric Garner in New York City to see the extent to which this is being played out in communities throughout the United States. When civilians in Ferguson and New York City spontaneously organized to denounce a white policeman's killing of an unarmed black youth and a defenseless black man, the immediate response was to militarize both areas with combat-style hardware and forces, including snipers. Americans now find themselves living in a society that is constantly under siege as narratives of endangerment and potential threats translate into conditions of intensified civic violation in which almost everyone is spied on and subjected to modes of state and corporate control whose power knows few limits. War as a "state of exception" has become normalized.[7] Moreover, society as a whole becomes increasingly militarized; political concessions to public interest groups become relics of long abandoned claims to democracy; and the welfare state is hollowed out to serve the interests of global markets. Any collective sense of ethical imagination and social responsibility toward those who are vulnerable or in need of care is now viewed as a scourge or pathology. Within this mindset, interventions that might benefit the disadvantaged are perversely deemed to be irresponsible acts that prevent individuals from learning to deal with their own suffering—even though, as we know, the forces that condition their plight remain beyond their control, let alone their ability to influence them to any degree.

What has intensified in this new historical conjuncture is the practice of disposability in which more and more individuals and groups are now considered dispensable, consigned to zones of abandonment, containment, surveillance, and incarceration. Moreover, the political maneuvers that target groups as disposable and enact their widespread disappearance cannot be divorced from the evisceration of the public commons more broadly. The collapse of public spheres necessary for the exercise of democracy is part of a larger process of systematic depoliticization, privatization, and militarization. Any semblance of political rights thus becomes suffocated by the weight of what Naomi Klein has called "disaster capitalism."[8]

Citizens are now reduced to market and surveillance data, consumers, and commodities, and as such inhabit identities in which they increasingly "become unknowables, with no human rights and with no one accountable for their condition."[9] Within this political assemblage, not only does ethical blindness and impunity prevail on the part of the financial elite, but the inner worlds of the oppressed are constantly being remade under the force of economic pressures and a culture of anxiety and precariousness. According to João Biehl, as the politics of disposability "comes into sharp visibility, tradition, collective memory, and public spheres are organized as phantasmagoric scenes [that] thrive on the 'energies of the dead,' who remain unaccounted for in numbers and law."[10]

Economists such as Robert Reich, Paul Krugman, and Doug Henwood have argued that we are living in a new Gilded Age, one that mimics a time when robber barons and strikebreakers ruled, and the government and economy were controlled by a cabal that was rich, powerful, and ruthless.[11] And, of course, communities of color, women, and the working class were told to mind their place in a society controlled by those already enriched. Often missing in these analyses is the fact that what is new in the second Gilded Age is not just the moral sanctioning of greed, the corruption of politics by corporatism, and the ruthlessness of a global capitalist class. What is also unique is the constant reconfiguration of the nation-state in the interests of a market that colonizes collective subjectivity with discourses of risk, insecurity, catastrophe, and inescapable endangerments. The second Gilded Age is then a boom time for elites, but for everyone else it's what psychologist Robert Jay Lifton rightly calls a "death-saturated age" in which matters of violence, survival, and trauma now infuse everyday life.[12]

Discarded by the corporate state, dispossessed of social provisions, and deprived of the economic, political, and social conditions that enable viable and critical modes of agency, more and more sectors of civilian society find themselves inhabiting what Biehl calls "zones of total social exclusion" marked by deep inequalities in power, wealth, and income. Such zones are sites of rapid disinvestment, places marked by endless spectacles of violence that materialize the neoliberal logics of containment, commodification, surveillance, militarization, cruelty, criminalization, and punishment.[13] These "zones of hardship" constitute a hallmark and intensification of the neoliberal politics of disposability, which is relentless in the material and symbolic violence it wages against society for the benefit of a financial minority.[14] What has become clear is that capitalist expropriation, dispossession, and disinvestment have reached a point where life has become completely unbearable for many living in the most prosperous of nations.[15] Areas of great affluence can often be found adjacent to, if not surrounded by, zones of great misery inhabited by impoverished immigrants, poor minorities, the homeless, young people living in debt, the long-term unemployed, workers, and the declining middle class, all of whom have been delivered by market forces into criminalized communities of violence, harassment, surveillance, and everyday humiliations and brutality.

Earlier promises of modernity regarding progress, freedom, and political affirmation have not been eliminated; they have been reconfigured, stripped of their emancipatory potential, and subordinated to a predatory market and a hyper-privatized society. Dispossession and disinvestment have invalidated social enrichment and have turned "progress" into a curse for the marginalized and a blessing for the privileged who constitute the smallest financial minority—the wealthy few. Modernity has thus reneged on its undertaking to fulfill the social contract, however disingenuous or limited, especially with regard to young people. Measuring everything through the metrics of private profit, the ideological and affective spaces of neoliberalism work hard to substitute individual gain for any concern for the public good. The savagery of neoliberalism is also on display in its attempts to fiscally snuff out institutions meant to help families find pathways out of the miseries of impoverishment, undernourishment, underemployment, criminalization, and lack of adequate housing. The social contract and the relations it once embodied are now replaced with unchecked power relations. Long-term social, educational, and ecological planning and the institutional structures that support it are now weakened, if not eliminated, by the urgencies of privatization, deregulation, and the extraction of short-term profits. Social bonds have given way under the collapse of social protections and are further subverted by the neoliberal insistence that there are only "individual solutions to socially produced problems."[16] One consequence is that neoliberalism has launched what Robert O. Self calls an assault on "the basic architecture of our collective responsibility to ensure that [we all] share in a decent life."[17] It is also an aggressive counter-force constantly antagonizing the formative cultures and modes of individual and collective agency that engender a connection between the democratic polis and the sustenance of economic, social, and political community.[18]

Neoliberalism's industries of disposability relentlessly enforce unchecked notions of the private that both dissolve social bonds and deter conditions of agency from the civilian landscape of responsibility and ethical considerations. Absorbed into privatized orbits of consumption, commodification, and display, inhabitants of neoliberal societies are entertained by the toxic pleasures of spectacles of violence which cannot be divorced from the parasitic presence of the corporate state, the concentration of power and money in the upper 1 percent of the population, the ongoing militarization of all aspects of society, and the relentless, aggressive depoliticization of the citizenry. In its current historical conjuncture, the nation-state is a nodal point of intersection—something that appears akin to a green zoning of the world, protecting and servicing a handful of billionaires.

The Silent Order of Battle
Governments have often openly extended the narrative of war both to provide a sense of urgency and to appeal to a sense of moral certainty when dealing with political problems.[19] The very act of securitization itself begins as an imperative to act

toward the alleviation of unnecessary suffering. While we have become all too familiar with the age-old discourses of war as applied to a range of issues including drugs, poverty, crime, and terror—the former two in particular being integral to the broadening and deepening of the security agenda in "human" terms—in practice, the focus on unnecessary suffering has all too easily shifted the blame onto the shoulders of the global poor. Indeed, while the expanded and seemingly ubiquitous language of warfare has created conditions that have long since dispensed with familiar orthodox demarcations such as friend and enemy, inside and outside, civilian space and battle space, along with times of peace and times of war, the discourse has become beholden to existing power relationships instead of eliciting critical engagement with complex social issues. The language of warfare as such, when internalized, turns emancipation into colonization, as it remains at the service of those who seek to condemn political differences, instead of those in whose name it is marshalled. What therefore appear to be benevolent wars on behalf of the disadvantaged all too easily turn into wars against the disadvantaged, as power inverts its own systemic failures and invests in carceral industries that profit from policing and criminalizing those it abandons. The United States, in particular, has not only made war one of society's highest ideals, but has reconstituted almost all public spheres as private zones that legitimate violence and militarization as the ultimate arbiter of social relations and problems. Education in disposable communities now often involves as many police as teachers, for schools that once served as pathways to a better life now act as pipelines to prison. In communities of color such as Ferguson, Missouri, the landscape of everyday life is criminalized as local police forces are deployed to civilian protests with military-grade weapons used in the Iraq and Afghanistan wars. More and more, everyday behaviors are targeted and criminalized, some as trivial as violating a dress code or panhandling in the streets.[20]

Neoliberal governance has been transformed into an instrument of social war and internal colonization. Violence and fear have become the motivational forces of societies successfully indoctrinated by notions of privatization, which sell competitive private interest at the expense of all else, beginning with such public interest values as community, cooperation, compassion, fairness, honesty, and care for others. It has become increasingly difficult in such self-regarding societies to trust anyone else, let alone raise critical ideas in the public realm.[21] In the United States, for example, massive inequality resulting from an unprecedented concentration of wealth, power, and money in the hands of the 1 percent has resulted in a culture of cruelty, a survival-of-the-fittest ethic, as well as "the massive intrusion of criminality into political processes [and] a style of politics which by itself is criminal."[22] As public values and social bonds are gutted, there is a retreat from both social responsibility and politics itself. Politics is eviscerated when it supports a market-driven view of society that turns its back on the idea, as expressed by Hannah Arendt, that "Humanity is never acquired in solitude."[23] That is, neoliberal societies have come undone in terms of the social contract, and in doing so have turned their support away from the public sphere that by definition provides conditions for democracy: free speech, social autonomy, cultural freedom, and political equality. This violence against the social not only hastens the death of the radical imagination, but also mimics a notion of the banality of evil made famous by Arendt who argued that at the root of widespread subjugation was a kind of thoughtlessness, an inability to think, and a type of outrageous ignorance in one's actions and thought processes in which "there's simply the reluctance ever to imagine what the other person is experiencing."[24]

Under neoliberalism, those considered redundant are now consigned to a veritable wasteland, deprived of the most basic social provisions, and ridiculed by those ruling elites who are responsible at a systemic level for their hardships and suffering. One only has to watch a brief segment of Fox News to experience the ways in which impoverished communities are continually blamed and criminalized for their plight. At the same time, the crisis of ethics, economics, and politics has been matched by a crisis of ideas, as the conditions for critical agency dissolve into the limited pleasures of instant gratification wrought through the use of technologies and consuming practices that deter, if not obliterate, the very possibility of thinking differently. This is immanence of the worst kind, for it abides by the private logics of neoliberal rule. What is particularly distinctive about this historical conjuncture is the way in which a vast number of citizens, especially young people of color in low-income communties, are increasingly denied any place in an already weakened social order and the degree to which supporting young people is no longer seen as central to how the society defines its future and intellectual capital.[25]

For instance, close to half of all Americans live on or beneath the poverty line, and "more than a million public school students are homeless in the United States; 57 percent of all children are in homes considered to be either low-income or impoverished, and half of all American children will be on food stamps at least once before they turn 18 years old."[26] At the same time, the 400 richest Americans "have as much wealth as 154 million Americans combined, that's 50 percent of the entire country, [while] the top economic 1 percent of the U.S. population now has more wealth than 90 percent of the population combined."[27] Within this system, the civic institutions that advance public interest ethics capable of countering such violence and suffering disappear, while targeted communities lose their privacy, dignity, bodies, housing, and material goods. The fear of losing everything, the horror of an engulfing and crippling precarity, the quest to merely survive, and the promise of violence and catastrophe (individual and collective) are increasingly becoming a "normal" way of life for the majority. As such, the response modeled by those in power toward people's suffering is anything but one of compassion; contempt, cruelty, surveillance, and incarceration have replaced community, social responsibility, and political courage. Karen Garcia captures well the underlying logic of disposability and its darker roots. She writes:

It's bad enough in the most drastic epoch of wealth disparity in American history that most people are suffering economically. What makes this particular era so heinous is that the hungry, the homeless, the unemployed, and the underemployed are being kicked when they're already down. They are being ground into human mulch for dumping in a vast neoliberal landfill. People are not only poor, their poverty and suffering have literally been deemed crimes by the elite class of sociopaths running the place.[28]

Nowhere is the severity of the consequences of this new era under neoliberalism more apparent than in the disposability of younger populations. In fact, this is the first generation, as Bauman argues, in which the "plight of the outcast may stretch to embrace a whole generation."[29] He rightly argues that today's youth have been "cast in a condition of liminal drift, with no way of knowing whether it is transitory or permanent."[30] Youth no longer occupy a privileged place of possibility that was offered to previous generations. Instead of symbolizing vibrant potential, many youth now represent and internalize a loss of faith in better times to come, echoing the catastrophic narratives in the dominant culture that paint the future as indeterminate, bleak, and insecure. Yet diminished prospects pale next to the normalization of market-driven government policies that have wiped out pensions, eliminated quality health care, raised college tuition, and produced a harsh world of joblessness, while giving billions to banks and the military. Students, in particular, now find themselves in a world in which heightened expectations have been replaced by dashed hopes and a miasma of onerous debt.[31]

What has changed for an entire generation of young people includes not only neoliberal society's disinvestment in the future of youth and the prospect of permanent downward mobility, but also the fact that youth live in a commercially carpet-bombed and commodified environment that is unlike anything experienced by their predecessors. Youth have become a marker for a mode of disposability in which their fate is defined largely through the registers of a society that readily discards resources, goods, and *people*. Nothing has prepared this generation for the inhospitable world of commodification, privatization, joblessness, frustrated hopes, surveillance, and stillborn projects.[32] The present generation has been born into a society dominated by casino capitalism in which players take a gamble on the unstable market economy with stakes that, for many, translate into life or death. Young people and their futures are viewed increasingly as a suitable wager to be risked and, if necessary, to be disposed of, especially if they do not generate value as workers, consumers, and commodities. In such conditions, young people who speak out about their troubling circumstances are dismissed as either naturally anxious as if by biological design or a source of trouble should they have the temerity to challenge orthodox reasoning. Instead of being viewed as "at risk," they are perceived as posing a risk to society and are subject to a range of punitive policies.

The structures of neoliberalism do more than disinvest in young people and commodify them; they also transform the protected space of childhood into a zone of disciplinary exclusion and cruelty. This is especially true for those young people further marginalized by race and class, who now inhabit a social landscape in which they are increasingly disparaged either as flawed consumers or as outsiders transgressing the acceptable boundaries of what it means to be a citizen. With no adequate role to play as consumers or citizens, many youth are now forced to inhabit "zones of social abandonment" extending from schools on the margins of financial existence to bulging detention centers to prisons.[33] These are zones where the needs of young people are generally ignored, and where many, especially poor minority youth, often find their appearance alone is sufficient to warrant criminalization. For example, with the hollowing out of the social state, the circuits of state repression, surveillance, and disposability increasingly "link the fate of blacks, Latinos, Native Americans, poor whites, and Asian Americans" to a youth-crime complex, which now serves as the default solution to major social problems.[34] Impoverished communities and low-income youth are thus viewed as out of step, place, and time; they are defined largely as "pathologies feeding on the body politic" and exiled to spheres of "terminal exclusion."[35]

We live in a historical moment in which everything that matters politically, ethically, and culturally is being erased—either ignored, turned into a commodity, or simply falsified. As the welfare state is hollowed out, a culture of compassion is replaced by a culture of brutality and atomization. Within the neoliberal historical conjuncture, there is a merging of violence and governance, accompanied by a systematic disinvestment in and breakdown of institutions and public spheres that have provided the minimal conditions for democracy. A generalized anxiety now shapes neoliberal societies—one that thrives on insecurity, dread of punishment, and a perception of constant lurking threats.

Such hysteria not only is politically debilitating but also feeds the growing militarization of society, culture, and everyday life. This trend is evident in the paramilitarizing of the police, who increasingly use high-tech scanners, surveillance cameras, and toxic chemicals on those who engage in peaceful protest against the warfare and corporate state. The war on terror has evolved into a war on democracy as local police are now being militarized with the latest combat-grade equipment imported straight from the battlefields of Iraq and Afghanistan to the streets of places like Ferguson, Missouri, and numerous other cities. In the United States, military technologies once used exclusively on the battlefield are now being supplied to police departments across the nation. Drones, machine-gun-equipped armored trucks, SWAT vehicles, and tanks now find themselves in the hands of local police and campus security forces, turning them into the normalized symbols of everyday violence that now plague the neoliberal state. Arming domestic police forces, with paramilitary weaponry ensures their systematic use even in the absence of a terrorist attack; moreover, such weapons will produce more aggressive modes of policing, if not violence, against young people, communities of color, and immigrant families. Criminalization and violence now proceed with a colonial vengeance on the part of the power elite, followed by the stigmatizing and humiliation of those considered disposable, beyond the pale of compassion, justice, and ethical concern.[36]

A state of permanent war requires modes of public pedagogy to form obedient subjects who abide by its values, ideology, and narratives of greed and violence. Such legitimation is largely provided through a market-driven culture that advocates for consumerism, militarism, and organized violence, circulated through various registers of popular culture extending from high fashion and Hollywood movies to the creation of violent video games sponsored by the Pentagon. The market-driven spectacle of war demands a culture of conformity, complicit intellectuals obedient to established relations of power and its version of history, and a passive republic of consumers. It also needs compliant subjects who through relentless marketing are cultured both to find pleasure in the spectacle of violence and to divorce its occurrence from political questions raised by personal ethics and social conscience.

As the pleasure principle reigns, unconstrained by an ethical compass guided by a respect for others, it is increasingly shaped by the need for intense excitement and a never-ending flood of heightened sensations. As brutality become more commonplace in entertainment, unfamiliar violence such as extreme images of torture and death—whether fictional or real—becomes banally familiar, while familiar violence that occurs daily is barely recognized and relegated to the realm of the unnoticed and unnoticeable. As an increasing volume of violence is pumped into the culture, yesterday's spine-chilling and nerve-wrenching violence loses its shock value. The desire for exhilaration from media violence grows more intense along with increasing indifference and desensitization to such images. Representations of ever-greater cruelty and suffering are offered up as fodder for sports, entertainment, news media, and other outlets for seeking pleasure. A "political culture of hyper punitiveness" appears tame by comparison; the normalization of violent spectacles thus renders political violence increasingly acceptable as it accelerates through the social order like a highly charged electric current.[37]

Punishment has become the ultimate form of entertainment as the pain of others, especially those stigmatized as alien and criminal, or simply unproductive and powerless, has become the subject not of compassion but of ridicule and amusement. The emphasis here is on the sadistic impulse and how it merges spectacles of violence and brutality with forms of collective pleasure that often lend support to and sway public opinion in favor of social policies and "lawful" practices that create zones of abandonment for youth and others viewed as expendable. No society can make a claim to being a democracy as long as it defines itself through shared trepidations rather than shared responsibilities, especially in regard to the future. Widespread violence now functions by turning the economy of genuine pleasure into a mode of sadism that creates the foundation for sapping democracy of any political vitality that might be capable of countering the politics of disposability.

A symptomatic example of the way in which violence has

saturated everyday life can be seen in the increasing criminalization of the behavior of young people in public schools. Transgressions that were normally handled by teachers, guidance counselors, and school administrators are now dealt with by the police and the criminal justice system. The consequences have been disastrous for young people. Not only do many schools now resemble the culture of prisons, young children are being arrested and subjected to court appearances for behaviors that can only be termed as trivial. This is not merely systematic abuse and oppression parading as reasoned political reform; it is also a blatant indicator of the degree to which sadism and the infatuation with violence have become standardized in a society that even commercializes acts of dehumanizing itself.

As politics is disconnected from its ethical and material moorings, it becomes easier to punish and imprison young people than to educate them. From the inflated rhetoric of the political classes to the market-driven media peddling spectacles of violence, the influence of the criminogenic in everyday life is undermining our collective sense of belonging by justifying cutbacks to social supports and restricting opportunities for democratic resistance. Rather than providing pathways out of oppression, the state wages war against its most vulnerable families and communities. Saturating mainstream discourses with anti-public narratives, the neoliberal machinery of disposability and the anti-public pundits who legitimate it effectively weaken public supports and prevent the emergence of much-needed new ways of thinking and speaking about politics. But there is more at work here than merely the neutralizing of collective opposition to the growing control and wealth of predatory financial elites and the violence they impose on marginalized and vulnerable populations. Concerted attempts have been made by the corporate state to validate malignant characterizations of marginalized groups so as to render them voiceless and thus powerless in the face of hardship and oppression.

The consolidation of military, corporate, academic, and cultural industries into a complex with unbridled power points to the need for strategies that address what is specific about contemporary neoliberalism and how multiple interests, social relations, public pedagogies, and economic configurations come together to shape its domestic politics, its catastrophic reasoning, the harshness of its survivalist narratives, and its mechanisms of disposability. Understanding this conjuncture is invaluable to us politically in that it provides a theoretical opening for making the practices of the neoliberal manipulation of civilian democracy visible. It also points to the conceptual power of making clear that history remains an open horizon that is not predetermined, despite its dismissal by those who claim we have come to "the end of history" or the end of ideology.[38] Without a more complex understanding of the current historical conjuncture, it will be difficult to motivate and organize successful resistance to neoliberal ideologies, policies, and modes of governance. It is precisely through the indeterminate nature of history that resistance becomes possible and politics refuses any guarantees and remains open.

Eviscerating the Human

We live at a time in which instrumental rationality appears increasingly divorced from the community-building values of democracy, public life, and education. Hannah Arendt understood better than most the links between technological progress and alienation. She prefaced her landmark study *The Human Condition* with a short meditation on the launch of the first satellite in 1957, which she compared to the "splitting of the atom." Arendt elucidated the metaphorical significance of what she interpreted as an attempt to escape from Earth. She suggested it represented both a form of internal completion that made us realize that the world was now full (inasmuch as speed had finally conquered space) and a new form of alienation as the flight from this world resulted in nothing less than a flight from the human condition. This "full possession" of our mortal dwelling thus created a situation wherein each person became as much an "inhabitant of the earth as of [his or her] own country." Rather, however, than making us feel at home, what occurred was a further amplification of the Cartesian doubts, as the world seemed fully accessible and yet unknowable in its full complex mastery at the very same moment. The flight into space symbolized not only a degree of technological progress, but also a refiguring of the self as under the control of a new kind of rationality rooted in a notion of progress tied not to matters of social and political responsibility but to the urge to conquer, control, and elevate matters of efficiency, science, and rationality beyond the constraints of the ethical imagination. It is precisely our exodus from the planetary domain that ends up being the source of our flight from ourselves, as metaphysical praxis is firmly displaced by a technologically driven gaze, whose wonder at the infinite is turned back in upon itself to produce the most suffocating of mindsets as we become alienated from the life-world system upon which we completely depend.

That worldly alienation has taken place, as Arendt foresaw, now seems very evident as both an empirical fact and a philosophical claim. Indeed, if the hallmarks of the previous century were both mass production and mass destruction, as the final outputs (whether the production of goods or the destruction of bodies) were removed from the immediate gaze, so the continued technological transformation from industrial to network-based societies has furthered our sense of alienation. That is to say, if the mask of mastery for twentieth-century modernity produced specialist workers blinded by the limits of their own expertise, as well as producing the remarkably disciplined, regimented, and deeply compartmentalized regimes of truth in which they were embedded, the world we now live in appears in all of its complex, adaptive, and unknowable permutations at

odds with any viable notion of solidarity and celebrates alienated orbits of privatization and the crumbling language of the
commodity. What masks the mastery of power today are modes
of technological interfacing that dispense with the very notion
of essential truths and a foundational belief in the fixed order of
things. Alienation as such is no longer a question of being alienated *from* a world that we strive to know and want to discover; it
is to be alienated as a result of its very completion, as the once
assumed promise of truth, security, and prosperity is replaced by
a global colonization of the imagination such that any vision of
worldly belonging is seen through the lens of crises, insecurity,
and unavoidable regression.

The everyday effects of this interior world of alienation,
atomization, and privatization are plain to see wherever we dare
to look. Simply step into a coffee shop or walk down any city
street to notice how many people are in some other place, as
their technological devices separate their physical presence from
their virtual attention. What we might term here the age of the
"disembodied self" is not limited to zones of affluence; it is the
prevailing norm, as globally distributed forms of connectivity
authenticate what are often termed "post-human" subjectivities ultimately devoid of any physical and ethical sense of location and connection. Being elsewhere defines the presentness
of the modern human condition such that distancing increasingly shapes the most mundane of social interactions. All the
while, we are sold the idea that to be "smart" simply requires the
purchase of a device that quite literally places the world in our
hands. The sense of frustration is palpable, as noted by the vast
increase in anxiety syndromes. Not only does physical interac-
tion appear more difficult as the removed sense of inhibition in
digitized worlds proves to be more comforting than the realities
of human encounters, we are equally reminded of the raw realities of global problems that deny us the chance of even identifying their source, let alone finding a lasting resolution. Nobody is

in control. And our alienated connectivities merely add anxiety to the uncertain drama of our times.

Little wonder that the lines between the reality of military combat and the reality of everyday violence have become so blurred that it is now difficult to respond or to understand the origins of the economic, political, and social formations that now rule neoliberal societies. Its predatory formations operate by denying things in plain sight as the omnipresent nature of threat naturalizes violence in ways that occlude once familiar modernist explanations. We know the tragedies still exist, yet we cannot write about their source or truth with any certainty or clarity. There is no truth other than the threat of disasters yet to materialize within our crises-laden life-world systems. Subjectivization as such is all about the internalization of violence in ways that render it an integral element of the human condition; it is presented as innate and natural to systematic designs. The human condition therefore becomes endangered by forms of threat so ubiquitous that they place the capacity for terror into the operative fabric of those very systems deemed vital to our perilous modes of existence.[39] Under such conditions, the crises of truth are also related more profoundly to metaphysical crises of the courage to speak the truth, a confluence that is having a profound impact upon the capacity for sustained political critique essential for political transformation.

What is particularly disturbing here is the current resurgence of a poisonous form of technical rationality in neoliberal societies, or what we might call the return of "data storms" that uncritically amass metrics, statistics, and empirical evidence at the expense of knowledge that signals the need for contextualization and interpretation in support of public values, the common good, and the ethical imagination. Data storms make an appeal to a decontextualized and allegedly pure description of facts, or what Herbert Marcuse called a "misplaced concreteness" regarding complex human behaviors, one that was particularly "prevalent in the social sciences, a pseudo-empiricism which . . . tended to make the objectivity of the social sciences a vehicle of apologetics and defense of the status quo."[40]

This obsession with metrics feeds an insatiable desire for control and lives in an eternal present, removed from matters of justice and historical memory. The novelist Anne Lamott is right when she explains to an interviewer that the frenzy over data is endangering "everything great and exciting that someone like me would dare to call grace. What this stuff steals is our aliveness. . . . Grids, spreadsheets, and algorithms take away the sensory connection to our lives, where our feet are, what we're seeing, all the raw materials of life, which by their very nature are disorganized." She extends her consideration of the subjective impact by explaining how a focus on data deprives people of a sense of autonomy and choice, "because if you're going by the data and the formula, there's only one way."[41] And that way is increasingly catastrophically framed.

The mode of rationality underlying the exaltation of data to unquestioned truth is antithetical to other modes of consciousness that recognize and value what cannot be measured as being essential to a poetic existence. It also ignores or diminishes the human experiences in which democratic values of social relations are rooted: the bonds of solidarity, community, friendship, compassion, and love. In doing so, it carries the weight of a deadly form of dehumanizing logic wedded to notions of control, violence, and ideological purity.[42] It is a form of rationality that serves the interests of the rich and obscures modes of thinking that are more capacious and reflective in their ability to address broader conceptions of identity, citizenship, and non-market values such as trust, cooperation, and confidence in one another.

It bears repeating: reality is now shaped by the culture's infatuation with a narrow, depoliticizing rationality, or a more complex version of what Frankfurt School theorist Max Horkheimer once called instrumental reason. It is the triumph of the technical vision of the world (techne) over its more poetic possibilities (poesis). Bruce Feiler, writing in the *New York Times*, argues that not only are we now awash in data, but "unquantifiable arenas like history, literature, religion, and the arts are receding from public life, replaced by technology, statistics, science, and math. Even the most elemental form of communication, the story, is being pushed aside by the list."[43] We see this in the pernicious intellectual violence of the likes of Richard Dawkins, who deemed the narration of fairy tales to children to be dangerous on account of the fact that it encourages worldviews that cannot be empirically verified—as if imagination must be scientifically quantified. Dawkins would do well to remember that a great mathematician who aliased as Lewis Carroll appreciated the importance of the imagination, and indeed the motivational impulse to reinvent the world that drives the poetics of technical scientism. Historical memory and public space are indeed the first casualties in this reign of technocratic suffocation, which models agency only on consumerism and value only on exchange value. The cult of the measurable is enthralled by instant statistical evaluation, and fervently believes that data hold the key to our collective fate. John Steppling sums up the brutal nature of this ideological colonization of the imagination and the monopoly it claims on the present. He writes:

> Today, the erasure of space is linked to the constant hum of data information, of social networking, and of the compulsive repetition of the same. There is no space for accumulation in narrative. Emotional or intellectual accumulation is destroyed by the hyper-branded reality of the Spectacle. So, the poor are stigmatized for sleep. It is a sign of laziness and sloth. Of lassitude and torpor. The ideal citizen is one at work all the time. Industrious and attentive to the screen image or the sound of command. Diligence has come to

mean a readiness to obey. A culture of shaming and reprimand is based on a model of reality in which there is no history to reflect upon. Today's mass culture only reinforces this. The "real" is a never-changing present. Plots revolve around the idea of disrupting this present, and then returning to this present. Actual tragedy, Chernobyl or Bhopal or Katrina, are simply ignored in terms of their material consequences. What matters are events that disrupt the Empire's carefully constructed present reality.[44]

Zygmunt Bauman and David Lyons have connected the philosophical implications of experiencing a reality defined by constant measurement to the fact that most people now allow their private expressions and activities to be monitored by the security-surveillance state.[45] No one is left unscathed. In the current historical conjuncture, neoliberalism's theater of violence joins forces with new technologies that can easily "colonize the private" even as it holds sacrosanct the notion that any "refusal to participate in the technological innovations and social networks (so indispensable for the exercise of social and political control) . . . becomes sufficient grounds to remove all those who lag behind in the globalization process (or have disavowed its sanctified idea) to the margins of society."[46] With people habituated to data gathering and number crunching, techno-fetishism has become not only permissible but laudatory—bolstered by a general ignorance of how a market-driven culture induces all of us to sacrifice our secrets, private lives, and very identities to social media, corporations, and the surveillance state.[47]

What we are witnessing with the Internet and social media is a new type of confessional in which all that matters is interviewing oneself endlessly and performing private acts as content for public consumption. Facebook "likes," lists of "friends," and other empty data reduce our lives to numbers and the illusions

of power that now define who we are. Technocratic rationality rules while thoughtful communication—translated into data
without feeling, meaning, or vision—withers. Lacking any sense
of larger purpose, it is not surprising that individuals become addicted to outrageous entertainment. Of course, the confessional
society does more than produce its own private data storm and
exhibit a narcissistic obsession with performing publicly the most
personal and intimate elements of the self; it also allows one to
flee from any sense of ethical responsibility or genuine friendship. Moreover, it is complicit with a surveillance state in which,
as Bauman observes, "social networks offer a cheaper, quicker,
more thorough and altogether easier way to identify and locate
current or potential dissidents than any of the traditional instruments of surveillance . . . a true windfall for every dictator and
his secret services."[48]

Hidden in Plain Sight

The lines between the spectacle of violence and the reality of
everyday violence have become blurred, making it difficult to
respond to, let alone understand, the economic, political, and
social formations that now rule neoliberal societies. Violence
has become so normalized and ingrained in our political imaginaries that it no longer has a history. In other words, even as
its underlying political and economic structures are shown to
be interwoven with the social fabric of neoliberal societies, the
painful memories it evokes disappear quickly among the bar-
rage of spectacles of violence and advertisements addressing us
not as ethical beings but as customers seeking new commodities,
instant pleasure, and ever more shocking thrills. At the same
time, such violence reinforces our preoccupation with surveillance, incarceration, and the consumer-level security industry
that profits from a general state of panic. As with our sense of
time and history, the impact upon our sense of space has been
dramatically altered as we witness a full-spectrum takeover of

public spaces by a culture of securitization. This is happening to whatever public spaces have not been sold off to the higher bidder by state power, as we now see a rapid growth of private military zones operating at the behest of corporate power and in the service of neoliberal rule.

Our societies have become addicted to violence, and this dependency is fostered by conditions of unending war that reach into the intimate depths of our societies. War in this instance is not how it is publicly represented: as the outgrowth of policies designed to protect the security and well-being of civilian populations (as if war is ever waged for the benefit of marginal groups within the social body). This state of permanent war, the continuance of which serves the interests of the corporate surveillance state, is possible because, as C. Wright Mills pointed out, it deploys a "military metaphysics"[49]—or a militarized definition of reality promoted by a complex of forces that includes corporations, defense industries, politicians, financial institutions, and universities. War provides jobs, profits, political payoffs, research funds, and forms of political and economic power that reach into every aspect of society. It is also one of the most honored virtues, as militaristic values now infuse almost every aspect of daily life. As war in the most privatized sense becomes the condition of possibility for political rule, it erodes the distinction between war and peace, fed by a sense of hysteria that makes shared anxieties about the potential for some catastrophe the primary register of social relations.

As Chris Hedges explains, a society commanded by a military metaphysics can only view "human and social problems as military problems."[50] This conceptual merging of war and everyday violence is most evident in the way the language of war saturates how policymakers talk about waging war on drugs, poverty, and the underclass. This militaristic language does more than promote a set of unifying symbols that embrace a survival-of-the-fittest ethic and elevate conformity over dissent, the strong over the weak, and fear over responsibility. It also gives rise to a failed democratic ethos in which violence becomes the most important mediating force in shaping all social relationships. Surely the looming failure of civilian democracy should make us all ask what has led to this radical turn toward a military mindset where insensitivity to cruelty is matched by prurient images of violence.

Part of this process is due to the fact that our societies are distorted by an unprecedented "huge volume of exposure to . . . images of human suffering."[51] Under regimes of neoliberalism, we are politically immobilized by a lethal mix of privatization, commodification, violence, and an individualized social order. This is made worse by the fact that what is distinct about neoliberalism's love affair with the spectacle of violence is that, as Étienne Balibar observes, "politics and violence now mutually inform each other in a new and more intense form of symbiosis" that embraces "the new visibility of extreme violence."[52] We would do well here to heed the warning of Bauman, who argues there are social costs that come with this immersion in a culture of staged and openly glorified violence. One possible consequence is that "the sheer numbers and monotony of images may have a 'wearing off' impact, [and] to stave off the 'viewing fatigue,' they must be increasingly gory, shocking, and otherwise 'inventive' to arouse any sentiments at all or indeed draw attention. The level of 'familiar' violence, below which the cruelty of cruel acts escapes attention, is constantly rising."[53] As with the horror movie genre and its endless sequels, the audience's appetite can only be quenched with more ingenious and sophisticated ways of killing those who are written into the plot as the already expendable. This raises a number of questions regarding ethical care and cultural sensitivity for the subject of violence in our media-saturated age. How, for instance, might we devise a meaningful critique of violence that would allow us to rethink its pedagogical imperatives?

The remarkable cinematic work of Michael Haneke offers a poignant example here. Haneke has gone on record to discuss his personal revulsion for witnessing violence and the fact that he finds the staging of violence to be a truly formidable challenge.[54] Indeed, for Haneke, the task of the film director is precisely to render violence intolerable, such that the witness cannot abide its performance. This is apparent throughout his body of work, for despite the fact that violence is a central theme to most of his films, it is largely noticeable by its absence from the cinematic script. And yet, in presenting violence in this way, the message in terms of its political and cultural qualities is amplified exponentially. As Max Silverman has duly noted, "in a number of his films, Haneke strips away the veneer of bourgeois society to reveal its violent underside which is hidden beneath."[55] Drawing particular attention to the disturbing movie *Funny Games*, in which a family retreat becomes the scene for cruel and harrowing brutality, Silverman explains, "bourgeois domestic space, and the banal format of the game or reality show, is transformed into the sadistic space of the torture chamber or concentration camp in which 'normal' social rules and ethics have been waived." Hence, what Haneke demonstrates throughout this sadistic play is that residents of "a world without law and ethics—do not inhabit a separate world but are deeply embedded in the structures of contemporary popular culture, and within the legal and ethical framework of modern democratic societies." Indeed, for Silverman, the subtlety and ethical care for the subject of violence evident in Haneke's work allows for a disturbing revelation:

> What is perhaps truly shocking here is the way in which we do not recognize the links between everyday life and the violent disposing of lives, the way in which we are blind to the true nature of this political reality. The family's inability to understand the "logic"

at play here is due to their blind attachment (and our own) to "normal" conventions which fail imaginatively to perceive the presence of a camp "logic" within the logic of bourgeois law and popular culture. . . . Haneke not only forces us to witness the real violence that is hidden by contemporary popular culture; we are also made to confront the possibility that that culture (our culture) is late capitalism's version of camp life and, what is more, that it is pleasurable as we consume it avidly on a daily basis.

THREE

THE DESTRUCTION OF HUMANITY

Casualties of War

One of the real casualties of the post-9/11 terror wars has been our belief that we can transform the world for the better. The effects of the violence have largely delegitimized the once comman belief that the wars were guided by the humanitarian principle of individual and social emancipation, just as the rule of law in the nations at war has given way to a perpetual state of martial emergency. *Humanitarian* war has destroyed the very concept of such a principle at a time when it has never appeared more urgent and necessary. The responsibility to protect has become hijacked by a militaristic ethos that results in the widespread slaughter of many of those whom it claims to be protecting. What therefore inevitably remains is an increasingly dystopian landscape that can only envision the future as ruinous and the coming of events that are endlessly catastrophic. There is little doubt that the decade that followed the September 11 attacks was marked by a real sense of resignation. Civilian politics felt merely illusionary as wars were carried out in our name, yet against our wishes. We watched the seemingly endless investment in military capacities for destruction, knowing full well that this debt would eventually burden us all. Allied casualties—not civilian deaths—became an ethically alarming gauge of how things were going. It simply did not matter how many innocent families and communities were destroyed as the military invasion and occupation pressed onward year after year. Moreover, providing commitment to the "end" took precedence over the madness of killing hundreds of thousands of people with little justification or regret.

There is a broader genealogy that must be accounted for here if we are to understand more fully the political stakes in a post-9/11 world. What happens in the post-9/11 moment cannot be neatly explained as some reaction to the violence of that fateful day. The appropriation of humanitarian discourse for the furtherance of war and military intervention was slowly maturing within neoliberal discourses and their calls for political intervention for some considerable time. Much of the post–Cold War humanitarian ethos can be dated in fact to the Ethiopian famine of the 1980s which created for the first time the idea of global witness and elicited a heart-wrenching desire to respond to and alleviate the suffering of strangers. Even here, however, with this most benevolent of causes, representations of the violence and suffering played into very familiar Western tropes as images of starvation and helplessness connected a seemingly apocalyptic situation with almost a redemption-like response. The standout image here was *TIME* magazine's "Famine" cover of December 21, 1987, which encapsulated the moment in remarkable representational similarity to Michelangelo's *Pietà* depicting Mary and Jesus after the crucifixion. Such redemptive iconography functioned politically. Indeed, it began what Mark Duffield calls "the requiem for the prophets"[1] as the potency of imagery was mobilized for political action and military interventions that spoke both to liberal rights and to the furtherance of neoliberal governance.

As the 1990s progressed, we witnessed the overt politicization of war images for the intention of justifying people's "liberation" through militarized violence that would eventuate the colonization and widespread transformation of entire societies. To echo the sentiments of Tony Blair, who carried this logic seamlessly through into the post-9/11 security terrain: "There is no compromise possible with such people, no meeting of minds, no point of understanding with such terror. Just a choice: defeat it or be defeated by it."[2] This was the discourse of certainty that thrived on militant ultimatums while abandoning any attempt at self-reflection or thoughtfulness. It has been argued that in such circumstances it is possible to maintain our civilizational credentials because war as we wage it always adheres to humanitarian principles.[3] Hence, alongside the emergence of the oxymoronic novelty "humanitarian war" we also encounter the official marketing of spin that pitches violence as a necessary thread in the fabric of humanitarianism, while casting aside excessive force and the raw realities of neoliberal violence as mere collateral damage.

The logic of violence at play here is a radical departure from the logic underpinning the mass violence of the twentieth century. There is no longer an effort made to draw upon a pre-existing "myth of nation" that people needed to defend and uphold. Such violence can no longer be connected to a project that is established and foundational. Humanity, instead, as Blair affirmed time and time again, is to be realized by the wars fought in its name. Its myth can only be realized by the violence of its very construction. What type of people then, we might ask, are produced when violence brings about their very realization? And what does this say about the poverty of our political imaginations when the only way humanity can be it seems unified is through a commitment to forms of violence that are empty of morality and unchecked in terms of their social costs?

It seems that there is little escape from a world that is fated to move from crisis to crisis. How this is understood and managed by the dominant cultural apparatuses of neoliberal power represents one mode of critical intervention. It is achieved, in part, by sanitizing public memory. Critical knowledge and oppositional struggles are all but erased from newspapers, radio, television, film, and increasingly from those educational and cultural institutions that engage in critical pedagogy by attempting to make sense of our present conjuncture in order to rethink the world anew. Historical consciousness has been transformed into narratives of ceaseless, unavoidable catastrophe, devoid of any engagement with wider structures of power and the underlying conditions of our ongoing oppression. As Theodor Adorno once put it, "The murdered are [now] cheated out of the single remaining thing that our powerlessness can offer them: remembrance."[4]

Critical thinking in such times becomes a burden, as being able to question the fundamental ontological and epistemological parameters in all their catastrophic permutations is tantamount to being at odds with the prevailing orthodoxy and the dystopian logics of rule contemporary neoliberalism thrives upon. One could go further and argue that thinking itself becomes dangerous. Not only do uncertainty and precariousness breed anxiety and insecurity, they are repackaged as the only viable way to envisage our political futures. Nowhere is this more evident today than in the doctrine of resilience, which has become a defining mode of subjectivity for an age that has normalized catastrophe and its promises of violence. Indeed, as argued elsewhere, while it is tempting to focus on the doctrine of resilience as originating within ecological circles, the humanities and social sciences reveal something more about the implicit political stakes.[5] One of the more perverse cases of this doctrine's symbolism is found in the recently "christened" USS *New York*. "Forged from the steel of the World Trade Center," this latest warship embodies the most potent expression of "bounce-backability." As former New York Governor George E. Pataki explained, "We're very proud that the twisted steel from the World Trade Center towers will soon be used to forge an even stronger national defense. . . . The USS *New York* will soon be defending freedom and combating terrorism around the globe, while also ensuring that the world never forgets the evil attacks of September 11, 2001, and the courage and strength New Yorkers showed in response to terror." As former New York Governor George E. Pataki explained, "We're very proud that the twisted steel from the World Trade Center towers will soon be used to forge an even stronger national defense. . . . The USS *New York* will soon be defending freedom and combating terrorism around the globe, while also ensuring that the world never forgets the evil attacks of September 11, 2001 and the courage and strength New Yorkers showed in response to terror."[6]

Politics in these "terrifyingly normal times" is now sapped of its democratic vitality just as the logic of disposability has seeped deeply into the economic and cultural structures of neoliberal societies. As nihilistic tendencies permeate all modes of governance and public policy, any semblance of social justice withers. It has become increasingly difficult for people to transform their struggles into questions of political literacy and social responsibility, while many of those engaged in intellectual work now speak their own language, which is rarely translated "back into the language of society."[7] Under these conditions, we are asked to abandon critical thought, disregard critical historical narratives, and surrender to pedagogies of cynicism. How can we explain the shameless denial of history by the likes of Dick Cheney and Tony Blair if not through the normalization of a deeply embedded cynicism wherein the political classes continue to distort even the most recent of memories? How often are we told that our recollection of events is somehow misguided, and that we must surrender to the intimidation of those in power? "There is no alternative" thus becomes more than some economic mantra; it conditions everything from the resort to violence to the embedding of political formations that benefit the few and marginalize the masses through the illusion of power.

In the place of intellectually energized critical education and politically vibrant public spheres, the immensely powerful corporations and entertainment industry offer up for mass consumption spectacles that encourage a flight from politics and interrogative context. Beyond the increasing violence entrenched in celluloid Hollywood spectacles, a televised shame culture features a host of programs that, when not focused on narcissistic confessionals, make a mockery of poverty and celebrate the corporate values embedded in survival-of-the-fittest "Reality" TV. As Zygmunt Bauman writes of the popular reality television program *Big Brother*:

> If the camps served as laboratories in which the limits of the totalitarian tendency endemic to modern society but "under normal circumstances" tamed and attenuated were tested, Big Brother shows do the same for the "new modernity"—our modernity. Unlike those experiments, though, the contemporary testing of tendencies is conducted publicly, in the limelight, in front of millions of spectators . . . letting the subjects play their own games and blame themselves in the event that the results are not up to their dreams.[8]

Reality TV thus presented is not so much a sick distortion of reality as a compensatory fantasy (of hyper-individualized agency) that could also be viewed as a microcosm of the larger social order—hence its function as a normalizing or "disimagining" force. It is little wonder that widespread cynicism has replaced political aspiration as public life is foreclosed by the ever-encroaching domain of the private. Social ills and human suffering become more difficult to identify and understand, let alone purposefully engage. What Bauman elsewhere describes as "the exit from politics and withdrawal behind the fortified walls of the private" has resulted in not only a society that has stopped questioning itself, but also the decline and disappearance of those discourses, social relations, and public spaces in which people can speak, exercise, and develop the capacities and skills necessary for critically encountering the world.[9] The result is that in "our contemporary world, post 9/11, crisis and exception [have] become routine, and war, deprivation, and [the machineries of death] intensify despite ever denser networks of humanitarian aid and ever more rights legislation."[10]

The depoliticization of the public sphere works in tandem with the spectacles of violence that increasingly permeate all aspects of society.[11] These spectacles curate and enforce modes of thinking that render challenges to the system—social and environment justice activism, for example—as dangerous, if not criminal. On both the domestic and foreign fronts, violence is the most prominent feature of neoliberal modes of political engagement. It is our greatest export industry. It is about all that we produce. Soldiers are idealized, and violence becomes an omnipresent form of entertainment pumped endlessly into the culture. When wars become the primary organizing principle for shaping relations abroad, at home a corrosive pathology becomes deeply rooted. The militaristic mindset becomes the mark not of a few individuals, but of a society that, as Erich Fromm once pointed out, becomes delirious and fixated with the promise of violence to come.[12] Arendt's deeply disturbing "dark times" thus appear in a new guise as the concentrated power of the corporate, political, cultural elite creates societies that have become a breeding ground for psychic disturbances and pathological behaviors now commonplace. Meanwhile, greed, inequality, and oppressive power relations wage an assault on all collective political imaginations.

As civilian societies become more militarized, civil liberties are displaced by security concerns and lockdown preparedness. In the United States, President Barack Obama has merely continued the violence initiated by the Bush administrations of the previous decade and even increased programs such as targeted assassinations and immigrant deportations as instruments of foreign policy. At the local level, police across the country have been expanding their powers by procuring and deploying the most advanced military technologies brought back from theaters of war, while going so far as to subject people to invasive body searches, even when they had only been stopped for minor traffic violations. One man in New Mexico was stopped for failing to come to a complete halt at a stop sign. On the baseless allegation that he might be harboring illegal narcotics, he was taken to a hospital and forced to undergo eight anal cavity searches, including a colonoscopy.[13] No illegal substances were found. When the police believe they have the right to issue warrants that allow doctors to perform enemas and colonoscopies without consent, and anyone they choose can be subjected to such invasive indignities, then genuinely felt "terror" takes on a new and perilous meaning. Entire neighborhoods inhabited by low-income families of color have been turned into war zones by paramilitarized police, reinforcing violence and criminalization as the default approach to all encounters with the inhabitants of these zones of disposability. Even within schools, those sites traditionally entrusted with the responsibility to nurture and safeguard students, young people are being arrested in record numbers.[14] Many U.S. schools have become little more than holding centers for youth from low-income communities of color whose profiling already attributes to them certain levels of disposition to criminality.[15]

The poor, homeless, and unemployed are continually blamed as if individual responsibility explains the ballooning gap in wealth, income, and power, or the growing state violence that supports it. Impoverished people end up in homeless shelters or in debtor's jail for not paying parking tickets or their bills, while the heads of banks, hedge funds, and other financial services who engage in all manner of fraud and predation are rarely prosecuted to the full extent of the law.[16] Surely if there were a crime against humanity worthy of the term, it has been the willful destruction of both the global economy and the environmental commons that continues, in a multitude of ways, to subject many of the world's citizens to the violence of the everyday.

Neoliberalism has no real language for promoting community-level democracy and the political freedoms, public well-being, and social responsibility it both depends on and advances. Increasingly, our social and cultural landscapes resemble an odd merger of the shopping mall and the prison. Contemporary life suffers from a socially disembodied version of possessive individualism, debilitating a viable notion of freedom with the catastrophe of privatization that no longer even hides its catastrophic nature. In fact, it thrives on its very possibility and occurrence. The inevitable outcome is a series of profiteering disasters and crises, matched by the rise of surveillance and the carceral state with its sophisticated architectures of criminalization and control. This all-encompassing reduction of society into a security enclave is justified at the outset by dread of those excess humans considered disposable, along with fear of anyone capable of questioning the prevailing wisdom. Indeed, while certain groups are invariably profiled more than others, not one of us is exempt as a potential suspect; surveillance, therefore, is now continuous, ubiquitous, and normal as pie.

The human capacity to tolerate mass violence and widespread systematic abuse, as Adorno, Arendt, Deleuze, and Foucault understood all too well, has a long shadow that refuses to simply disappear into the pages of a fixed and often forgotten history. Such violence has never been a static entity capable of being defeated by political or economic forces such as neoliberalism. And it now permeates the biopolitical practices of our societies as the promotion of neoliberal ways of living is upheld by the vagaries of the market; the continual use of technology such as drones to engage in old and new methods of torture and killing at home and abroad; propaganda campaigns and the use of force to undermine civil liberties; prosecutions of whistle-blowers who speak out against the abuses of the state or powerful corporations; and the rise of mass incarceration that is shamefully reminiscent of fascist regimes of the past. Even now, it would be possible to write the history of twenty-first-century fascism. But it would be misguided to simply focus our attention on the resurrection of chauvinistic nationalism and the claims to national supremacy being made by right-wing political parties in many countries across the globe. The desire for and abuse of power are as multifarious as the changing nature of regimes of control.

The Predatory Formations of Neoliberalism

It has long since been explained how capitalists exploit whatever offers the potential for surplus value. Limit conditions have only been recognized by its advocates in order to be transgressed and purposefully commodified. Indeed, the history of capitalistic development has been one of continued expropriation and plunder of the world's resources—including its people. Neoliberalism, however, as its frontmen from Hayek to Friedman have openly testified, represents something that is much more than a system of economic organization and reasoning. It makes overt political, ethical, moral, and cultural claims to authenticate forms of individual subjectivity premised on the purity of profit maximization rationales, along with claims to rightful stewardship over the global domain and its resources as no less than a matter of security, peace, and prosperity. From this perspective, neoliberalism has always been about governance, not merely the virtues of a self-regulating invisible hand (although Adam Smith's divine connotations here should be duly noted, as advocates of the "free market" no doubt makes distinct theological claims).

Neoliberalism is a predatory formation—or what Deleuze and Guattari have termed a "war machine"—that is willing to appropriate, manipulate, or fabricate whatever vocabulary or discourse is necessary to enforce its rule and justify its expansion, thereby continually adapting its principles in whatever ways will maintain power given the conditions of the times. Notions of freedom, individualism, autonomy, justice, and democracy itself are now mediated through the irrational belief that economic rationality extends into all domains, modes of agency, and institutions of society. What now gets transformed under neoliberalism is not merely the economy, but the whole of social life as the market becomes the template for curating which issues, communities, and people are acknowledged, which are exploited, which are criminalized, and which are simply ignored.

Many authors have noted how the lines between neoliberalism and classical liberal theory today have blurred beyond all recognition. Neoliberal societies are those that have been colonized by the dictates of the market, such that the very basis of subjectivity itself is shaped and defined by a consumerist ethos and its modes of authentication and disqualification. Nowhere has this been more apparent than in the militarization of every aspect of the public realm—not least, the civic idea that we have all too "human" obligations to one another. Under such circumstances, militarized community replaces democratic community. Every war for the past two decades has been presented to us as a humanitarian war in which the desire to save strangers and build lasting capacities for peace has been tied to discourses of security, rights, and justice—but far from producing any of these noble ends, they leave us witness instead to the widespread transformation of local societies by the effective imposition of neoliberal regimes of militarized governance and occupation.[17]

There is an important genealogy to map out here in terms of war and violence and how they conform to neoliberal rationalities and their dystopic visions. During the wars of the past decade, in particular, two visions of combat have emerged. The first was premised on the logic that sophisticated technology could replace the need to suffer human casualties. The second was premised on a more humanitarian ethos, which demanded local knowledge and engagement with dangerous populations.

For a brief period in the 1990s, for example, the United Nations attempted to use the humanitarian plight of war-affected populations to broker peace among state and non-state perpetrators. The narcissistic violence of the global terror wars has put this secondary vision into lasting crises as the violence of liberal encounters has inevitably dispensed with any universal commitment to rights and justice. Not only did we appear to be the principal authors of violence, thereby challenging the notion that underdevelopment and impoverishment were the true causes of social endangerment worldwide, but populations within liberal consumer societies lost faith in the belief that it was possible to engage in war for the purpose of creating lasting peace. Among the casualties of the terror wars, then, has been the belief that we might engage and transform the world and its peoples for the better. Proactivism is thus firmly displaced by a catastrophic reasoning that both enforces inactivism and literally places us at the point of extinction.

As war by assassination disappears into the background, citizens and professionals who have nothing to hide are now expected to enact their innocence by living openly under the electronic gaze. On the one hand, to be connected means to have access to the only rights that seemingly matter—the smart rights of digital passage and consumer spending privileges. Disconnection, on the other hand, is not only pathologically inexplicable; it is a dumb state that is cause enough for suspicion, alarm, and disposability. Hence, while violence continues to be packaged for Western media consumption, its transmission into people's homes and now personal devices blurs any possible distinction between the realms of a civic and a militaristic order such that the interconnected subject actively embraces a technological mindset that privatizes everything—violence included. As the previous campaign to stop Joseph Kony, the Ugandan warlord, suggested, we are all now invited to be mercenaries. The call to violence is but a "like" click away from the composition of a digitized frame that is less about contents than about the immediacy and potency of affective registers that defy more considered deliberation.

There is an important point to emphasize here regarding the political and social function of technologies. No technology can be removed or abstracted from regimes of power. Indeed, while we are well aware that the creative impetus for technological innovation gestures towards the poetic, its veritable appropriation and application all too quickly turns autonomous potentiality into the force of reason. With this in mind, the technologies we produce are always and already revealing of the desires that circulate within any given political and social order. They might reveal an individual's desire for flight from the conventional order of things; they might also reveal the changing cartographies of power and violence as the ubiquitous nature of certain technological outputs prove to be paradigmatic in the construction of entirely new social morphologies that radically alter the ontological configurations of life-world systems. Nowhere is this more evident than in the militarized investment in technological innovations. Not only have such products been integral to inducing profound social transformations (the Internet being the obvious contemporary example), but they have subsequently proven to be remarkably diagnostic of prevailing political fortunes as they appear to animate both the productive and destructive qualities of power.

Drone violence is particularly diagnostic, as it reveals a *retreat* from the world of people and the strategic move toward *violence at a distance*.[18] While the first recorded drone strike was authorized by President George Bush in Pakistan on June 18, 2004, under Barack Obama it has become the more favored method for dealing with troublesome elements. Indeed, while the Bush administration favored extraordinary rendition and indefinite detention, the Obama policy for preventing the growth of inmate population in camps such as Guantánamo has been to prioritize execution over capture. In this case, has inhumane torture and barbarity been replaced by the more "dignified" method of targeted assassination, as some would argue? Much of the debate on drone violence tends to question its legality, as it doesn't fit within established rules of war and suffers from poor democratic accountability. This point is made by Derek Gregory, who writes: "Although the Obama administration insists that its targeting procedures adhere to the laws of armed conflict, the covert nature of a war conducted by a clandestine agency ensures that most of its victims are wrapped in blankets of secrecy. Accountability is limited enough in the case of a declared war; in an undeclared war it all but disappears."[19]

Proponents have countered Gregory's claim by insisting that concerns regarding a lack of oversight are widely overstated. Amitai Etzioni, for instance, has argued that while there are good enough reasons to maintain levels of secrecy here, there is enough information available in the public domain to reassure us that "drones are preferable to most instruments of warfare."[20] Such arguments invariably adopt a familiar techno-moralizing tone, as questions of legal status are subordinated to the technology's alleged humane qualities, in that targeted precision, they assert, ensures that only those worthy of being killed succumb to the fate of the aerial assault.

Authors such as Michael Boyle have attempted to move beyond such debates and focus on the policy failure caused by the technology itself. Boyle begins his analysis by following the accusation that Obama in particular has abandoned his liberal sensibilities and election promises by being "just as ruthless and indifferent to the rule of law as his predecessor." He explains: "while President Bush issued a call to arms to defend 'civilization' against the threat of terrorism, Obama has waged his war on terror in the shadows, using drone strikes, special operations, and sophisticated surveillance to fight a brutal covert war against Al-Qaeda and other Islamist networks." What Boyle refers to as "the Obama approach" features little congressional oversight, with attacks taking place in Afghanistan, Pakistan, Somalia, and Yemen, all the while "most Americans remain unaware of the scale of the drone programme operating in these countries and of the destruction it has caused in their name." Crucially, for Boyle, it is of little consequence whether drone violence is morally or legally right, or whether the technology itself succeeds or fails in its mission. What matters is whether the policy underlying its use is as effective as its proponents claim. He argues it fails to achieve the goals of being a more humane and less destructive form of intervention when, in fact, "drone strikes corrode the stability and legitimacy of local governments, deepen anti-American sentiment and create new recruits for Islamist networks aiming to overthrow these governments."[21]

While Boyle's analysis does offer a more honest reflection of the way violence is thought about at the policy level, he pays little attention to the wider context or the ways drone warfare connects to social and technological dynamics integral to contemporary forms of neoliberal rule. Whereas Bush launched a trend-breaking, one-sided territorial assault on Iraq and Afghanistan in order to defend "civilization," with the return of liberal inhibition following what were effectively U.S. ground defeats, Obama has waged a technologically mediated war in the deregulated atmospheric shadows where U.S. technological supremacy allows for the continuation of uninhibited forms of violence. Ostensibly out of respect for public sensibilities, a "precise" or "surgical" form of violence is delivered remotely to distant adversaries. Moreover, this violence is occluded or absent not simply because it often remains classified or hidden. Select information regarding drone attacks is released to the public, as Etzioni has pointed out, but that is not the key issue at stake here. Rather, our concern is that the technologies, infrastructures, and design used in remote warfare are essentially the same as those that support the economy and consumer society.

Markets, far from the mythology of being "free" and de-regulated, are regulated differently in a neoliberal age. Increasingly, their social arrangements are shaped by military ideologies and formations. The military not only secures markets crucial to its interests—ones that both generate profit and legitimize the ongoing militarization of society—but also produces a culture of fear supporting an inflated military budget that defies justi-fication, whether economically, politically, or ethically. As David Theo Goldberg observes, "the logics of militarization—its order(ing) of things, the modes of organization . . . its wars of thinking and doing . . . are fused with military structure, truth, temporality." The militaristic mindset operates alongside a militarized economic and social order, or what President Dwight Eisenhower termed "the military-industrial complex," in order to legitimate the ongoing militarization of society by producing modes of regulation and discipline that shape both domestic and foreign policies in the interests of those who hold power. [22] Both military drone strikes and commercial marketing systems rely on the same data-driven objectifying ideology, instrumentalized values, computer-based technologies, and algorithmic sense-making tools. For example, how Amazon.com mechanically suggests your next book purchase is not fundamentally different from how adversarial behavioral patterns are isolated and anticipated as the state curates whom to target for killing and whom to target just for surveillance. America's drones have not only become President Obama's private air force;[23] they have become a symbol of a new kind of lawful violence in the making, defined through a martial notion of permanent warfare and state of emergency that produces both a kind of micro-militarism enforced in small cultural spaces and a foreign policy marked by a kind of targeted violence that offers no testimony on its victims.[24]

Sickness of Reason

Mass violence is poorly understood if it simply refers to casualties on battlefields or continues to be framed through conventional notions of warfare. What we need is a sober and honest reflection on the memory of violence so that we are better equipped to understand its more subtle and sinister qualities. This reflection must go beyond memorialization of traumatic and horrifying world events, which alone can give the mistaken impression that we now live in more secure and peaceful times. What is required is a new vocabulary that can interrogate the disposability of entire populations in order to reveal its historical complexities and its novel and contemporary forms. As Adriana Cavarero rightly observes, "violence against the helpless is becoming global in ever more ferocious forms, [and] language . . . tends to mask it."[25] Such a task requires us to explore more fully how the violence of reason—its veritable sickness—connects to the spectacles of violence and their role in the formation of cultural and political communities.

How does a society become complicit in the disposal of entire communities in such a way that its spectacular display is enjoyed and openly celebrated? The threatening nature of the sickness of reason suggests more than simply ignorance, a lapse of alertness, or a lack of awareness. It points to what David L. Clark calls the breeding of horrors.due to "an inattentiveness to the never-ending task of critique, the failures of conscience, the wars against thought, and the flirtations with irrationality that lie at the heart of the triumph of everyday aggression, the withering of political life, and the withdrawal into private obsessions."[26]

In developing a framework for the complex modes through which mass violence is enacted in our time, we can turn to Michel Foucault's useful concept of the "biopolitical," which can be understood as what happens when power takes life itself to be the principal referent object for political strategies. Foucault introduced the term as a way to denounce the illusion of institutional peace and the inevitability of freedom despite the existence of free-flowing power relations. As he put the question, "When, how, and why did someone come up with the idea that it is a sort of uninterrupted battle that shapes peace, and that the civil order—its basis, its essence, its essential mechanisms—is basically an order of battle?"[27] There are two important aspects to this concept that must be dealt with here. First, when Foucault refers to "killing" in a biopolitical sense he does not simply refer to the vicious and criminal act of physically taking a life: "When I say 'killing,' I obviously do not mean simply murder as such, but also every form of indirect murder: the fact of exposing someone to death, increasing the risk of death for some people, or, quite simply, political death, expulsion, rejection and so on."[28] And second, despite the semblance of peace, it is incumbent upon the critical cartographer to bring into question normalized practices of human disposability so as to reveal the hidden order of politics.[29]

This represents an important shift in our understanding of violence. No longer simply content with exploring extra-judicial forms of violent abuse, Foucault turns our attention instead toward those forms of violence that take place in the name of human progress and the emancipatory subject. This type of violence permeates a hidden order of politics, a silent battle, concealed beneath the circuits of state- and corporate-sanctioned vocabularies of truth, civility, and prosperity. We have already argued that the dominant institutions that promoted social progress in the past, such as universities, are no longer sovereign in any popular sense of the term today. At the national level, state sovereignty has now been compromised by unrestricted corporate sovereignty, just as state power now more closely resembles the workings of an imprisoning state. At the same time, power now circulates in global networks, exceeding the bounded governance of the nation-state and indifferent to the specificity of its practices and outcomes. Power and violence have been elevated into the global space of flows, unchecked by state-based regulations or the pressures, however weakened, of democratic state responsibility and accountability to a citizenry.[30] The most evident development of this has been the "capitalization of peace" in which the global ravages of poverty, war, and violence are tied to neoliberal policies that proceed in the name of human togetherness/progress/unity yet conceal an inner logic of biopolitical separation and social containment.[31]

As politics is emptied of its ability to control global power, the moral bankruptcy of neoliberalism becomes evident in the hollowing out of the social state and the increasing force of the dominant discourses and policies that legitimate its extinction. For example, when the Bush and Obama administrations argued that the banks were too big to fail, we were presented with more than just another neoliberal conceit regarding supply-side economics and its practice of ensuring that the distribution of wealth and income continues to shift away from the poor and middle class toward the already enriched. The more dangerous conceit paved the way for the destruction of even the most minimal conditions for a sustainable democracy. While this subterfuge at one level argues that the victims of capitalism are guilty of waging class warfare, at the same time the ruling elite destroy all those public spheres capable of providing even minimal conditions for individuals to engage the capacities to think, feel, and act as engaged citizens. And they do it in the midst of a decrepit and weakened state of politics that holds corporate power unaccountable while endlessly repeating the poisonous mantra of deregulation, privatization, and commodification. The banking elite and the mega–financial services openly serve the rich, engage in widespread ecological devastation, and destroy the safety nets that serve the rest of society—low-income people and the middle class. But since the banking sector is seen to be integral to the vision of planetary stability and peace, it demands securing as a matter of human survivability.

The ruinous logic of militarization now provides global finance with the machinery of violence needed to dispense with the power of reason and the demands of global social responsibility. To put it another way, since the enforcement of global deregulation and security are central to the neoliberal project, we should be under no illusions about where military allegiance lies. George Bush certainly didn't send troops into Iraq and Afghanistan for the betterment of the victims of market fundamentalism at home or those Iraqis suffering under the ruthless dictatorship of Saddam Hussein. Neither was the more recent securitization of the London Olympics carried out to protect immigrant populations living on the margins in the capital's run-down areas. There is therefore no hegemonic discourse in any conventional sovereign geo-strategic sense of the term. Instead, what appears is a neoliberal will to rule that is upheld by a formidable school of intellectual thought and takes direct aim at the critically minded as a potentially dangerous community to be deterred or criminalized and vanquished. Reason in this sense is unmoored from its emancipatory trappings, reduced to a legitimating discourse for a notion of progress that operates in the service of repression and the militarization of thought itself.[32] How else to explain the ruthless attacks under neoliberal regimes, especially in the United States and the United Kingdom, on low-income populations, the welfare state, unions, public schools, the unemployed, and any institution or government policy that benefits the "undeserving" poor, young people, veterans, and the elderly? Though neoliberal rationality may strive for coherence in its economic worldview, it becomes clear in its treatment of human beings, especially society's most disadvantaged, that its mode of reasoning dissolves into nothing more than a politics of contempt and a culture of cruelty. More recently, the culture of cruelty has appeared full-blown in the United States through the savage expression of anti-immigrant fervor aimed at immigrant women and children during a protest in Murietta, California.

Bearing an eerie resemblance to the white protesters in Boston, Massachusetts, and Selma, Alabama, who attempted to prevent school integration, the Murietta protesters "with their faces contorted in hatred, screaming vile things at children" exhibited a racism and hate on a scale one would associate with the Ku Klux Klan and other extremist right-wing groups.[33] In this instance, the sickness of neoliberal reason and its dehumanizing economic calculus reveals a dark affinity with the kind of zealous appeals to social purity that evoke white militia, neo-Nazi political parties, violent thugs, and the darkest side of twentieth-century fascistic violence based on a pure hatred for the Other.

The contemporary sickness of neoliberal reason is not exclusively tied to state power and now works within expansive market-based modes of governance and the growing banking and financial sectors that exercise power. Reason embraces tyranny through the logic of the market and its principle of risk. It is most revealing to find that economic agencies are at the forefront of this policy that has made economic questions of prime political significance. During the 1990s organizations such as the World Bank increasingly became interested in political concerns, as the focus of their work (along with economics more generally) changed from the managed recoveries of national crises to the active promotion of better lives.[34] Transforming their remit from economic management to security governance, such organizations became moral agents in their own right, advocating economic solutions to the ravages of civil wars, criminality, shadow economies, poverty, endemic cultural violence, and political corruption. Neoliberalism thus became a source of political and financial legitimacy, determined not only to institute market-based structural reforms but also to establish the conditions for producing particular types of agency, subjects, and social relations—ones that would thrive by embracing an ethos of risk that essentially accepted social and economic insecurity as a trade-off for political security.

The unchecked celebration of a neoliberal subject who is willing to take market-based risks—through either financial speculation or acts of consumption—does more than provide a rationale for the corrupt trading practices of investment bankers and hedge fund power brokers; it also points to the closer connection between those considered the producers of capital and those who are now the new "at risk" disposable populations. The financial elite now view themselves as corporate missionaries promoting policies, practices, and ideas that are not only designated as universal but purported to take their inspiration from the divine. How else to interpret Goldman Sachs chief executive Lloyd Blankfein's comment that he is just a banker "doing God's work"?[35] Needless to say, those individuals and populations who are outside the accumulation, possession, and flow of capital are considered the new parasites whose simple presence threatens their host. That is, those negligent consumers (the poor), "enemy combatants," unpatriotic dissidents, youth of color, low-income white kids, immigrants, and others inhabiting the margins of global capital and its ecosystem of vast inequality and ruthless practices of disposability.

Neoliberal capitalism is not only wedded to the production of profits but also invested in a form of intellectual violence that legitimates its savage market-driven practices and the exercise of ruthless power. When applied to the intellectual terrain, to paraphrase C. Wright Mills, the violence of neoliberalism strives for nothing less than the breakdown of democracy, the disappearance of critical thought, and "the collapse of those public spheres which offer a sense of critical agency and social imagination."[36] Since the 1970s, we have witnessed the forces of market fundamentalism take aim at education, stripping it of its public values, critical content, and civic responsibilities as part of a broader goal of creating new subjects wedded to the logic of privatization, efficiency, flexibility, consumerism, and the destruction of the social state. The sickness of predatory neoliberalism is evident in its attempt to colonize not only education and other vital institutions, but the more intimate realms of consciousness, desire, and identity itself. Its stranglehold on the intellect seeks to suffocate agency by reducing it to a commodity and transforming all social relations into commercial transactions. Consciousness and desire in neoliberal regimes serve the market and produce subjects whose understanding of citizenship is diminished to consumerism and whose relationships to themselves and others are alienated into orbits of self-interest.

Bound largely by instrumental purposes and measurable paradigms, many institutions of higher education are now committed almost exclusively to economic growth, instrumental rationality, and the narrow, civically empty task of preparing students for paying off their massive student loans by immediately entering the workforce. The question of what kind of education is needed for students to be informed and active citizens is now rarely asked.[37] Hence it is no surprise, for example, to read that "Thomas College, a liberal arts college in Maine, advertises itself as Home of the Guaranteed Job!"[38] Within this market-centered discourse and model of the university, faculty are largely understood as a subaltern class of low-skilled entrepreneurs, removed from the powers of governance and subordinated to strictly instrumental policies, values, and practices.[39] Within both higher education and the educational force of the broader cultural apparatus—with its networks of knowledge production in the old and new media—we are witnessing the emergence and ascendance of powerful and ruthless market-driven notions of governance, teaching, learning, freedom, agency, and responsibility. Such modes of education do not foster a sense of organized responsibility central to a democracy, and they actively work to corrupt any commitment to critical pedagogy. As David Harvey insists, "the academy is being subjected to neoliberal disciplinary apparatuses of various kinds [while] also becoming a place where neoliberal ideas are being spread."[40]

Bringing the War Home

Many still prefer to deal with these emotional registers at the level of the individual as if they can somehow be abstracted from reasonable thought. This is unfortunate. More than absolving power of its affective qualities, it precludes any serious attempt at understanding how emotion has political and social signifi-cance. Pleasure and desire are in fact social categories. All desire, as Deleuze and Guattari argue, once properly evaluated is *assem-bled*. Importantly, however, the social ordering of desire under particular circumstances "gives desire a fascistic determina-tion."[41] The problem, as Eugene Holland puts it, is to question what exactly are the assemblages that produce the "thousand little monomanias [and] self-evident truths . . . giving any and everybody the mission of self-appointed judge, dispenser of jus-tice, policeman, neighborhood SS man."[42] Hence, to understand the relationship between the individual subject and its fascistic and narcissistic influences, we must interrogate the specific ways that regimes of power articulate desire and forms of pleasure that actively encourage self-subjugation and the willful oppres-sion of others to the point of their effective normalization.

When images of degradation and human suffering are marketed for their entertainment value, the body is no longer a sovereign space but a site of objectification and vulnerabili-ty, "the location of violence, crime, and social pathology."[43] As decadence and despair are made palatable in the wider culture by dominant forces that share the benefit, if not always the in-tent, of removing all dissent, people are increasingly alienated from one another and reduced to their own narrow spheres of existence. As a result, any viable notion of the democratic social sphere is subordinated to the violence of a deregulated market economy and its ongoing production of cultures of cruelty.[44] Representations of violence against people and communities cannot therefore be abstracted from a broader neoliberal regime in which the machinery of consumption endlessly trades in the production of sensationalist images designed for entertainment. This is especially true for spectacles of violence that are now not only stylistically extraordinary but also grotesque depictions of the culture that produced them. No longer mere bystanders to "every act of violence and violation," the public eagerly sacrifices any sense of ethical responsibility in order to experience sensations of pleasure from images of human suffering.[45] How else to explain the insistent demand by many that the U.S. government should have released the grisly yet openly celebrated images of Osama Bin Laden's corpse, even though the fact of his assassination was never in doubt? How might we understand the growing support, among the American populace in particular, for state-sanctioned torture and the lack of moral outrage in response to images that reveal its horrible injustices? Just as torture for many in the Western world has become an acceptable measure to take against potential "enemies," the spectacle of violence spreads through the culture with ever-greater intensity.

Terry Eagleton comments on the political implications and social costs of the neoliberal ordering of desire and its visceral sensations. He writes: "Sensation in such conditions becomes a matter of commodified shock-value regardless of content: everything can now become pleasure, just as the desensitized morphine addict will grab indiscriminately at any drug. To posit the body and its pleasures as an unquestionably affirmative category is a dangerous illusion, in a social order which reifies and regulates corporeal pleasure for its own ends just as relentlessly as it colonizes the mind."[46] This explains how controlling pleasure as both a normative and a performative practice is such an effective tool used by neoliberal public pedagogy in its campaign against democratic sensibilities. The entertainment-amusement complex, or "cultural apparatus" as C. Wright Mills called it, no longer merely traffics between popular culture and authority.[47] This apparatus and its public pedagogy have now been enlisted by neoliberalism's combination of market and politics in order to acclimatize the public to real violence through a commercialization of violence itself. Victims no longer have to be looked in the eye, since they often appear as just dots on an electronic screen. But more than merely neutralizing the horror of violence, spectacles now seduce their audiences, though not unproblematically, through both a new register and economy of pleasure and a machinery of affect rooted in the spectacle of hyper-violence. Staged violence is now anticipated with bated breath by viewers who all too willingly displace moral criteria with "the aesthetically spaced world, structured by the relevancies of [intense excitement], pleasure-potential, [and] interest arousal."[48]

The result of having our desires shaped in such intimate ways by our private acts of consumption is that real life increasingly mimics and reinforces the power of the staged spectacle. With the rise of new and highly advanced computer-generated digital and screen technologies, the space between images and the consequences of real violence becomes wider and less meaningful, just as the exercise of real violence becomes easier to perform. Video games, for instance, do more than indulge young participants in cartoonish orgies of violence, slaughter, and mayhem. They are also viewed as a source of valuable training by the U.S. Defense Department, which hires young people with video game skills to sit in secluded rooms in California and manipulate drone aircraft designed to target and kill America's "enemies" in countries such as Yemen, Iraq, Somalia, Pakistan, and Afghanistan. Killing becomes entirely removed from ethical responsibility, while humane actions are reduced to computer errors. Real-life cruel acts and their representations often escape critical attention because they make their first appearance in "unofficial" sites that operate outside of dominant broadcast culture. Going "viral," videos of such acts incite repeat viewing even as their mode of consumption through privatized technologies makes engaging in public discourse about them more challenging.

The now famous *Collateral Murder* video released by WikiLeaks is a "graphic video from Baghdad [that] shows a July 2007 attack in which U.S. forces, firing from helicopter gunships, wounded two children and killed more than a dozen Iraqis, including two Reuters employees."[49] The video verifies the presence of two photographers and a man who, though severely wounded, was later purposely killed along with the civilians who tried to rescue him. The voices of the soldiers on the recording are merciless, intense, and clearly excited by the pleasure gained from pursuing the targeted and reckless killings. Cruelty manifests itself in a depravity that is marketed for pleasure and incited by the possibility of a kill, regardless of whether the latter involves a fictional character in a video game or innocent victims such as women and children living in Iraq and Afghanistan. So how might we begin to ethically think of alternatives to the growing commercialization of violence?

Jacques Rancière argues that "the main procedure of political or critical art consists in setting out the encounter and possibly the clash of heterogeneous elements. The clash of these heterogeneous elements is supposed to provoke a break in our perception, to disclose some secret connection of things hidden behind the everyday reality."[50] Art thus functions here in a way that allows us to grasp the hidden depths of any given situation, to question what is not being questioned yet remains implicit in any given state of affairs. In this regard, critical art makes visible that which is hidden in plain sight. This is not in any way suggestive of an underlying conspiracy. It is to challenge directly the regime of truth that connects forms of violence with particular narratives such that an alternative angle of vision might be crafted.

For Rancière what is of importance here is not simply the quantity of any given representational genre.[51] We are already drowned in images of suffering that lack political context. It is how the image might function politically to give voice or not to the people who are victimized by power. As he explains, "the issue is not whether it is necessary to show the horrors suffered by the victims of some particular violence. It revolves around the construction of the victim as an element in a certain distribution of the visible."[52] What Rancière calls the "dispositif of visibility" thus points to a "spatiotemporal system in which words and visible forms are assembled into shared data, shared ways of perceiving, being affected, and imparting meaning."[53] It is all about producing or countering models of representation, reality, and meaning. Rancière points here to the earlier work of Martha Rosler whose "Bringing the War Home" series juxtaposed the violence of the Vietnam War with the tranquil domesticity of the American household. These images, he maintained, produced a dual effect by creating an "awareness of the system of domination that connected American domestic happiness to the violence of imperialist war, but also a feeling of guilty complicity in this system."[54] Building on this analysis, Michael Shapiro suggests that Rosler's photomontages disrupt familiar sequences of time as they "combine the longer-term historical moment of the increasing commoditization of the home and the shorter historical moment of the Vietnam War. As a result, the juxtaposition of the dual events gives a surcharge to the kind of distraction the images evoke because they disturb the complacency one ordinarily achieves by consummating the significance of an experience by naming it."[55]

We should acknowledge here that Rancière's contribution to political aesthetics owes considerable intellectual debt to Deleuze and Guattari. Indeed, he acknowledges the influence their work has had by informing his understanding of the importance of poetics and the political valence of art. Rancière cites directly a compelling passage from their book *What Is Philosophy?*:

The writer twists language, makes it vibrate, seizes hold of it, and rends it in order to wrest the percept from perceptions, the affect from affections, the sensation from opinion—in view, one hopes, of that still missing people. . . . This is precisely, the task of all art and, from colors and sounds, both music and painting similarly extract new harmonies, new plastic or melodic landscapes, and new rhythmic characters that raise them to the height of the earth's song and the cry of humanity.[56]

It is well documented that Deleuze had a passion for cinema and the movement-image. Indeed, perhaps in contrast to Susan Sontag, who spoke consistently of the depth made possible by the photographic still (as it concentrates one's attention due to an apparent suspension of time), for Deleuze cinema allowed for the critical production of "conceptual personas" so integral to rethinking and reimagining the world.

Shapiro has developed his critical analysis of images (art and cinema) through a geopolitical lens, bringing to light the complex political messages behind aesthetic representation in meaningful ways through his transdisciplinary methods that have awakened the discipline of international politics from its dogmatic slumber. Most significantly, his analysis in *Cinematic Geopolitics* counters one-dimensional readings of cinema as pure propaganda to reveal the resistive potential within the genre that often proves far more potent than any public sermon offered by a politician. Central to Shapiro's work is the concept of the "cinematic heterotopia," which provides the space for counter-representations and counter-narratives so often precluded from dominant media and mediatized landscapes of prime time television. As he writes, "Contemporary technologies now render the ethico-political relevance of cinema pervasively present. . . . The world of injustice can receive perpetual recognition because, to invoke Walter Benjamin's terms, its objects can be continually reactivated."[57]

We are reminded here of a remarkable contribution to international collaborative film titled *11, 09, 01*. Our interest is the 11 minute, 9 second segment directed by Samira Makhmalbaf and Ken Loach. Makhmalbaf's Iranian-set narrative shows the real tragedy of lives soon to be overtaken by "a very important global incident" to which they have no possible means of relating. The scene begins with Afghan refugees in Iran building a brick shelter to protect them from what they believe to be an inevitable violent response on part of the United States following 9/11. A local teacher subsequently appears and instructs the children who are helping with the building to go to school, noting, "Whatever happens to them will happen to you too. You can't stop atomic bombs with bricks. Send the children to class." It is the masterful use of child actors in this particular scene that allows Makhmalbaf to produce a form of criticality that works on a number of levels by: a) exposing the real poverty and violence of their local plight with the key actors remaining noticeably "nameless" throughout the montage; b) addressing the intellectual violence and pedagogical catastrophe of the situation as seen through the critical dualism in the discourse between teacher and pupil; and c) presenting the situation as absurd and yet devastatingly foreboding as the community imagines the worst to come. Aside from a remarkably haunting final scene when the young children are asked to stand in silence underneath a burning kiln tower, thereby tasking them with the impossibility of imagining what it must have felt like to stand at ground zero in Manhattan as the skyline was slowly consumed by the terrifying clouds of destruction, it is the illogical narratives of violence as seen through the children's reasoning and discourse that allow for a truly potent critique.

The contribution by Ken Loach exemplifies what Shapiro has termed "critical transversality," in which atrocities of the past are used to critique the violence of the present. Loach's meditation narrates a letter from a Chilean survivor of the U.S.-

supported toppling of the socialist Allende government on September 11, 1973—the date signified in the film as the first 9/11. In this personal description of the events addressed directly to the citizens of New York City, past and future collide through the shared experience of suffering. What is particularly compelling here is the fictional realism of the format as the tales of slaughter and barbarity are overlaid with the raw and unmediated footage of the atrocities. The real strength, however, is the compassionate tone that doesn't in any way seek to justify the violence; rather, it functions to connect the personal with the systematic and the past with the present such that the experience of September 11, 2001, cannot be reduced in meaning to a singular event and a singular atrocity. Situated in this broader historical context, the memory of 9/11 demands a broader frame of reference that denies us the simple comfort that the "original sin" of globalization narratives suggest.

FOUR

A PROMISE OF VIOLENCE

The Enemies Within

Two remarkable magazine covers appeared within the space of a few days that revealed a larger message about how society now perceives violence. On the face of it, the *TIME* magazine cover dedicated to Trayvon Martin and the *Rolling Stone* cover picturing the Boston Marathon bombing suspect Dzhokhar Tsarnaev have nothing in common except for some relation to a violent act. *TIME* magazine's "After Trayvon" edition that appeared on July 29, 2013, was presented as a response to a personal tragedy. The *Rolling Stone* "Boston Bomber" cover instead asked why a promising and popular student ended up becoming a "monster." While both covers caused some reaction, the latter in particular for its apparent glamorizing of the terrorist, neither has been compared and discussed in the broader context of the violence of our times. That is to say, the political contextualization of Trayvon's killing is altogether removed, while the politics of the bomber is effectively reduced to parental deficiencies and personality defects that made this more "whitened" embodiment ultimately the source of endangerment. Decontexualized, the images collapse the historical and the political into the private. As Robin D. G. Kelley points out in another context, this kind of representation "focusing on the *personal* obscures what is really at stake: ideas, ideology, the nature of change, the realities of power, and the evisceration of our critical faculties under the veil of corporate celebrity culture."[1] But what is actually going on with these forms of representation that might reveal more about the wider logics of power? And how do they speak to the present historical conjuncture?

Let's first examine the case of the "After Trayvon" issue of *TIME*. What is remarkably striking here is the form of the cover itself. The body of Trayvon Martin is altogether removed from the composition, replaced instead by an x-rayed hoodie top so reminiscent of airport style security. This image functions in two ways. First, we are left in no doubt that the guilty party here was, as a direct result of his affordable attire that invokes all too familiar stereotypes about the behaviors of the under-privileged, in fact the murdered youth. He is objectified as a se-curity concern in the most visible and obvious of ways. Second, the fact that Trayvon's body is removed from the composition effectively eliminates the question of race from the analytical arena. "After Trayvon" becomes in the clearest of pictorial ar-ticulations an example of what David Theo Goldberg calls "see-ing through racism." Joe Klein's accompanying article is a sure testament to this fact. While Klein acknowledges the verdict left many unanswered questions, he was nevertheless compelled to argue that "this is not the 1980s; race isn't the issue it was 30 years ago. It isn't binary—black and white—anymore. It was not beyond a reasonable doubt that Zimmerman was overacting in self-defense. Martin's death is an outrage, but it is not Emmett Till or Medgar Evers." Hence, for Klein, while there "will al-ways be injustices like the murder of Trayvon Martin," it is our color-blindness that will ensure that as far as a racial divide is concerned, "we are moving beyond all that."[2]

Complex issues get lost when spectacular events are taken over by a media frenzy that feeds on sound bites and simpli-fied answers. Media coverage focused an intense spotlight on the personal defects of the two men involved, with the result that important issues such as the social and human costs of a corpo-rate-driven gun culture, the privatization of security forces, the price paid by poor minority youth whose every act is criminal-ized, and the crimes motivated by an all-embracing racism are shrouded in darkness, pushed off stage, or rendered invisible. To bolster the outlandish claim that we live in a post-racial society, crimes such as the murder of Trayvon Martin are often isolat-ed from a larger set of socio-economic forces that might pro-vide a broader understanding of both the needless death of the 17-year-old black youth and its relationship to a virulently ra-cialized, all-encompassing war on youth that is causing massive suffering and needless deaths of many young people in America. The events of Ferguson thus appear here to be a mere flashpoint in the ongoing violence against the disenfranchised.

This brings us to the controversial *Rolling Stone* cover of Boston bombing suspect Dzhokhar Tsarnaev, whose appearance resembles that of a handsome rock star rebel. Beyond the so-called glamorization effect, consternation regarding the cover was undoubtedly caused by its divergence from the familiar modes of representation used to depict fanatical Islamists. Gone from the image were the familiar Talibanesque dressings and the obligatory AK-47, and in their place we find a laid-back youth with a hairstyle and pose eerily reminiscent of the magazine's fa-mous Jim Morrison cover. This is an image of quintessential col-lege youth, American-style—tolerated white radicality. Could it actually be the case that what so perturbed people here was pre-cisely that Dzhokhar Tsarnaev was not visually demonized and looked like one of "us," even a face you'd see in a GAP clothing ad? And while white societies have learned to fear and criminal-ize youth of color like Trayvon, the representation of Tsarnaev points to a wider logic of power that fears the potential of youth to challenge authority and imagine different futures.

Dzhokhar Tsarnaev's violence was abhorrent. But what can we conclude about a society in which young people of color are shot down in the streets across America, while moves toward demonizing youth as "enemies within" are seldom questioned?

Nobody is suggesting here that the experience of youths is in any way uniform. Yet what we do experience is a deep suspicion of youths that allows for multi-leveled modes of profiling such that people of color can be routinely killed by the police with near perfect impunity. Hence if we truly want to understand the Trayvon Martin case, there is also a need to come to terms with a broader set of complex power logics that are interwoven with profoundly unsettling emotions toward an entire generation of young people.

Today's youths now find themselves in a world in which sociality has been reduced to an economic battleground over materialistic needs waged by an army of nomadic individuals, just as more and more people find their behavior pathologized, criminalized, and subject to state violence. This is a social order in which bonds of trust have been replaced by bonds of anxiety. As Zygmunt Bauman puts it: "Trust is replaced by universal suspicion. All bonds are assumed to be untrustworthy, unreliable, trap-and-ambush-like—until proven otherwise."[3] All forms of social solidarity are now directly undermined by a private market logic that has individualized responsibility and reduced civic values to the obligations of a consumer-driven self-interest advanced against all other interests. How else to explain the fate of generations of Americans, especially young people in impoverished communities, who find themselves in a society in which 500,000 young people are incarcerated and 2.5 million are arrested annually, a society in which, by the age of 23, "almost a third of Americans have been arrested for a crime"?[4] What kind of society allows 1.6 million kids to be homeless at any given time in a year? What social order allows massive inequalities in wealth and income to produce a politically and morally dysfunctional system in which "45 percent of U.S. residents live in households that struggle to make ends meet, [which] breaks down to 39 percent of all adults and 55 percent of all children"?[5] What is clear is that many people now live in societies that invest more in what Étienne Balibar calls "the death zones of human-ity" than in life itself, especially when it comes to poor youth.[6]

Comprehending such a pervasive fear of youth allows us to better explain the militarization of education in the United States today. Schools have become the testing grounds for new modes of security and military-style authority, treating students largely as if they are detainees subject to a variety of egregious disciplinary practices, ranging from repressive zero-tolerance policies to the criminalization of what are often trivial infrac-tions such as dress code violations. The war on youth is most obvious in the ways in which young people marginalized by class and color are now largely seen as disposable populations, whose behaviors are largely governed through a youth-crime complex. In fact, in cities such as Chicago, military academies have become the institutions of choice in dealing with students marginalized by race and class. School for many young people has become simply a pipeline into the criminal justice and cor-rectional system. In an incident that offers a modern twist to the convict-leasing system, a few years ago two judges in Luzerne County, Pennsylvania, accepted over $2.6 million in kickbacks for sentencing hundreds of kids to a for-profit, privately owned juvenile detention center.[7]

State-sanctioned violence and the formative culture that makes it possible have increasingly tainted higher education. While there is a long history of higher education taking on research funds and projects that serve the military-industrial complex, such projects were typically hidden from public view. When they do become public, they are often the object of stu-dent protests and opposition, especially since the 1960s. What is new today is that more research projects in higher education than ever before are being funded by various branches of the military, but either no one is paying attention or no one seems to care about it.[8] Ethical and political considerations regarding the role of the university in a democratic society have given way to a hyper-pragmatism couched in the language of austerity and largely driven by a decrease in state funding for higher education. Nearly every social sciences program is now influenced by the seductions of military research dollars. While war has always required embedded academics who can wage an intellectual fight against a disbelieving public and critical voices, what makes the current moment different from the past is the way the very survival of university departments is tied to raising external research income.

This external funding is often contingent on impact/policy agendas such that critical thought translates into providing the impetus for doing war—and selling war—better. In addition, higher education is being militarized in ways more directly related to the sinister role militarization plays in the larger society. Many universities are now beefing up their security forces and turning them on peaceful youthful dissenters such as the pepper-spraying of protesters at UC Davis. Moreover, they are importing combat weapons from the battlefields of Iraq and Afghanistan and incorporating them into the arsenals of campus police. For instance, Ohio State University campus police recently acquired a Mine-Resistant Ambush-Protected vehicle.[9] The message here is clear. Bringing high-powered weaponry onto college campuses speaks less to the demands for student safety than to the production of a culture of fear around and among the students. Such an environment is the antithesis of what a university should be. Faced with the prospect of a massive security machine being used against them, the message is clear: students who even think about questioning authority or engage in peaceful demonstrations do so at their own risk.

The Racial Present

The problem of race today is considerably different from the moment in which W. E. B. Du Bois famously argued, "the problem of the 20th century is the problem of the color line."[10] This is not to suggest that race has declined in significance, or that the racial conditions, structural inequalities, and practices that provided the context for Du Bois's prophecy have been overcome. Rather, today's forms of racism and racialization have transformed, mutated, and recycled forms of the past, and have taken on new and in many instances more covert modes of expression.[11] Du Bois, to his credit, recognized that the color line was not fixed—its modes of expression changed over time, as a response to different contexts and struggles—and that one of the great challenges facing future generations would be not only to engage the complex structural legacy of race but also to take note of the plethora of forms in which it was both expressed and experienced in everyday life. Indeed, we live in a period today that, despite claiming to be "post-racial" and "post-colonial," is in fact continually marked by what Derek Gregory has aptly termed "the Colonial Present"—that is, a setting in which the reproduction of "imagined geographies" of domination/oppression, superiority/inferiority, civility/backwardness still transpires but has been transformed by its global expressions. Given this condition, the concept of race as biologically determined has been subsumed within religious and cultural narratives such that biology is seen as an outdated measure of superiority or inferiority. On a global scale, the notion of race has been transmuted (especially in the post-9/11 moment) into broader discourses of development and deliverance that conceal relations of power and speak with the deceptive eloquence of a humanitarian voice.

Representations of race have undoubtedly become far more subtle and complicated in recent times. The supposedly race-transcendent public policy touted by neoliberal societies is in fact complicated by ongoing public debates over affirmative action, welfare, crime, and the prison-industrial complex. This suggests that although the "color line" has been modified and dismantled in a few instances, race and racial hierarchies still exercise a profound influence on how most people in the world experience their daily lives.[12] Despite popular discomfort with discussions of race, rather than disappearing, race retains its power as a key signifier in structuring all aspects of life. As Michael Omi keenly observed: "Despite legal guarantees of formal equality and access, race continues to be a fundamental organizing principle of individual identity and collective action. I would argue that, far from declining in significance, the racial dimensions of politics and culture have proliferated."[13]

Representations of race and difference are everywhere in neoliberal societies, and yet racism as both a symbol and a condition of life is now either ignored or relegated to an utterly privatized discourse—typified in references to individual prejudices or psychopathic dispositions such as expressions of "hate." As politics becomes more racialized, the discourse about race becomes more privatized. While the realities of race permeate public life, they are engaged less as discourses and sites in which differences are produced within iniquitous relations of power than as either unobjectionable cultural signifiers or desirable commodities. Similarly, as corporate power undermines all notions of the public good and increasingly privatizes public space, it obliterates those public spheres where criticism might emerge that acknowledges the tensions wrought by a pervasive racism functioning as "one of the deep, abiding currents in everyday life, in both the simplest and the most complex interactions of whites and blacks."[14] Indifference and cynicism breed outright contempt and social resentment as racial hierarchies now collapse into evasive strategies to assert power over certain racial and economic groups, such as blaming subjugated communities for not working hard enough, or for failing to exercise sufficient initiative, or for having the audacity to make visible the scourge of racism.

In play here are forms of racism that refuse to "translate private sufferings into public issues,"[15] a normalized racism that works hard to remove issues of power and equity from broader social concerns. Ultimately, it imagines the only obstacle to effective citizenship and agency being each person's lack of principled self-help and ethical responsibility. This translates into a veritable politics of denial that is not merely about the failure of public memory or the refusal to know, but an active, ongoing attempt on the part of many conservatives, liberals, and others to rewrite the discourse of race so as to deny its valence as a force for ongoing discrimination and exclusion. Despite objections that talking about race relations causes racial antagonism, the refusal to speak of the idea of race relations, along with the conditions of racism that have real political effects, operates only to make those effects harder to recognize and critically challenge.

Bauman rightly anticipated how the elimination of public space and the subordination of democratic values to commercial interests would narrow the discursive possibilities for supporting notions of the public good and create the conditions for "suspicion against others, the intolerance of difference, the resentment of strangers, and the demands to separate and banish them, as well as the hysterical, paranoiac concern with 'law and order.'"[16] Positioned within the emergence of neoliberalism as the dominant economic and political philosophy of our times, structural racism can be understood as part of a broader attack against not only difference, but the value of public memory, public goods, and democracy itself. Racism today thus occurs within a larger economic order in which the principle of winner-take-all translates into the losers finding themselves living with few options in a heavily policed but otherwise abandoned social wasteland.

Unlike the old racism, which defined racial differences in terms of fixed biological categories organized hierarchically, racism today operates in various guises, proclaiming among other things race-neutrality, culture as a marker of racial difference, or race as merely a private matter. Unlike the crude racism with biological referents and pseudo-scientific legitimations buttressing its appeal to white racial superiority, the new racism cynically recodes itself within the vocabulary of the Civil Rights movement, invoking the language of Martin Luther King Jr. to argue that individuals should be judged by the "content of their character" and not by the color of their skin. This argument, of course, reflects the early version of King's philosophy, exemplified by the inspiring "I Have a Dream" speech, not the later, more insurgent King whose critical association of "poverty, racism and militarism" violently sealed his fate.

Racism today, as Amy Ansell explains, also "utilizes themes related to culture and nation as a replacement for the now discredited biological referents of the old racism. It is concerned less with notions of racial superiority in the narrow sense than with the alleged 'threat' people of color pose—either because of their mere presence or because of their demand for 'special privileges'—to economic, socio-political, and cultural vitality of the dominant (white) society."[17] The implications of this are, as David Theo Goldberg explains, "the devaluation of any individuals considered not white, or white-like, the trashing or trampling of their rights and possibilities, for the sake of preserving the right to *private* 'rational discrimination' of whites. . . . [Thus] racist discrimination becomes privatized, and in terms of liberal legality state-protected in its privacy."[18]

Structural racism operates through the changing nature of language and other modes of representation. One of the most sanitized and yet pervasive forms of racism today is evident in the language of color-blindness. Within this approach, it is argued that racial conflict and discrimination are a thing of the past and that race has no bearing on an individual's or group's location or standing in contemporary neoliberal societies. Color-blindness does not deny the existence of race, but denies the claim that race is responsible for alleged injustices that reproduce group inequalities, privilege whites, and negatively impact economic mobility, the possession of social resources, and the acquisition of political power. Put differently, inherent in the logic of color-blindness is the central assumption that race has no valence as a marker of identity or power when factored into the social vocabulary of everyday life and the capacity for exercising individual and social agency. As Charles Gallagher observes: "Within the color-blind perspective it is not race per se which determines upward mobility but how much an individual chooses to pay attention to race that determines one's fate. Within this perspective race is only as important as you allow it to be."[19] Veiled then by a denial of how racial histories accrue political, economic, and cultural weight, color-blindness deletes the relationship among racial differences, relations of power, and forms of violence; in doing so, it reinforces the legacy of colonial privileges as the arbiter of value for judging difference against a normative notion of homogeneity.

Historical consciousness matters more than ever because it illuminates and offers a different narrative of our present condition. It also provides the context for holding up to critical scrutiny those forms of tyranny and modes of suffocation that now parade as common sense, popular wisdom, or just plain certainty. It evidences the political bonds of solidarity, community building, friendship, mutual aid, and compassion, along with the poetic qualities possessed by the most affirmative and critical of minds so often derided as dangerous at the time. Hence, as we diagnose the complex organization of systemic violence, suffering, and domestic warfare in our current moment, so we also imagine a world that might be radically different. There are, however, no guarantees. The logical trade in commodities of violence penetrates all aspects of life, while the most important concerns driving society no longer seem to be about political subjectivities, equity, social justice, or advancing a better future with critical confidence. The most important choice now facing most people is less about living a life with dignity and freedom, and more about making the grim choice between survival and dying. Indeed, tales of survival seem to be the only narratives available in the dominant culture for explaining the contemporary human condition and the ebb and flow of its regressing fate.

As social institutions give way to systems of mass surveillance and containment, social provisions disappear and exclusionary logics use ethnic, racial, and religious divisions to render more communities disposable. Racism disguised as neoliberal "color-blindness" works in tandem with the politics of disposability to rationalize the confinement of all those considered "problems" in the privatized hell of the prison-industrial complex. Angela Y. Davis captures this brilliantly in her comment that "according to this logic the prison becomes a way of disappearing people in the false hope of disappearing the underlying social problems they represent."[20] Excluded from public life—languishing in prisons, exploitative working conditions, or the deepening chasm of poverty—they are prevented from engaging in politics as a means to change the conditions of their lives. Any meaningful action that could challenge the vast human suffering, misfortune, and misery caused by social problems becomes increasingly difficult as public discourse is now replaced with vapid neoliberal sentiments regarding personal safety and individual responsibility. The complexity of decentered forms of global power feeds the sense of political inertia, if not complicity, that supports neoliberal orthodoxy. Under such circumstances, politics seems to take place elsewhere—in globalized regimes of power that are indifferent to traditional political geographies such as the nation-state and hostile to any notion of collective responsibility that might address preventable suffering and social injustice.[21]

Racism without Content

To get a real handle on the pernicious nature of racism today, we need to move beyond the post-racial debates of conventional political discourse to explain how widely questions of race have become detached from broader questions of systemic prejudice and the profiling of others. Key here are the ways in which the

race question has been appropriated by popular culture to narrate a particular reading of the racial moment, while in fact denying us the possibility of rigorously questioning the conditions
that give rise to and normalize the subjugation of people who
are deemed to be biologically or culturally inferior. That is to
say, the flattening of the question of race—such that we all now
appear to be potentially racist—is part of a broader logic that
internalizes the problem without addressing the conditions that
allow prejudice to thrive and prosper. We are not denying here
Hannah Arendt's, Wilhelm Reich's, and Zygmunt Bauman's assertion that each one of us could become fascistic if certain conditions were to prevail. None of us knows how we would react in
certain conditions that seem to us in the present moment to be
beyond our comprehension. To reason otherwise is to fly in the
face of the history of oppression by reducing the desire for power to the actions of a few brutal tyrants. Yet to articulate a theory
of race without questioning the conditions that make such an
eventuality possible is tantamount to the same intellectual de-
ceit. Whereas former self-serving analysis against state racism
preferred to focus on structure while absolving the agency of the
masses of any complicity, what we find in the contemporary moment is a focus on agency without the complexity of structure.
Racism, then, without the content!

Nowhere is this more evident than in Paul Haggis's widely
acclaimed Oscar-winning debut film *Crash* (2006). In step with
the marketing of the film as "a provocative, unflinching look at
the complexities of racial conflict in America," critics in general
lined up to praise Haggis's dramaturgical economy, technical acu-
men, and political courage. David Denby of the *New Yorker* suggested that *Crash* "makes previous movie treatments of prejudice
seem like easy and self-congratulatory liberalizing,"[22] and Ella
Taylor of the *Los Angeles Times* hailed it as "one of the best Hollywood movies about race."[23] Another interpretation, however, is
that the movie effectively renders overt racist expression visible,

only to banish its more subtle articulations to invisibility, along with its deep structural and institutional dimensions. Theorizing racism as a function of private discrimination—a matter of individual attitude or psychology—denies its role as a systemic political force with often dire material consequences. In this regard, *Crash* operates precisely to affirm a politics of denial wherein the all too human tendency toward misunderstanding and fear reflects the kind of schizophrenia that marks the politics of race in the post–Civil Rights era. Hence, while Haggis may be credited for moving beyond the black/white dichotomies often imposed on the radical heterogeneity of contemporary U.S. cities by his inclusion of Mexican, Chinese, and Iranian populations, these largely ascriptive identities function to explain away the motivations and aspirations of others both historically and newly raced.

With the formal dismantling of institutional and legal segregation, most people in the United States believe that racism is an unfortunate—and bygone—episode in American history, a past that has been more than adequately redressed and is now best forgotten. If inequality persists today, so mainstream opinion goes, it is a function not of structural disadvantage (that is, dilapidated, dysfunctional schools; rampant unemployment or underemployment; unequal access to loans and mortgages; police harassment and profiling or mass incarceration, etc.), but rather of poor character. Reinforced by the neoliberal mantra that negotiating life's problems is solely an individual challenge, cultural forms of racist expression and exclusion are denied their social origin and content even as informal, market-based resegregation proliferates in the private sector. The roles of the state, political economy, segregation, colonialism, capital, class exploitation, and imperialism are excised from public memory and from accounts of political conflict. Politics, in short, becomes "culturalized," as Mahmood Mamdani explains, such that "every culture has a tangible essence that defines it and then explains politics as a consequence of that essence."[24]

Wendy Brown has observed that when emotional and personal vocabularies are substituted for political ones, when historically conditioned suffering and humiliation are reduced to "difference" or "offense," calls for "tolerance" or "respect for others" are substituted for political transformation in the interests of social justice. Political action devolves into sensitivity training, and the possibilities for political redress dissolve into self-help therapy.[25] Paving the way for the onset of what Vanessa Pupavac has called "therapeutic governance," such care for the self not only naturalizes trauma as part of everyday existence, but presumes the inherent fallibility of everybody in ways that further authenticate neoliberal notions of ontology that rest upon individualizing the causes of social failure. *Crash* operates precisely at this level with its insistence that we are all somehow flawed in our relations to others, yet this demands no wider critique of the system that produces tension and resentment—let alone bringing systemic conditions into the dialogue.

Like *Magnolia* (1999), *Amores Perros* (2000), *21 Grams* (2003), *Syriana* (2005), and *Babel* (2006), among other celebrated films, *Crash* maps a series of interlocking stories with random characters linked by the gravity of racism and by the diverse ways in which they inhabit, mediate, reproduce, and modify its toxic values, practices, and effects. Episodic encounters reveal not just a wellspring of seething resentment and universal prejudice, but also a vision of humanity marked by internal contradictions as characters exhibit values and behaviors at odds with the vile racism that more often than not offers them an outlet for their pent-up fear and hatred. Put on full display, racism is complicated by and pitted against the possibility of a polity enriched by its diversity, a possibility that increasingly appears as a utopian fantasy as the film comes to a conclusion. However, while Haggis considers the power of racial stereotyping and how it complicates the lives of the perpetrators and the victims, he does very little to explore the historical, political, and economic conditions that produce racist practices and exclusions. *Crash* foregrounds racism only to mimic the logic of color-blindness currently embraced by both conservatives and liberals by shifting the criticism to "flawed humanity" in an attempt to complicate the individual characters who allow deeply felt prejudices to govern their lives.

Haggis explains away his own confusion about the constitutive elements of the new racism—who perpetuates it and under what conditions—by powerfully organizing *Crash* around the central motif that everyone has a bad day every once in a while, and occasionally that means indulging in some form of prejudice that cannot be helped. As Haggis explains in an interview for *LA Weekly*: "We are each such bundles of contradictions. . . . You can conduct your life with decency most of your days, only to be amazed by what will come out of your mouth in the wrong situation. Are you a racist? No—but you sure were in that situation! . . . Our contradictions define us."

In other words, Haggis vapidly argues that some racists can be decent, caring human beings, and some decent caring human beings can also be racists. In this equal-opportunity scenario, racism assumes the public face of a deeper rage, fear, and frustration that appears universally shared and enacted by all of L.A.'s urban residents. This free-floating rage and fear, in Haggis's worldview are the driving force behind racist expression and exclusion. Thus racism is reduced to individual prejudice, a kind of psychological mechanism for negotiating interpersonal conflict and situational difficulties made manifest in emotional outbursts and irrational fears. What such a definition of racism cannot account for is precisely racism's collusion with rationality, the very "logical" use to which racism has historically been put to legitimize the consolidation of economic and political power in favor of white interests. In addition to recognizing its psychological dimensions, recognizing racism's logic requires an engagement with a 400-year history of racist oppression enacted in the interests of white supremacy; without this historical consciousness, it becomes too easy to identify all forms of racism as a matter of bad taste, personal prejudice, or extremist.

Haggis's model of prejudice as a universal flaw has very little to say about racism as a site of power operating within the larger structural conditions that enforce it. *Crash*'s delineation of racial conflict both privatizes and depoliticizes race, drowning out those discourses that reveal how it is mobilized "around material resources regarding education, employment conditions, and political power."[26] Within this equal-opportunity view of racism, the primary "insight" of the film trades in the worst banalities: there is good and bad in everyone, or as Stephen Hunter puts it, "nobody's truly innocent and the other side of the argument is that nobody's truly guilty."[27] Forcefully arguing against this position, David Edelstein, a film critic for *Slate*, observes:

> In the end, *Crash* says, when you push a vicious racist, you get a caring human, but when you push a caring human you get a vicious racist. . . . All the coincidences—there are more, involving Persian and Chinese families—make for one economical narrative: Haggis wants to distill all the resentment and hypocrisy among races into a fierce parable. But the old-fashioned carpentry (evocative of '30s socially conscious melodrama) makes this portrait of How We Live Now seem preposterous at every turn. A universe in which we're all racist puppets is finally just as simple-minded and predictable as one in which we're all smiling multicolored zombies in a rainbow coalition.[28]

While the movie throughout offers a pertinent exposition of the all too neoliberalized notion of the always flawed self, the final scene in particular is most striking. In this scene, Anthony, the black youth catalyst for the violent car-jacking at the start of the plot, ends up discovering his more "human" side by releasing Chinese migrants held captive in a pick-up truck he sequestered and was intent on selling. This directly links the redemptive moment to a commoditized ending such that living with racism can be at least tempered as one enters into the streets, now less paved with gold but certainly appealing in their fluorescent splendor. Here freedom is conflated with the neoliberal condition of choice, while the principal message is that although our societies are populated by deeply prejudiced peoples, at least we owe something to the system for providing us with the freedom not to be prejudicial as we open ourselves up to the enrichment of foreigners. Everybody is welcome in the melting pot of individualized discrimination.

Confronting the Spectacle of Militarized Racism

If there were any doubt about the real violence associated with racism in the United States and beyond, one need only focus for the briefest of moments on the killing of an unarmed 18-year-old African-American, Michael Brown, in Ferguson, Missouri, in August 2014. This act of homicide by a white police officer has made visible how a racist military culture now dominates American society. Brown was shot six times even though his hands were held high above his head, only for his corpse to be left on the sidewalk for several hours before being collected. A reminder of the same treatment given to the low-income victims of Katrina, many of whose bodies, rendered worthless and undeserving of compassion, were left to float with other debris in flooded streets after the hurricane pounded New Orleans. How else does this neglect function if not to serve as a warning to others that they too might be disposed of at any given moment? That Brown underwent a subsequent demonization by the media only confirmed how the act of killing finds its entrance into the public consciousness as a form of spectacularized entertainment.

Violence now mediates all relationships, and extreme violence not only informs daily politics but merges entertainment with a culture of fear such that the line between them is increasingly disappearing. Extreme violence now moves from a Hollywood production to real life as the police have been turned into soldiers who view the inhabitants of the neighborhoods in which they operate as enemy combatants. Outfitted with full riot gear, submachine guns, armored vehicles, and other lethal weapons imported from the combat zones of Iraq and Afghanistan, their mission is to assume a battle-ready posture. Such violence has to be situated within the broader racial context we have already outlined. As Gary Younge observed: "There are places in America where young people are not supposed to die. Movie theaters. Schools. College campuses. Their deaths prompt great moral panic if little change. And then there are areas where they are expected to die. The shooting of a teenager in poor black neighborhoods often earns little more than a paragraph in the local paper. Beyond their communities, their passing prompts little more than a weary sigh. To exist as a working-class African American is to be vulnerable: to live in a poor, black area simply renders you collateral."[29]

When fear and terror become the organizing principles of a society in which the tyranny of the state consolidates with the despotism of an unaccountable market, violence becomes the only valid form of control. The system has not failed. As Jeffrey St. Clair has pointed out, it is doing exactly what it is supposed to do, which is to punish those it considers dangerous or disposable—a massive and ever-growing group. Hannah Arendt was right in arguing that "if lawfulness is the essence of non-tyrannical government and lawlessness is the essence of tyranny, then terror is the essence of totalitarian domination."[30] In an age when an utterly commodified and privatized culture erases all vestiges of memory and commitment, it is easy for a society to remove itself from those sordid memories that reveal the systemic injustices belying the presence of violence.

Not only do the dangerous memories of bodies being lynched, beaten, tortured, and murdered disappear in the fog of celebrity culture and the 24/7 entertainment/news cycle, but the historical flashpoints that once revealed the horrors of unaccountable power and acts of systemic barbarism are disconnected from any broader understanding of domination and vanish into a past that no longer has any connection to the present.[31] The murder of Emmett Till; the killing of the four young black girls, Addie Mae Collins, Cynthia Wesley, Carole Robertson and Denise McNair, in the 1963 church bombing in Birmingham, Alabama; the assassination of Dr. Martin Luther King Jr.; the killing by four officers of Amadou Diallo; and the recent killing of Eric Garner by a police officer using an illegal chokehold are not isolated expressions of marginalized failures of a system; they are the system, a system of disposability that has intensified without apology.

We believe that cultural critic bell hooks is right when she states that "the point of lynching historically was not to kill individuals but to let everybody know: 'This could happen to you.'" This is how regimes of violence control people. They individualize fear and insecurity and undercut the formation of solidarity and collective struggle. Fear of punishment, of being killed, tortured, or reduced to the mere level of survival has become the government's weapon of choice. This leads to the manufacturing of ignorance and relies on induced isolation and privatization to depoliticize the population. Without the ability to translate private troubles into public issues, neoliberal societies face a crisis of individual and collective agency as well as a historical crisis. This is captured in images of the police spraying tear gas into the crowds of peaceful protesters in New York City. It can be seen in reports of the police choking students, firing hundreds of rounds of bullets into the cars of civilians, beating a defenseless mentally ill woman, and in the ongoing comments of neoliberal advocates who instill moral panic over the presence of immigrants, protest movements, and any other form of resistance to state-sanctioned oppression.

The events in Ferguson and the egregious killing of Eric Garner sweep away any viable claim of a post-racial society. Even national media such as *Time*, *Bloomberg*, the *New York Times*, and the *New Yorker* were forced to headline the violence in ways that exposed the realities of racism perpetrated in the United States today. It is of course further revealing that the photographer for two of the most striking covers, Scott Olson, was arrested because he committed the allegedly egregious crime of "being a member of the press in a public place and mingling with the public, rather than [staying] in a pen where officials had hoped to confine the press."[32] We have all become familiar with the powerful images from Birmingham, Alabama, during 1963, when the brutality of legal apartheid in the United States appeared in full view. And yet the image of civilian youth flanked by militarized personnel in combat fatigues, with sniper assault weapons locked on their unarmed targets in a way that indicates a willingness to kill, ensures more than just that the state suppression of protest in Ferguson stays long in the memory. It marks a new moment in the enforcement of race and class divisions wherein low-intensity warfare is losing its ability to remain part of the hidden order of politics, but is forced, due to popular uprisings and collective struggles for justice, to take place in the open.

It would be a mistake, however, to simply focus here on the militarization of the police and their racist actions in suppressing free speech and community outrage over the killing of Michael Brown. What we witness with this brutal killing and mobilization of state violence is the impunity with which the neoliberal system conducts business by one set of rules while subjecting the population to another. By doing so, the system not only establishes that there is, in fact, a low-intensity war being waged against civilian society, but also furnishes the justification for insurrectional politics of the type anticipated by and coded into the Declaration of Independence itself.

What Ferguson and the Garner killing show is that neoliberal states can no longer justify and legitimate their exercise of ruthless power without inciting rebellion. Moreover, as Slavoj Žižek argues, "worldwide capitalism can no longer sustain or tolerate . . . global equality. It is just too much."[33] From this perspective, it is misguided to talk about the militarization of local police forces without recognizing that the metaphor of "war zone" is apt for a global politics in which the state and public spheres have been replaced by the machinery of finance; the militarization of entire societies, not just the police; and the widespread use of punishment that extends from the prison to the schools to the streets. Some have rightly argued that these tactics have been going on in the black community for a long time and are not new. What is new is that the intensity of violence and the level of military-style machinery of death being employed is much more sophisticated and deadly. For instance, as Kevin Zeese and Margaret Flowers point out, the militarization of the police in the United States is a relatively recent phenomenon dating back to 1971. They write:

> The militarization of police is a more recent phenomenon [and marks] the rapid rise of Police Paramilitary Units (PPUs, informally SWAT teams) which are modeled after special operations teams in the military. PPUs did not exist anywhere until 1971, when Los Angeles under the leadership of the infamous police chief Daryl Gates, formed the first one and used it for demolishing homes with tanks equipped with battering rams. By 2000, there were 30,000 police SWAT teams, [and] by the late 1990s, 89% of police departments in cities of over 50,000 had PPUs, almost double the mid-'80s figure; and in smaller towns of be-

tween 25,000 and 50,000 by 2007, 80% had a PPU quadrupling from 20% in the mid-'80s. [Moreover,] SWAT teams were active with 45,000 deployments in 2007 compared to 3,000 in the early '80s. The most common use . . . was for serving drug search warrants where they were used 80% of the time, but they were also increasingly used for patrolling neighborhoods.[34]

At the same time, the impact of the rapid militarization of local police forces on communities of color is nothing short of terrifying and symptomatic of the violence that takes place in advanced genocidal states. For instance, according to a recent report titled "Operation Ghetto Storm," produced by the Malcolm X Grassroots Movement, "police officers, security guards, or self-appointed vigilantes extrajudicially killed at least 313 African-Americans in 2012. . . . This means a black person was killed by a security officer every 28 hours." The report suggests that "the real number could be much higher."[35]

We would do well then to remember that the murders of Michael Brown and Eric Garner were in no way extraordinary occurrences. They represent a state of normality faced by many communities deemed to be disposable by a system that looks upon them with prejudice and hostility. What is unique here, however, is the local population's rebellion against the impunity with which the system uses violence, and the division of race, class, and power that such violence enforces in the process. This is significant. For it is not the case that the Ferguson response and the massive demonstrations all over the United States over the failure to indict the police officer who killed Eric Garner were related to some exceptional moment. The police had already been trained to harass, abuse, humiliate, and injure young black men viewed as a threat to public order. At the same time, in the case of the Ferguson uprisings, the military hardware had already been stockpiled and was ready for deployment by the local police department. Using combat-grade assault weapons to face down a challenge to the impunity of their violence would have been normal if the local community had not declared it otherwise. Thus, it is the rebellion of the Ferguson citizenry that is significant, rebellion which confronts the spectacle of violence and refuses to accept the racialized militarization of communities in America today.

The emergence of the paramilitary cop and the surveillance state go hand in hand and are indicative not only of state-sanctioned racism but also of a new phase in the politics of disposability wherein containment alone is no longer sufficient to deter challenges to the neoliberal system's authority. Brutality mixed with attacks on freedom of speech, dissent, and peaceful protest evokes memories of past brutal regimes in the American South as much as of dictatorships in Latin America in the 1970s and 1980s. The events in Ferguson speak to a history of repression in both the United States and abroad that Americans choose to forget at their own risk. In spite of his generally right-wing political views, Rand Paul got it right in arguing that "when you couple this militarization of law enforcement with an erosion of civil liberties and due process that allows the police to become judge and jury—national security letters, no-knock searches, broad general warrants, pre-conviction forfeiture—we begin to have a very serious problem on our hands." What he does not name is the problem, which is a society that is not simply on the precipice of outright militarization of local zones of crisis, but has fallen over the edge into a state of permanent warfare.

Under the current regime of neoliberalism, the circle of those considered disposable and subject to state violence is now expanding. The heavy hand of the state is not only racist; it is also part of a new mode of governance which is willing to use violence—and the threat of violence—to deter, criminalize, or eliminate whatever threatens the private interests at stake in its core. The United States' domestic deployment of military-grade weapons at the community level adds a grade of seamlessness to the system's grid of power and enforcement. As once-civilian authorities become increasingly militarized and networked with the Department of Homeland Security, the Border Patrol, and the National Security Agency, only collective mobilizations of rebellion, like that in Ferguson, seem to create openings in national discourse to successfully mount challenges to the consolidation of national military and surveillance power at the most local level.

Amid the growing intensity of state terrorism, violence becomes the DNA of a society that refuses to deal with larger structural issues such as massive inequality in wealth and power, a government that now unapologetically serves the rich and powerful corporate interests, and makes violence the organizing principle of governance. None of this would have been lost on Foucault, who once noted:

> While colonization, with its techniques and its political and juridical weapons, obviously transported European models to other continents, it also had a considerable boomerang effect on the mechanisms of power in the West, and on the apparatuses, institutions, and techniques of power. A whole series of colonial models was brought back to the West, and the result was that the West could practice something resembling colonization, or an internal colonialism, on itself.

The worldwide response to what is happening in Ferguson and in demonstrations against indiscriminate violence by the police shines a light on the racist and militarized nature of American society so as to make its claim to democracy seem both hypocritical and politically insipid. The criminalization of more and more elements of the population is too obvious to ignore. Communities of color are increasingly targeted by armed state authorities that view them as hostile. Blacks are increasingly killed in the street by cops, while prisons continue to overflow with people of color, children are being inducted into the criminal justice system for trivial infractions, and Wall Street bankers commit with impunity crimes of economic mass destruction that siphon vast wealth from the many to the few.

Political life has come alive once again in the United States, waking in fits and starts from the trance imposed through commercial culture, continuous marketing, and entertainment. The time has come to recognize that Ferguson and the ongoing murder of black men is not only about the reinforcement of age-old racial divisions in one town, but also about the consolidation of corporate media, police-state politics, militarism, and social disposability as instruments of neoliberal social control nationally, and beyond. The mass demonstrations that have taken place across the United States coupled with the events in Ferguson prompt us to rethink the meaning of politics and to begin to think not about reform but about a major restructuring of our values, institutions, and notions of what a real democracy might look like. "Ferguson is a wake-up call," writes Mumia Abu-Jamal, "a call to build social, radical, revolutionary movements for change."

The events in Ferguson and the killing of Eric Garner are flashpoints that have mobilized people all over the country. Many people are beginning to realize that the ongoing killing of black people is not even the most serious issue, however horrible and tragic. The biggest problem is the existence of the militarized finance state that operates as the repressive apparatus of the financial elite. The demonstrations must continue full force, and as a first step criminal charges must be brought against rogue cops and lawless police departments that believe that they can engage in racist repression, brutalizing black neighborhoods by treating them as war zones. Exposing the racist ideologies, institutions, and language as part of a systemic project of disposability, harassment, and expulsion constitutes the first step toward opposing the brutalizing and in some cases killing of young black men with impunity. But then the hard work begins. Let's hope the killing of Michael Brown, Tamir Rice, and Eric Garner provide the beginning of a political and social movement to fight what has become a dark and gruesome political state of governance in the United States.

The impunity surrounding the killings of Eric Garner in New York and Michael Brown in Ferguson remind us that we should organize to resist the normalization of violence. These events also tell us that the political and ethical imagination is still alive. When pushed far enough, people still organize, resist, and rebel. When such social energies are cultured and sustained through deep solidarities with other struggles, the seduction of neoliberalism loses its spectacular power and the prospect of social justice and democracy comes back into play. The people of Ferguson, along with the young people demonstrating for racial justice, like those in Palestine and Zapatista Chiapas, show us that human dignity and community-level organizing can stand up to military coercion and the neoliberal politics of disposability. Their rebellions against oblivion not only challenge the everyday spectacles of violence within which they live, but offer diverse counter-narratives of participation, liberation, historical memory, community, and autonomy, all of which show the humanity of struggle in ways that the logic of the market—which is the logic of violence—is incapable of understanding.

FIVE

CRIME AND PUNISHMENT

The Force of Law

Michel Foucault's landmark text *Discipline & Punish* remains the seminal study of violence in relation to the modern incarceration system.[1] Foucault's analysis starts with the spectacle of the scaffold. Once the preserve of the sovereign right to kill, the scaffold was slowly appropriated by the masses as a way to show popular dissent. *La guillotine* thus becomes, as Foucault intimated, a leveling mechanism turned back against power as the spectacles of violence that hallmarked the ancien régime were inverted for both vengeance and possible emancipation. This, however, was only the start of a process that in many ways signaled the threshold of modernity. For it was through a shift from the sovereign right to kill through the all too public spectacles of violence to the advent of the punishing state that the body was inscribed with more complex markers of suspicion and presumed guilt on account of a person's and a wider population's profiles. It is through these markers that we are able to detect the links among crime, punishment, and the production of subjectivities whose very bodies become sites for continual intervention on account of their alleged deviancy and recalcitrant natures. The significance of this move and its impact upon political subjectivity was fully appreciated by Judith Butler who writes:

> *Discipline and Punish* can be read as Foucault's effort to reconceive Nietzsche's doctrine of internalization as

a language of inscription. In the context of prisoners, Foucault writes, the strategy has not been to enforce a repression of their criminal impulse, but to compel their bodies to signify the prohibitive law as their manifest essence, style, and necessity. That law is not literally internalized, but incorporated on bodies; there the law is manifest as a sign of the essence of their selves, the meaning of their soul, their conscience, the law of their desire. In effect, the law is fully dissimulated into the body as such; it is the principle that confers intelligibility on that body, the sign by which it is socially known.[2]

It would be a mistake, however, to understand the emergence of the prison-industrial complex as a move away from spectacles of violence. As Foucault intimated, while the violence of discipline may be internalized, power's disciplinary apparatus nevertheless develops a sophisticated panopticon that continually gazes upon society as inmates within its grid of control. In a neoliberal setting, violence operates both through traditional enclosures, through the colonization of needs and desires, as well as through the production of diverse modes of public pedagogy. The registers of violence are no longer modeled after the heavy hand of repression but now work through circuits as diverse as the traditional media, ever-evolving digital technologies, social media, and the Internet. It is for this reason that Foucault once said that the prison "begins well outside of its gates. From the moment you leave your house!"

Every law, Derrida explains, is a response to a particular crisis that centers on human behavior. Understood from the perspective of the dangerous subject, it is taken within law that some lives are more prone to transgression, or, more dangerous still, to exposing already existing crises more than others. The force of law as such has never been divorced from power politics. Nor has it been divorced in the modern period from the biopolitical production of subjectivities that work to authenticate/disqualify the meaning of lives. Law remains a strategic tool in social and racial wars of the twenty-first century, used to continually inscribe notions of guilt upon certain lives before any crimes have been committed, merely on account of their potentiality.

Hence, modes of punishment leave distinct markings upon the body that affix particular meanings upon the subjugated. Such markings prove to be far more complex than familiar notions of political enmity, as the scars of violence can inscribe qualities of complicity, shaming, inferiority, and, of course, disposability. We are particularly concerned here with the multiple ways in which the spectacle of violence functions or performs politically such that the violated body is continuously marked with deeper meaning and significance beyond the tortuous scars that are routinely showcased for public display. That is to say, certain bodies are inscribed with meaning such that they can logically and reasonably be disposed of within the everyday order of things. In this regard, the study of disposability takes political aim at the systematic production of disposable lives and the complex bodily inscriptions that manifest in oppression and its affective relations. The production of disposable lives as such takes us into the vexed terrain of identity politics—not simply identity of birthplace, but identity rooted in political distinctions that appear self-evident, thereby affirming which bodies are to be protected and which are to be protected against. In communities of color across the United States, the lines are clear. "Black lives matter!" protesters say in solidarity with the people of Ferguson ever since the night since it was announced no charges would be brought against the cop that killed an unarmed black youth from their community. The "I can't breathe" slogan taken up by demonstrators across the United States after the killing of Eric Garner also makes clear that communities of color are under siege, and the violence incurred here is one driven by the spirit of racial genocide consistent with that which all but exterminated indigenous nations, languages, and memories from their conquered homeland.

The politics of disposability and the lack of critical attention it has received demand new ways of thinking about the question of performativity as it relates to predatory formations. Judith Butler remains one of the most celebrated theorists in this area. Highlighting the ways that our identities are constructed in terms of social norms and questions of unacceptable deviance, she explains how life "appears" in constant negotiation with regimes of power which compel the subject to live in conformist ways.[3] Butler reconciles this with notions of precarity, inequality, and vulnerability to illustrate the violence of the performative act that naturalizes conditions of oppression and exploitation.[4] Following very much in the thought of Michel Foucault, normative violence for Butler both authenticates and disqualifies the meaning of lives. Normative violence sets out what can live and what must be killed for the social order to be maintained. Unless the norm is adhered to, violence can be sanctioned to force compliance. Such violence for Butler doesn't always need to be physical, although the body is undeniably "marked" with signs that often have devastating consequences for those deemed to be abnormal. Normative violence thus understood is restrictive in terms of denying those lives their very modes of existence, and yet prescriptive in terms of affirming through the violence of denial those qualities necessary for a more acceptable character. This is what Foucault referred to as the dual process of "making live and letting die": "to *foster* life or *disallow* it to the point of death."[5]

Butler is fully appreciative here of the significance of the spectacle for establishing normalization. She accounts for this in terms of the framing of different subjectivities: "The 'frames' that work to differentiate the lives we can apprehend from those we cannot (or that produce lives across a continuum of life) not only organize visual experience but also generate specific ontologies of the subject. Subjects are constituted through norms which, in their reiteration, produce and shift the terms through which subjects are recognized."[6] Importantly, for Butler, since what matters is the subsequent production of truthful (hence authentic) subjectivities out of the ashes of devastation, we must bring into question the normative framing of life as an objective ontological and epistemological fact: "To call the frame into question is to show that the frame never quite contained the scene it was meant to limn, that something was already outside, which made the very sense of the inside possible, recognizable. The frame never quite determined precisely what it is we see, think, recognize, and apprehend. Something exceeds the frame that troubles our sense of reality; in other words, something occurs that does not conform to our established understanding of things."[7] Butler counters this by calling for a break with the dominating frames of the time. This is more than an attempt to draw attention to the multiplicity of the experiences of events. It is a call to open up the space for alternative political mediations by breaking apart the myth of the universal experience of truth. Butler, in this case, makes clear that at the heart of the production of violence is the construction of particular identities, desires, and modes of identification that operate within unequal relations of power. Normalizing the framing mechanisms that make some lives privileged over others is fundamentally what makes the political educative at its core and demands an unraveling of its performative capacities and effects.

While understanding the spectacle of violence as a continuous performance is convincing, we nevertheless depart from Butler in one particular and deeply important ontological way. Butler's entire project is premised upon the fundamental assertion that life is by definition ontologically vulnerable. This allows her to explain the human condition through various degrees of precariousness. It also allows her to develop a concept of the political that emerges from the universality of the vulnerable subject—most notably embodied in the tragic figure of Antigone. Our preference is for the pedagogy of oppression. This is not simply semantics. It is central to how we understand and advance formations of (non)violence. Not only does the universalization of vulnerable subjectivities diminish the potency of oppression as carried out by those who create insecurities by political design, but it undermines the confidence of those whose dignity and courage to resist—especially with non-violent means—modes of critical awareness transforms the world for the better. That is not to suggest that people don't feel vulnerable when they are exposed and threatened. There is however a marked difference between the creation of conditions of vulnerability out of systemic oppression and positing ontological vulnerability when understanding the political and the capacity for meaningful change. What is more, should we take the performative nature of violence seriously, what is demanded is not accepting the inevitability of injustice, but a pedagogical confidence to imagine another world is both possible and desirable.

Oppressive power does not fear vulnerable subjects. It produces them. What it fears is the courage to counter its spectacles of violence with the belief, despite the horror, that there are still enough reasons to believe in this world and transform it for the better. Holding on to that confidence seems key to our critique of violence today.

What is distinctive about the performative nature of neoliberal violence is that it not only absorbs the state as a proxy for violence, but also relegates entire populations to spaces of invisibility and disposability. In this regard we can agree with Jacques Rancière when he argues that, despite the proliferation of daily spectacles of violence, the mediation of suffering provides an effective mask to police what we are exposed to. As he writes, "we must challenge the received opinion that this system drowns us in a flood of images in general, and images of horror in particular, thereby rendering us insensitive to the banalized reality of these horrors."[8] What matters more in "rendering us insensitive," for Rancière, is "the politics specific to its image" inasmuch as the selection and mediation of the form allows for reductionist interpretations that affirm particular political discourses and deny others:

> The dominant media by no means drown us in a torrent of images testifying to massacres, massive population transfers and the other horrors that go to make up the planets present. Quite the reverse, they reduce their number, taking good care to select and order them. They eliminate from them anything that might exceed the simple superfluous illustration of their meaning.[9]

Let's take as an example here the cruelty displayed within popular Hollywood films such as *Fast Five* (2011) and *Acts of Valor* (2012). These films, only two examples of an increasingly militarized popular culture, drench the screen in lawlessness and provide fast-rising volumes of sledgehammer blood feasts. The producers of *Acts of Valor* boast that the film uses live ammunition and shamelessly tout it as an avenue for recruiting Navy Seals and other soldiers needed for special operations missions in the age of unending crises.[10] Gender by no means acts as a buffer from these dynamics. For instance, films such as *Let Me In* (2010), *Hannah* (2011), and *Sucker Punch* (2011) move from celebrating hyper-violent women to fetishizing hyper-violent young girls.[11] Rather than being depicted as gaining stature through a coming-of-age process that unfolds amid representations of innocence and complicated negotiations with the world, young girls are now valorized for their ability to produce high body counts and their dexterity as killing machines in training.

Taking this fetish for violence to a more explicit pornographic level, Hollywood films such as the *Saw* series transcend the typical slasher fare and offer viewers endless, super-charged representations of torture, rape, animal cruelty, revenge, genital mutilation, graphic death blows, and much more. Whatever bleeds here—gratuitously and luxuriously—brings in box office profits and dominates media headlines, despite often being presented without any viable political context or ethical responsibility for making sense of the imagery or any critical commentary that might undercut or rupture the pleasure viewers are invited to derive from such images.

Representations of hyper-violence and human tragedy thus merge seamlessly with modes of forgetting that mediate the aesthetics of suffering. On the one hand they structure social relations through the exposure to violence. And yet, on the other hand, they attempt to remove from sight the systemic nature of such violence by relegating it to a personal and individualized experience. This is the true mask of mastery for contemporary neoliberal regimes of power. For as the quantitative assault of representations of anxiety overwhelm all qualitative deliberation on the meaning of their content, so we are taught to accept that things are fundamentally insecure, and thus we have no reason to struggle to identify the source of our suffering, let alone transform our conditions for the better.

In this regard, the more brutal and consuming the entertainment becomes, the less we are forced to consider the true depths of suffering faced by many on a daily basis. Hollywood films along with other elements of neoliberal screen culture have contributed to a violence-saturated culture that inordinately invests in and legitimates a grim pleasure in the pain of others, especially those considered marginal and disposable. The media thus increase their hold on the imagination, decentered and disconnected from any ethical criteria for the politics of their content and effectively disallowing a wider critique of the conditions that produce disposable lives in the first instance. Such mediation of aesthetic regimes of suffering and violence, coupled with the search for ever more intense levels of sensation and excitation become the reigning pedagogical and performative forces in shaping individual and collective identities. Within this context, the elevation of cruelty to a structuring principle of society is matched by the privatization of pain, and it is precisely through the depravity of imagery encouraged by neoliberal capitalism that the pleasure of humiliation and violence is maximized and safely ensconced in a metaphysics of everyday militarization that attempts to makes us all obedient consumers or criminals.

We are not of course suggesting that questions of justice and rights are of no consequence here. On the contrary, implicit in the idea of the force of law is the constitution of new notions of right that are fully in keeping with Derrida's commitment to the democratic people to come. In fact, if we follow the call of Howard Zinn to conduct a people's history of rights and justice, we discover that it is precisely the people who should be seen as constitutive of a political order and not the order that constitutes a people. This was one of the failures, modernity that has now been extended into neoliberal thought and practice. For instead of conceiving of the body politic as the ongoing process of a people's community, democracy, and dignity, we are still tied to the top-down logic that the structure has the martial right to authenticate a people. As a result, it comes as no surprise that we continue to witness the transformation of the fundamental prejudices of modern states into new structures of power and domination, for they manage to seamlessly re-create the very logics that naturalize and enforce hierarchy to enrich and secure the few at the expense of everyone else. Law as such remains a key strategy in waging class war against the masses.

Poverty of Guilt

Our allusion to Fyodor Dostoyevsky's classical text in the title of this chapter is purposefully made. While a dominant trope to continually emerge from *Crime and Punishment* focuses on the right to violence in order to overcome social injustice and to achieve a higher political purpose, the narrative also works beautifully to expose the poverty of the burden of guilt as to what constitutes a crime, and the deserved punishment remains framed within social and class-based parameters. As Dostoyevsky recounts the trials and tribulations of his lead character, Rodion Raskolnikov, the call to violence may appear to be both a metaphor and a genuine sense of rage for the injustices of the world that force the subject to accept that conditions forever remain beyond one's control. It even works to force the impoverished to internalize the guilt such that any political motive is replaced by the notion of the innate savagery of the underclass, which becomes normalized and accepted. As a result, the focus turns more to the actions and psychology of the individual, instead of the structural violence that gave birth to the violent act in the first instance. Incarceration thus becomes the only way to conceive of moral redemption for a crime whose punishment works to strip the perpetrator of all collective notions of agency.

It is common to explain the juridical state apparatus as a series of material processes that appear to us in highly structured and deeply embedded social ways. We are encouraged to think of justice as a complex network that seamlessly connects the original scene of the crime, the forensic evidence, the legal and professional bodies, the courthouses, the armed transportation systems, and the penitentiary system itself. While these are no doubt integral to our understanding of the prison system, incarceration is nevertheless better critiqued by examining its effects at the level of life itself. Only then does it become possible to connect structural violence with power politics in ways that allow us to gain better tangible purchase on the micro-specific details of contemporary forms of punishment, especially their spectacles of violence that are actively produced for those both within and beyond the confining walls.

Imagery representing this setting often serves the forces of ethical tranquilization as it produces and enforces endless degrading and humiliating narratives of impoverished communities, dangerous protesters, and others considered disposable. Viewed as unworthy of civic inclusion, immigrants, protesters, and others deemed alien or hostile to the mechanizations of privatization, consumption, and commodification are erased from any viable historical and political context. Such groups now fill a landscape of criminalization that relegates them to those spaces that accelerate their invisibility while exposing them to the harsh machinery of a political and social death. Catherine Clement is right in insisting that "somewhere every culture has an imaginary zone for what it excludes, and it is that zone we must try to remember today."[12]

The politics of disposability, with its zones of abandonment and carceral industries of surveillance and containment, presents a new historical conjuncture and must be addressed within the emergence of a ruthless market economy which is not only a financial system, but also a dis-imaginative pedagogical force rewriting the meaning of agency, desire, and politics itself. Neoliberalism must then be subject to the kind of civic memory work in which the past is claimed as a site of injustice and the notion of learning becomes a matter of remembering differently.[13]

What appears worse here is the ritual humiliation of people that now takes place against the global poor and disadvantaged as if they are not only responsible for their suffering but deserve such hardships, and this in spite of the fact they are not accountable for the difficulties in which they find themselves. Those with little power or wealth are now not only seen as socially degenerate but are viewed as disposable, subject to the mercies of the market, and outside any consideration of compassion or justice. This contemptuous attitude toward the downtrodden has become commonplace enough that it now produces its own spectacles for consumption—what Gerry Mooney and Lynn

Hancock call "poverty porn," in which not only are people experiencing poverty blamed for their problems but viewers take pleasure in seeing them as objects of scorn, humiliation, and disdain. They write:

> Central to our understanding of the contemporary valorisations of "the poor" as "problem population" are a series of anti-welfare narratives and ideologies which are working not only to construct people in poverty as "other," but which operate in different ways to harden public attitudes to poverty and to those experiencing it, as well as paving the way for much tougher and punitive welfare policies. Hardly a week goes by without some media story which purports to depict some episode or crisis around social welfare in some form or another.[14]

Chris Hedges is partly right when he argues that, "any state that has the capacity to monitor all its citizenry, any state that has the ability to snuff out factual public debate through [the] control of information, any state that has the tools to instantly shut down all dissent is totalitarian."[15] While Hedges is aware that this disciplinary culture of fear and repression is rooted in a political economy that treats people as objects and makes the accumulation of capital the subject of history, he underestimates the oppressive nature of neoliberalism in the contemporary period. That is, what is novel about existing registers of discipline and control is that they operate in a new historical conjuncture in which the relationship of political power, cultural institutions, and everyday life has become more powerful and intense in its ability to undermine the radical imagination and the capacity of individuals to resist repression and make the crucial decisions necessary to take control over the forces that shape their lives. Yet, in an atmosphere of unrelenting repression and surveillance, the contradictions of neoliberalism become more exaggerated and obvious, and one consequence is that more and more people are organizing to resist its oppressive ideology, policies, and modes of governance. Domination is never so overwhelming or sutured as to make our imaginations believe that power can only be defined by oppression and the omnipotence of those with the most money and weapons. As David Graeber writes:

> Objections to such [neoliberal] arrangements are to be met with truncheons, lasers, and police dogs. It's no coincidence that marketization has been accompanied by a new ethos where challenge is met with an instant appeal to violence. In the end, despite endless protests to the contrary, our rulers understand that the market is not a natural social arrangement. It has always had to be imposed at the point of a gun. The university is dead. The question to ask now is not, how do we bring it back. That's impossible and quite undesirable. The question is what new forms of genuinely democratic self-organization might rise from its ashes? To even begin to ask this question we must first of all get rid of the police.[16]

The police have become the new private armies at the service of the global rich, designed to keep the public obedient, compliant, and deferential to the armed authority of the neoliberalized state. Conformity has become the order of the day and perpetual anxiety the new norm, reinforced by intellectual violence against all possible vestiges of protest or critique. One consequence is the emergence of a kind of anti-politics in which the discourses of privatization, possessive individualism, and crass materialism inundate every aspect of social life, making it easy for people to lose their faith in the critical function of education and the possibility for political change. In such instances, as Wendy Brown has noted, an ideology of depoliticization works its way through the social order, removing social relations from the configurations of power that shape them and substituting "emotional and personal vocabularies for political ones in formulating solutions to political problems."[17] The implications are twofold.

First, we are starting to see the emergence of new forms of violence that lack all political ambition. While the question remains as to why there isn't more revolutionary organizing in continental Europe while crippling austerity measures destroy the lives of millions and the fate of an entire generation of youths, it is also troubling that recent cases of riotous behavior seemingly mimic the nihilism of neoliberal materialism and its reduction of all value to consumer desires. The British riots of 2011 are a case point here. As Zygmunt Bauman observed, "These are not hunger or bread riots. These are riots of defective and disqualified consumers."[18] Central to Bauman's observation was the "humiliation" felt by disaffected youths who are taught by a society that self-worth and valuation are realized through one's material corporeality: "The objects of desire, whose absence is most violently resented, are nowadays many and varied—and their numbers, as well as the temptation to have them, grow by the day. And so grows the wrath, humiliation, spite, and grudge aroused by *not* having them—as well as the urge to destroy what you can't have." Hence, not only did the looting of shops "derive from the same impulsion and gratify the same longing" as that compelled by consumer capitalism, but the violence represented the "absence of dignity" by those who felt the battle for such political value was already lost, those who had accepted the designation of "non-entity" on account of their "good-for-nothingness."

Second, where political qualities and questions of agency do exist, the violence is often pathologized and stripped of any critical meaning, appearing merely barbarous or purely economical. A case point here is the frequent violence witnessed in the urban ghettos of Paris and port cities in southern France. The notorious *banlieues* as featured in Mathieu Kassovitz's compelling movie *La Haine* (*Hate*, 1995) evince most clearly how the social engineering of migrant populations can lead to deeply structured forms of poverty and conditions of violence that blur any neat demarcations between incarceration and wretched policies of urban containment. While the poverty and endemic crime of these areas often has leftist sociologists lamenting the lack of social provision to the inhabitants—all the while providing further ammunition to the right's insistence that multiculturalism has failed—the historical question that would link the violence of these Arab (notably Algerian) youths to the history of French colonial brutality, racial prejudice, and political marginalization as a result of the neoliberal embrace is seldom posed. And yet, as the case of Mohamed Merah in the southern city of Toulouse shows in the most horrifying ways, when regimes of oppression fail to address the political question of the times, the spectacle of violence evinces a terrifying mimicry. As Merah executed three French soldiers, the Rabbi Jonathan Sandler, and his 3- and 5-year-old sons, and then proceeded to chase an 8-year-old girl across a playground before shooting her in the head—while filming it all on a GoPro motorcycle head-cam—there was something else going on than simply state neglect and willful abandonment. We see in such horrors a toxic mix of neoliberalism, colonial heritage, and racial and class subjugation, along with the veritable death of hope that is condemning entire populations to ghettoized despair. As the character Vinz from Kassovitz's script recalls in a place where the billboards read "The World Is Yours": "It's about a society on its way down. And as it falls, it keeps telling itself, 'So far so good . . . so far so good . . . so far so good.' It's not how you fall that matters. It's how you land."

The Punishing State

Every once in a while certain events become visible that convey a society's failure to come to grips with the myriad conditions that produce human suffering while signaling a most frightening truth about the emergence of both a brutalizing culture of cruelty and the spectre of authoritarian tendencies. In the United States, such flashpoints have been evident in the aftermath of Hurricane Katrina, particularly the handling of the devastation and the abandonment of low-income communities caught in the ravages of the storm. The reach of state violence and the punishing state is also obvious in the rise of debtor prisons, the school-to-prison pipeline, the criminalizing of social behavior, the militarization of local police forces, and the outsourcing of school discipline to police personnel. The war on poverty and drugs has morphed into a war on the poor and largely on communities of color. Under the punishing state, police power and state violence are increasingly being used in ways that, as Chase Madar points out, turn every sphere of American life into a matter of policing and control, just as violence has now entered the DNA of American life. He writes:

> By now, the militarization of the police has advanced to the point where "the War on Crime" and "the War on Drugs" are no longer metaphors but bland understatements. There is the proliferation of heavily armed SWAT teams, even in small towns; the use of shock-and-awe tactics to bust small-time bookies; the no-knock raids to recover trace amounts of drugs that often result in the killing of family dogs, if not family members; and in communities where drug treatment programs once were key, the waging of a drug version of counterinsurgency war. (All of this is ably reported on journalist Radley Balko's blog and in his book, *The Rise of the Warrior Cop*.) But American over-

policing involves far more than the widely reported up-armoring of your local precinct. It's also the way police power has entered the DNA of social policy, turning just about every sphere of American life into a police matter.[19]

The increasing proliferation of the punishing, surveillance, and warfare state makes everyone a potential target and enemy combatant. As shared fears replace shared notions of trust, the poison of suspicion morphs into a culture of subterfuge, mistrust, and the fear to dare to think freely with a sense of dignity, courage, conviction, and outrage. Whistle-blowers are treated like traitors; immigrants are housed in overcrowded jails; school children are charged with a felony for throwing peanuts at a bus.[20] Moreover, as more police are deployed in schools, there has been "a surge in arrests or misdemeanor charges for essentially nonviolent behavior—including scuffles, truancy, and cursing at teachers—that sends children into the criminal courts."[21] In some school districts, kids as young as 5 years old are punished by being locked in what are called seclusion rooms. In one reported incident, Heather Locke's 10-year-old son, Carson, was punished by being placed in a room that had "cinder block walls, a dim light, and a fan in the ceiling that rattled so insistently her son would beg them to silence it."[22] It is no coincidence that Carson's punishment resembled a practice associated more with a prison than a school. How a society treats its youth provides a context for understanding the tension between the rise of the police state, democratic values, and the reality of despair and suffering that many children face daily.

The effects of the emerging police state can also be seen in the criminalization of poverty. This is particularly clear given the thousands of poor people jailed each year because they could not pay parking fines, truancy fines, or fines imposed for other trivial violations. For instance, an investigation launched by National

Public Radio found that "a 19-year-old was jailed for three days after catching a small-mouth bass during rock bass season, because he couldn't pay the fine; a homeless man [was] sentenced to a year in jail over $2,600 in penalties incurred by shoplifting a $2 can of beer; a recovering drug user [was] sent to jail three times for being unable to make payments on nearly $10,000 in court costs."[23] In one tragic incident "a mother of seven died in a Pennsylvania [jail] while serving a two-day sentence . . . because she could not pay the thousands of dollars in fines relating to her children's truancy from schools in the Reading, PA, area."[24] There is more at work here than a travesty of justice. There is also a culture of cruelty reinforced by a survival-of-the-fittest neoliberal ethic coupled with the weakening of the social state and the rise of a police state that gains newfound legitimacy through appeals to law and order, security, and a culture of fear. Instead of protecting its most vulnerable, the state now legislates policies that deny the poor food stamps, defunds public schools, empties the public treasury of funds for social provisions by lowering taxes on the rich and corporations, dismantles Medicaid, and aggressively attempts to eliminate any social program that provides a measure of security for those who are unemployed, sick, poor, or disabled.

With the social contract suspended, if not altogether abandoned, the state no longer feels obligated to take measures that prevent hardship, suffering, and death. Neoliberalism has produced what might be called the end of the era of political concessions. Economics now drives politics. In such a society, the ethical imagination loses its leverage, as profit-making and financial advantage undermine every vestige of community building, solidarity, and democracy itself. The state no longer protects its own disadvantaged citizens; they are already seen as having no value within the global economic/political framework. Specific populations now occupy a political space that effectively invalidates the categories of "citizen" and "democratic representation," categories once integral to the nation-state system. In the past, people who were once marginalized by class and race at least were supported by the government, because of the social contract or because they still had some value as part of a reserve army of the unemployed. That is no longer true. These slow forms of violence are conditioned by a permanent state of deepening crisis in which "vast populations are subject to conditions of life conferring upon them the status of living dead."[25] The populations are largely invisible in the global media or, when disruptively present, defined as redundant, pathological, and dangerous. Within this wasteland of disposability, whole enclaves of people are relegated to what Bauman calls "social homelessness."[26] While elite classes maintain lifestyles produced through vast inequalities of symbolic and material capital, the "free market" provides neither social protection and security nor hope to those who are disadvantaged by inadequate income, housing, health care, nutrition, and education.

Disposability in its current forms has produced slow forms of violence reinforced by a commercially curated media landscape in which social movements, dissenters, impoverished communities, the elderly, the infirm, and criminalized populations all share a common fate of disappearing from public view. Rendered invisible in deindustrialized communities far removed from the suburbs, barred from the tourist-laden sections of major cities, locked in understaffed nursing homes, interned in bulging prisons located in remote farm communities, hidden in decaying schools in rundown neighbourhoods that bear the look of third world slums, populations of poor black and brown citizens exist outside of the view of most Americans. They have become the waste products of a utopian dream, if not modernity itself, as Bauman has argued for some time.[27] The disposable populations serve as an unwelcome reminder that the once vaunted social state no longer exists, the living dead now an apt personification of the death of the social contract in the United States and its decline in other neoliberal societies. Having fallen through the large fissures in any remaining social safety nets, America's disposable men, women, and children reflect a government agenda that has continuously cut costs associated with helping impoverished families and communities. That these are largely people of color undermines the nation's post–Civil Rights era commitments; race continues to be the "major reason America treats its poor more harshly than any other advanced country."[28]

Perhaps no more stark example exists than the fallout from Hurricane Katrina—one of the worst storms in U.S. history. The response following Katrina shamed the American public into seeing the plight of impoverished communities. In less than 48 hours, Katrina ruptured the pristine image of America as the largely white, middle-class country endlessly marketed and put on display by its corporate media and entertainment industries. Janet Pelz was right in arguing that Katrina showed us the murky quicksand beneath the hype about the values and virtues of the alleged free market. She writes:

> Hurricane Katrina showed us faces the Republicans never wanted us to see—the elderly, the infirm, the poor. The ones with no car to get them out of the city before the storm hit, the ones unable to pay for hotel rooms until the waters receded. The ones with no health insurance to recover from the ravages of insulin shock, kidney failure or dehydration. The ones lying face down in the cesspool or dying of heatstroke in the Superdome. . . . As long as the poor remained out of sight, they could be described in whatever undeserving light the Republicans chose, and the rest of us would be unwilling to challenge them. This second Bush administration was to be the conservatives' crowning glory. They would finish slicing government to the bone, sacrificing environmental protections, critical

infrastructure investments, health and human services, all to massive tax cuts. Yes, the long climb back from the precipice of the New Deal was within reach. That is, until the poor came out of hiding and shamed us into seeing them. The [neoliberals] had sold us their theory—each of us should take care of ourselves. Citizens (at least those morally upstanding enough to be wealthy) could do better for ourselves than the government could do for us.[29]

Pedagogies by the Oppressed

Gayatri Spivak once asked, "Can the subaltern speak?"[30] That is to say, under what circumstances do those on the margins of the neoliberal grid have the ability to exercise agency on their own terms, having the power to speak with an authentic voice such that their political subjectivities are affirmed? This question leads the way to others. First, what are the criteria that should be met such that the disempowered of the world are given a voice through cultural productions? Second, in what ways are the subaltern speaking on their own terms, thereby allowing us to rethink, challenge, and work beyond neoliberalism's vapid spectacle?

A wonderful example is provided in David Simon's HBO series *The Wire*. The setting, the destitute and bleak landscape of post-industrial Baltimore, highlights the violence of community impoverishment and segregation, and the intersection of seemingly disparate worlds. Michael Shapiro, for instance, writes how the series explores the meaningful and complex articulation of new urban domains: "Although the frontier in *The Wire*— primarily a racial frontier—is more fixed, with political and policing forces on the one side and the criminal and delinquent assemblages on the other, many of the relationships are unstable, both within and between the two assemblages."[31] Indeed, drawing upon Foucault's biopolitical reading of spatiality, Shapiro reminds that, in this setting, fixed and clearly demarcated binaries tell us little, as "policing agencies and the 'delinquent milieu' (in this case drug gangs and users) are intimately connected, as the police produce and make use of informants to render 'delinquency' useful." What is more, since the interlocking narratives that benefit from the format's longer temporality eschew a "single ethico-political perspective" (let alone imposing moral condemnation) so often associated with "verbal ideological centres," they move away from the master-narrative sequencing to critically connect "the dramatic cleavage between Baltimore's macropolitical process in the central and western section of the city and the micropolitics of survival in East Baltimore."

Certainly one of the most compelling scenes that allows for a cultured critique worthy of the name appears in the Season 1 episode "The Buys," as the narcotics-selling street youths end up discussing the logic and complexities of the game of chess. In the episode titled "The King Always Stays the King," we encounter a subtle and sophisticated use of the chess metaphor to reveal more than a surface reading might suggest. The scene begins with two of the characters, Bodie and Wallace, misusing a chessboard to play a game of checkers. This sets up the dialogue, as D'Angelo, the nephew of the notorious local drug lord Avon, works the metaphor by identifying their inability to grasp the real rules of the game. Hence the question "Why y'all playing checkers on a chess set?" immediately sets the scene for a different type of discourse, as the level playing field assumed by all pieces on a checkers board is cast aside. What follows is worth repeating, not least the dissent eventually shown by Bodie, who refuses to accept that this different logic is any more valid:

> **D'Angelo Barksdale**: Now look, check it, it's simple, it's simple. See this? This the kingpin, a'ight? And he the man. You get the other dude's king, you got the game. But he trying to get your king too, so you gotta

protect it. Now, the king, he move one space any direction he damn choose, 'cause he's the king. Like this, this, this, a'ight? But he ain't got no hustle. But the rest of these motherfuckers on the team, they got his back. And they run so deep, he really ain't gotta do shit.

Preston 'Bodie' Broadus: Like your uncle.

D'Angelo: Yeah, like my uncle. You see this? This the queen. She smart, she fast. She move any way she want, as far as she want. And she is the go-get-shit-done piece.

Wallace: Remind me of Stringer.

D'Angelo: And this over here is the castle. Like the stash. It can move like this, and like this.

Wallace: Dog, stash don't move, man.

D'Angelo: C'mon, yo, think. How many time we move the stash house this week? Right? And every time we move the stash, we gotta move a little muscle with it, right? To protect it.

Bodie: True, true, you right. All right, what about them little baldheaded bitches right there?

D'Angelo: These right here, these are the pawns. They like the soldiers. They move like this, one space forward only. Except when they fight, then it's like this. And they like the front lines, they be out in the field.

Wallace: So how do you get to be the king?

D'Angelo: It ain't like that. See, the king stay the king, a'ight? Everything stay who he is. Except for the pawns. Now, if the pawn make it all the way down to the other dude's side, he get to be queen. And like I said, the queen ain't no bitch. She got all the moves.

Bodie: A'ight, so if I make it to the other end, I win.

D'Angelo: If you catch the other dude's king and trap it, then you win.

Bodie: A'ight, but if I make it to the end, I'm top dog.

D'Angelo: Nah, yo, it ain't like that. Look, the pawns, man, in the game, they get capped quick. They be out the game early.
Bodie: Unless they some smart-ass pawns.

While it is tempting to read this scene as a commentary on their local status and identities as dangerous youths, having no prospects other than to conform to their illicit plight, situated in the broader screenplay that connects all of Baltimore's seemingly disparate worlds, it can be seen as a further example of Simon's exemplary ability to allow the youth to both explain their position within local relations of power, and gesture toward the wider social conditions that allow them to speak to power on their terms. The game of chess has always provided useful metaphors to political thinkers and strategists concerned with explaining relations of power. That these dangerously profiled youths operating in "the pit" can evidence such levels of political understanding should not then be seen as incidental. It attempts to narrate the ways the most marginal are still acutely aware of their political agency, and are able to relate to questions of power on their own terms, using their own interpretations, while connecting to broader logics of power that end up looking remarkably familiar. Such transposition of logics between worlds is one of the real strengths of this series. Indeed, the ability to disrupt conventional political assumptions is continuously affirmed as corrupt local financiers, lawyers and public officials court the drug "kings" as one of their own. As Russell "Stringer" Bell articulates to D'Angelo's uncle Avon:

You know, Avon, you gotta think about what we got in this game for, man. Huh? Was it the rep? Was it so our names could ring out on some fucking ghetto street corner, man? Naw, man. There's games beyond the fucking game.

SIX

FASCINATING FASCISM REVISITED

The Spectacle of Fascism

Fascism is not simply a historical problem. Neither is it simply tied to twentieth-century ideological moorings now largely undone by political modernity. Such analysis not only prevents a rigorous assessment of power—especially the power of economy; it denies us the ability to understand more clearly both its desiring qualities and the spectacles of violence it often produces. This is what Michel Foucault has identified to be "fascism in all its forms": "not only historical fascism, the fascism of Hitler and Mussolini—which was able to use the desire of the masses so effectively—but also the fascism in us all, in our heads, and in our everyday behavior, the fascism that causes us to love power, to desire the very thing that dominates and exploits us." Such fascism cannot be represented as a historically constituted regime, a particular system of power relations, or incipient ideology. Fascism is as diffuse as the phenomenon of power itself. That does not in any way mean that fascism is somehow beyond representation. The problem of fascism, in all its contemporary forms, demands representation, naming, critical diagnoses, and resistance.

Susan Sontag believed that capitalist societies require the recurring motif of fascist imagery in order to infiltrate the culture of everyday life, legitimate official power, and anesthetize people through visual spectacles.[1] Such images also enable the circulation of information along with militaristic modes of surveillance and control. Sontag argued in her later work that war and photography have become inseparable, and as a result of that fusion, representations of violence no longer compel occasions for self and social critique. Rather, shocking images have increasingly emerged as a mode of commercialized entertainment, advancing the machinery of consumption and undermining democratic community and social formations. She was particularly concerned about an aesthetics of depravity—that is, the marketing of images that package representations of dehumanization with elements used in advertising, design, film, and art—thus serving in the main to "bleach out a moral response to what is shown."[2] For Sontag and many other critical theorists, an aesthetics of depravity reveals itself when it takes as its "transcendent" object the misery of others, murderous displays of torture, mutilated bodies, and intense suffering, while simultaneously erasing the names, histories, and voices of the victims of such brutal and horrible acts.

What is worth noting, especially in the current historical context, is that there seemed to be a perverse pleasure to be had in the erasure of the victims' names, voices, and histories. "Hasn't the universality of the extermination of bodies," asks Paul Virilio, "as well as of the environment from AUSCHWITZ to CHERNOBYL, succeeded in dehumanizing us from without by shattering our ethic and aesthetic bearings, our very perception of our surroundings?"[3] That is to say, not only has the spectacle of violence become the defining order of all appearances, it has infected our very ability to perceive and ethically interpret and respond to the destruction being waged around us, upon us, between us, and even within us. Marked instead by a virulent notion of hardness and aggressive masculinity, pain, humiliation, and abuse are condensed into digestible screen shots endlessly circulated through extreme sports, Reality TV, video games, YouTube postings, and proliferating forms of the new and old media. Neoliberal indoctrination through commercial entertainment includes extreme images of violence, human suffering, and torture splashed across giant movie screens, some in 3-D, offering viewers every imaginable portrayal of violent acts, each more shocking and brutal than the last. Nothing exemplifies this better than the senseless and highly profitable *Saw* movie series, which excels in providing more sophisticated means for torture and violence for our entertainment with each passing installment.

The growing taste for sadism can be seen in the remarkable fascination on the part of the media with Peter Moskos's book *In Defense of Flogging*, in which the author seriously proposed that prisoners be given a choice between a standard sentence and a number of lashes administered in public.[4] In the name of reform, Moskos argued, without any irony, that public flogging is a more honest and sure-fire way of reducing the prison population. Not only was this book given massive air time in the mainstream media throughout the United States, its advocacy of corporal punishment and flogging was treated as though it were a legitimate proposal for reform. Mind-crushing punishment could be presented as the only choice left for prisoners outside of serving their sentences. Moreover, this return to the types of punishment that openly inflicts pain on the body is legitimate as part of a public spectacle. Leaving aside the ethical implications of this type of policy advocacy, Moskos also seems to tragically miss how the legacy of slavery informs his proposal, given that flogging was one of the preferred punishments handed out to slaves and that 70 percent of all current prisoners in the United States are people of color. Surely, the next step on would be a Reality TV franchise in which millions tune in to watch public floggings. This is not merely violence parading as reform—it is also a blatant indicator of the degree to which sadism and the infatuation with spectacles of violence have become normalized in a society that seems to take delight in dehumanizing itself.

The problem of course is that reality tends to bite back.

Reality TV shamelessly sells itself as a form of democratization through the interactions now made possible by digital media. This has had a number of telling implications. Every form of spectacle is now served up for public consumption. We are even asked to actively participate as our "smart devices" replace the agora of the political with the networked ideas of connectivity made possible by "shared viewing platforms." But reality, for better or worse, on occasion has this remarkable ability to produce the untimely event that shatters the simulacrum of existence. We have only to recall here the reaction of Zinedine Zidane in the soccer World Cup of 2006. Against all the commercialization of this global media spectacle, which many pundits believed to be so corporate that the qualities of the games were of a pitiful standard, Zidane's momentary rage that came from a history of racial abuse suffered due to his Algerian ancestry stands apart as a form of violence that is sometimes difficult to condemn. Perhaps it is no coincidence then that Zidane's outrage, like Diego Maradona's infamous "Hand of God" twenty years earlier, became "the event" of the tournament, as it was to the viewing audience the only true act of spontaneity and dignified as a result. Likewise, the widespread disobedience that erupted in dozens of U.S. cities after the Ferguson grand jury decision not to indict a cop for shooting a black teenager to death shows the same spontaneity in the political and social arena.

Such localized outrage has a more sobering and tragic side. From 9/11 onwards we have become increasingly accustomed to the digital projection of images of violence that make the global real to us through the so-called democratizing media. Indeed, after being widely broadcast in the media and on the Internet, the brutal and digitally captured shooting rampage on the Canadian Parliament and murder of Canadian soldier Nathan Cirillo on October 22, 2014, by Michael Zehaf-Bibeau, a longtime crack addict, served as a convenient excuse to whip up moral panic and contrived hysteria in the service of justifying the police state at home and terror wars abroad.[5] Soon after the shooting and killing, conservative prime minister Stephen Harper claimed that this singular attack by a lone mentally unstable man was officially deemed to be an act of terror waged upon the entire fabric of society. Under such circumstances, the actually number of casualties is no longer of importance. It is the number of viewers of the message and the effects it produces that hallmark the spectacles of violence today. Such violence therefore conforms to current marketization strategies as it works by individualizing the tragedy such that we all bear witness and find the inertia palpable as our democratic processes seem incapable of securing us from their devastating effects. All that remains is the notion that we must partake in a world that increasingly appears to be terribly violent with each passing spectacle that now comes to us instantaneously and with decreasing possibility for purposeful collective reflection and response. After all, the instantaneousness of action demands an instantaneous response. One inevitable danger here is the birth of a new global vigilantism which, as the Kony episode suggested, holds the possibility for legitimating violence through the displacement of the ballot by the arbitrariness of the "like" button. Spectacle upon spectacle, violence upon violence, fashioned to render the only thing that remains of the "public" no more than a shared sense of vulnerability.

Rituals of Humiliation

Judith Butler's *Gender Trouble* (1990) disrupted conventional notions of the self by emphasizing how subjectivities are culturally constructed through the repetition of stylized acts in time. It is repetition that establishes the appearance of an essential "ontological core." This was developed in a later work, *Bodies That Matter*, where she emphasizes how performativity must be understood in the process of iterability—that is, a regularized and constrained repetition of norms. This notion of iterability is useful in that as it implies that the real strength of a social performance is not a singular act or event, but a ritualized production: "a ritual reiterated under and through constraint, under and through the force of prohibition and taboo, with the threat of ostracism and even death controlling and compelling the shape of the production."[6] This focus on the normal instead of the exceptional offers a different angle of vision here for thinking about spectacles of violence. In short, it forces us to consider the extent to which the most abhorrent acts of violence reveal a continuum of ritualistic acts which, akin to the more uncomfortable scenes in Pasolini's *Salò*, make humiliation central to the spectacle as a desired state of affairs. Indeed, it is the ritualization of humiliation that reveals the singularity of violence as a means for inscribing upon the body the most dehumanizing forms of markers, which designate the expendability and disposability of the subject.

In the spring of 2004, a set of images appeared that challenged the mythic representations of the global terror wars with the release of hundreds of gruesome photographs and videos documenting the torture, sexual humiliation, and abuse of Iraqi prisoners by American soldiers at the Abu Ghraib prison facility. They were first broadcast on the television series *60 Minutes II* and later leaked to the press, becoming something of a nightly feature in the weeks and months that ensued. Abu Ghraib prison was one of the most notorious sites used by the regime of the deposed Saddam Hussein to inflict unspeakable horrors on those Iraqis considered disposable for various political reasons, ironically reinforcing the growing perception in the Arab world that one tyrant had simply replaced another. In sharp contrast to the all too familiar and officially sanctioned images of the liberating soldier patrolling dangerous Iraqi neighborhoods, caring for wounded soldiers, or passing out candy to young Iraqi children, the newly discovered photos depicted Iraqi detainees being humiliated and assaulted. The success of the invasion was soon recast by a number of sadistic images, including now infamous photos depicting the insipid, grinning faces of Specialist Charles A. Graner and Private Lynndie R. England flashing a thumbs-up behind a pyramid of seven naked detainees, a kneeling Iraqi posing as if he is performing oral sex on another hooded male detainee, a terrified Iraqi man trying to ward off an attack dog being handled by American soldiers, and a U.S. soldier grinning next to the body of a dead man packed in ice.

The sheer horror of these images has led some commentators to invoke comparisons with the photographs of lynched black men and women in the American South and the torture of Jewish people in Nazi death camps.[7] One of the most haunting images depicts a hooded man standing on a box, with his arms outstretched in Christ-like fashion, electric wires attached to his hands and genitals, and another revealed a smiling England holding a leash attached to a naked Iraqi man lying on the floor of the prison.[8] In February 2006, previously unpublished pictures of prisoner abuse were broadcast by an Australian television station. These new images show an Iraqi prisoner having his "head slammed into a wall. . . . a naked detainee with multiple injuries to his buttocks, [and] a naked male prisoners forced to masturbate in front of the camera."[9]

This was more than an isolated event. These pictures followed video images released only a week earlier that showed British soldiers beating an Iraqi youth who had been dragged from a street demonstration into a fenced-in area and had been "pulled to the ground and beaten by at least five alleged British soldiers with batons and fists."[10] In 2007, retired U.S. Army general Anthony Taguba, who had written the initial and one of the most thorough reports on the torture and abuses at Abu Ghraib prison, told Seymour Hersh in an interview published in the *New Yorker* that some of the most disturbing images and videos still have not been released. These included "an Iraqi woman detainee baring her breasts . . . a video of a male American soldier in uniform sodomizing a female detainee," and a father forced to have sex with his son.[11] Like Oscar Wilde's infamous picture of Dorian Gray, the portrait of American patriotism was irrevocably transformed into the opposite of the ideal image it sought to present to the world. The fight for Iraqi "hearts and minds" was irreparably damaged as the war on terror appeared to produce only more terror, mimicking the very crimes it claimed to have eliminated.

As Susan Sontag pointed out, the leaked photographs include both the victims and their gloating assailants. For Sontag, the images from Abu Ghraib are not only "representative of the fundamental corruptions of any foreign occupation," which serve as "a perfect recipe for the cruelties and crimes committed against the thousands incarcerated without charges or access to lawyers in American-run prisons," but are also like "lynching photographs [that] were souvenirs of a collective action whose participants felt perfectly justified in what they had done."[12] Reminiscent of photos taken by whites who lynched blacks after Reconstruction, the images were circulated as trophy shots to be passed around and sent out to friends. For Sontag and others, Abu Ghraib could not be understood outside of the racism and brutality that accompanied the exercise of power both at home and abroad. Indeed, as time passed, it became clear that the instances of abuse and torture that took place at Abu Ghraib were extensive, systematic, and part of a larger pattern of criminal behavior that had taken place in other prisons in both Iraq and Afghanistan—not to mention the thousands of civilian prisons, jails, and detention centers in the United States.[13] Patterns of mistreatment by interventionist forces had also taken place in Camp Bucca, a U.S.-run detention center in southern Iraq, as well as in an overseas CIA interrogation center at the Bagram airbase in Afghanistan, where the deaths of three detainees were labeled homicide by U.S. military doctors.[14]

Consuming Violence

The images from Abu Ghraib were not at all exceptional in terms of their shock appeal. Since the early 1990s, Benetton, the famous clothing manufacturer, has proven that trafficking in pain and human suffering is not only good for business but also good for providing a patina of legitimacy to the company as an artsy brand with philanthropic concerns.[15] Benetton's United Colors campaign appropriated shocking and visually arresting representations of violence and pain in order to sell clothes and attract global attention to its brand. In doing so, Benetton did more than attempt to conjoin the worlds of glamour and suffering; it also pushed a mode of commercial advertising in which the subjects of often horrendous misfortunes and acts of suffering were deployed as part of a technique for product marketing. For example, Benetton used the colorized image of David Kirby, a dying AIDS patient, to sell jumpers. A more poignant example of the exploitation of images of suffering can be found in an unpublished interview in which Jacqueline Lichtenstein recounts her experience visiting the museum at Auschwitz. She writes:

> When I visited the Museum at Auschwitz, I stood in front of the display cases. What I saw there were images from contemporary art and I found that absolutely terrifying. Looking at the exhibits of suitcases, prosthetics, children's toys, I didn't feel frightened. I didn't collapse. I wasn't completely overcome the way I had been walking around the camp. No. In the Museum, I suddenly had the impression I was in a museum of contemporary art. I took the train back, telling myself that they had won! They had won since they'd produced forms of perception that are all of a piece with a mode of destruction they made their own.[16]

Such exhibitions give credence to Walter Benjamin's claim that in late modernity the mesmerizing and seductive language of power underlies captivating spectacles that inextricably fuse sophisticated design elements with a fascist politics.[17] To his credit Benjamin recognized the affective force of aesthetics and its at times perverse ability to "privilege cultural forms over ethical norms" while mobilizing emotions, desires, and pleasures that delight in human suffering and become parasitic upon the pain of others.[18] Benjamin's understanding of fascism's use of imagery is important, in spite of appearing deterministic, because it highlights how fascist spectacles use the force of sensations and serve to privilege the emotive and visceral at the expense of thoughtful engagement. In his analysis of Benjamin, Lutz Koepnick develops this point further by exploring how the fascist spectacle "mobilizes people's feelings primarily to neutralize their senses, massaging minds and emotions so that the individual succumbs to the charisma of vitalistic power."[19] There is an important point to be made here: fascism is better understood not through the lens of political ideology, but as an economy of power that suffocates the political in the most narcissistic yet publicly celebrated fashions. How else do people come to desire their own oppression if not through this micro-specific play of emotions which taps directly into personal anxieties to normalize violence?

Inglorious Bastards
Toward the final stages of the inglorious withdrawal from Afghanistan, a number of photographs surfaced depicting grotesque acts of violence and murder by a select group of American soldiers. These images were first released by the German weekly *Der Spiegel* and later by *Rolling Stone* magazine in the United States. The images in *Rolling Stone* focused on the murderous actions of twelve U.S. soldiers in Afghanistan who decided to kill Afghan civilians allegedly for sport. They used the moniker

the "Kill Team" to refer to themselves, aptly registering both the group's motivation and its monstrous actions. The soldiers' acts exhibited not only their immersion in a death-driven culture that we have been concerned to expose here. Their actions were neither isolated nor individualized but reflect their evident belief that killing for sport in such a culture could take place with impunity. Proudly naming themselves the "Kill Team" also registers "the pure depravity of the alleged crimes."[20] In the five months during which these soldiers went on a murderous rampage in Kandahar province, writes one reporter "they engaged in routine substance abuse and brutality toward Afghan locals that led to four premeditated murders of innocent civilians, the ritual mutilation of corpses (some of the soldiers reportedly severed fingers from their victims to keep as trophies), and the snapping of celebratory photographs alongside the deceased as if they were bagged deer."[21] In one particularly disturbing photo celebrating a kill, one of the soldiers, Jeremy Morlock, is shown posing with the body of Gul Mudin, a 15-year-old Afghan boy. With a grin on his face and a thumbs-up sign, Morlock is kneeling on the ground next to Mudin's bloody and half-naked corpse, grabbing a handful of hair to lift up his bloodied face.

The platoon's squad leader, Staff Sgt. Calvin Gibbs, was so pleased with the kill that he butchered the young boy's dead body for a souvenir, severing one of his fingers. Mark Boal quotes one soldier's account of the incident: "'It was like another day at the office for him'. . . . Gibbs started 'messing around with the kid, moving his arms and mouth and acting like the kid was talking.'" Boal adds, "then, using a pair of razor-sharp medic's shears, [Gibbs] reportedly sliced off the dead boy's pinky finger and gave it to [the soldier], as a trophy for killing his first Afghan."[22] Gibbs's instinct for barbarism appears utterly ruthless and lacking in any sense of ethical consideration or self-reflection—to say nothing of the political and social costs incurred by the U.S.-led mission. The staff sergeant was so intent on killing

Afghan civilians that he actually boasted about it, telling one soldier, "Come down to the line and we'll find someone to kill."[23]

Gibbs reportedly told his soldiers that all Afghans were savages and talked to his squad about how they might be inventive in killing civilians. In one almost unbelievable scenario, the soldiers considered throwing "candy out of a Stryker vehicle as they drove through a village and shoot[ing] the children who came running to pick up the sweets. According to one soldier, they also talked about a second scenario in which they 'would throw candy out in front and in the rear of the Stryker; the Stryker would then run the children over.'"[24] This is a very different atrocity from what occurred several years earlier at Abu Ghraib prison, to which it is dismissively compared.

What is revealing about the "Kill Team" photos is that they received very little attention in the American media, despite the atrocity of the crimes committed by this group of U.S. soldiers. Attempts by the U.S. media to explain the indefensible actions of these soldiers fell back on the usual laconic explanations, even though these crimes were different in a number of ways from previously reported atrocities. For example, Seymour Hersh claimed that "these soldiers had come to accept the killing of civilians—recklessly, as payback, or just at random—as a facet of modern unconventional warfare. In other words, killing itself, whether in a firefight with the Taliban or in sport with innocent bystanders in a strange land with a strange language and strange customs, has become ordinary."[25]

According to Hersh, such heinous barbarity is part of the social cost that comes with paying young people to wage war. Writing for the *New York Times*, Luke Mogelson argued that "American soldiers have become increasingly more willing to kill."[26] This position echoes the comments of one older American officer formerly in charge of training Marines going to war, who pointed less to how young people are trained to kill by the armed forces than to the larger mechanisms of indoctrination at work that increasingly culture an inability to identify with others, an instinct to use violence in response to problems, and the willingness to take pleasure in the act of slaughter. This officer stated: "I used to do this job in the '70s during the war in Vietnam. In those years it took six months to train a young person to be prepared to kill a human being. Now I am doing the same job in Iraq, but things have changed. The young men come here already trained. They come here ready to kill."[27] The editors of *Rolling Stone* and staff writer Mark Boal suggested that the killing of innocent civilians is partly due to the failure of military leadership as well as the martial conditioning achieved through the training that recruits receive before being shipped off to war. David Carr of the *New York Times* echoed this sentiment in his claim that photos taken in wartime "carry the full freight of war and its collateral damage."[28] All of these responses look directly into the face of what is an almost unimaginable horror, but in the end they shrink from it by failing to address both what is unique about the "Kill Team" photographs and more importantly what they reveal about the current state of American society. These responses ignore that the pleasure of killing is not just normalized in war but increasingly indoctrinated into American society as a result of relentless visual marketing and commercial culturalization of killing, atrocity, abuse, and cruelty.

Unlike the Abu Ghraib prison photos that were designed to humiliate detainees, the "Kill Team" photos suggest a deeper depravity, an intense pleasure in acts of violence that are pre-planned and carried out with no impending threat, culminating in the sadistic collection of body parts of the slain victims as trophies. The "Kill Team" was after more than humiliation and the objectification of the other; it harbored a deep desire to feel intense excitement through pathological acts of murder and then captured the savagery in photos that served as mementos, so they could revisit and experience once again the delight that comes with descending into the sordid pornographic hell that connects violence, pleasure, and death. The smiles on the faces of the young soldiers as they posed among their trophy killings are not the snapshots of privatized violence, but images of sadism that are symptoms of a social pathology in which shared pleasure in violence is now commonplace. As David L. Clark points out, the smiles on the faces of these soldiers suggest something perverse and alarming. He writes, "This isn't Hannibal Lecter, after all, but G.I. Joe, [and these photos appear as] symptomatic evidence of a certain public enjoyment of violence for the sake of violence, i.e., not the smile of shared pleasures between intimates (one form of the everyday), but a smile that marks a broader acceptance and affirmation of cruelty, killing for sport. Those smiles register a knowing pleasure in that violence, and say that it is okay to kill, and okay to take pleasure in that killing."[29]

The "Kill Team" photographs register a deepening of what can be called a failed sociality. In this instance, the social does not disappear as much as it is overwritten by a sociality of shared violence—a sociality marked by the injurious violence not of the lone sociopath, but increasingly by groups of sociopaths. The "Kill Team" photographs offer a glimpse into a larger set of social conditions in a winner-take-all society in which it becomes increasingly difficult to imagine pleasure except in terms of spectacle and violence. The actions of the "Kill Team" tell us something about how the dehumanizing attitudes, values, and actions of neoliberalism migrate from its spectacles and commercial products and serve to culture criminal depravity. What is it about these photos that reveals the smear of the pornographic, a titillation grounded in maximizing the pleasure of violence? What are the political, economic, and social forces bearing down on American society that so easily undercut its potential to raise critical questions about war, violence, morality, and human suffering? How is it that the very category of the image is reconstituted as part of a wider acculturation of consumption and spectacle of violence, transformed in the end to culture predation and depravity?

The "Kill Team" is revealing of the changing contours of mass violence in the contemporary period, which homes in on the individual, often to the veritable occlusion of the wider political regimes of which they are part. From the streets of Manhattan which joyously welcomed Bin Laden's fateful demise, to the streets of Sirte where grotesque pictures of a tortured Gaddafi had politicians reminding us instead of the horrors that had been attributed to the man, never in fact has the death of individuals looked quite so carnivalesque. The assassination of Osama Bin Laden is particularly telling. No longer did we have to decide whether to try him in a military or criminal court; whether to put him on trial for crimes against humanity in the Hague or for crimes against citizens of the United States; whether the content of the trial itself would be open to public broadcast; whether we would allow him to use it as a forum to discuss our once sympathetic past; whether the event would simply be a formal procession in order to condemn a man already deemed to be guilty as charged; whether it would descend into a media circus as the crime of the century went digital; whether this would lead to greater cultural polarization and vilification of Islamic culture; whether it would lead to further radicalization, especially if a publicly sanctioned execution took place seemingly with our approval; or whether in the process of eventually putting him to death we would have been endangered further. These questions no longer needed to be addressed. Neither did we have to come to terms with the prospect of another Nuremburg in which the horrifying likes of Hermann Goering proved to be far too intellectually sophisticated for the legal process. On both counts real justice would be denied. But maybe that is the precise point. Could it be that we didn't want to pursue this line of action precisely because it reveals to us the structural limits of our very notions of justice? Notions that are shrouded in universalistic discourses, yet tell us nothing about the particularity of suffering felt by the victims of crimes so murderous there cannot be any satisfaction or personal closure from a guilty verdict. Let alone a way to seek political solutions to political problems and open the violence of our societies up to critical interrogation.

Every war that passes we hope to be the last. Unfortunately we know the reality is "where next"? Despite the failures of Iraq and Afghanistan, Western leaders' appetites for war haven't been dampened. There has admittedly been more soul-searching about what the public is willing to tolerate. This, however, is carried out so that we can fight wars better. As Michael Shapiro observes:

> While the GI Joe doll was once the appropriate avatar of the warrior, a battlefield soldier skilled in hand-to-hand combat, it is now more appropriate to fashion an avatar of a video game–playing teenager—for example, the one described by Peter Singer, a nineteen-year-old high school dropout who wanted to join the army to be a helicopter mechanic. Although he turned out to be unqualified for that role, once the army recognized his video game prowess, he was recruited as a "drone pilot" instead. He joined a group of warriors who go to war at their computer consoles—often in their own homes—from which they guide weaponized drones (pilotless aircraft) and fire missiles at suspected antagonists. Singer describes a scenario in which a video warrior is helping his children with their homework at the dining table in a city in Arizona, shortly after firing lethal weapons at targets in Afghanistan.[30]

The Mimetic Rage

The violence of 9/11 broke new ground in that the actions of a handful of nameable individuals managed to create the image of a global security crisis. This was only possible as a result of the global witnessing of the event made altogether likely due to the nature of the target. Since then, we have become accustomed to the most horrific spectacles of violence ready made for public broadcast and personal consumption. Indeed, while soldiers' head-cam footage has become a new form of pornographic currency for adrenaline-seeking military junkies high on the thrill of a violent encounter, so often fetishizing the military hardware at their disposal, for insurgents the move has been away from the spectacular explosion to micro-politics of the most terrifying and brutal of kinds. While the mediation of the images of 9/11 managed largely to remove the personal loss of life from the media frame, it is now precisely the mutilation of the individual body that hallmarks the violence of our times.

Something further has happened on this front in the decade since 9/11 as the broadcasting of violence against individuals has taken a more sinister and counter-dialectical turn. Previous forms of violence on all sides largely rested upon the mediation of images made possible by the control of the medium for production and distribution. The advent of the smart phone and other high-tech devices that are capable of instant dissemination has radicalized this completely. Indeed, whereas military head-cams still offer a certain censorship, in that distance erases the enemy from the frame, not only are violent insurgents increasingly evident in the composition of their violent productions, they openly rely upon the fact that the public will now fulfill the task of the broadcast media in ways that pervert the democratic ethos—albeit in a fashion that is not too dissimilar from the NSA's perverted attempts to level the playing field by arming everybody in the most militaristic sense of any notion of justice.

In a pivotal moment on the afternoon of May 22, 2013,

British Army Solider Lee Rigby was slain in broad daylight outside his military barracks streets of Woolwich in South London.
What was remarkable in this instance was the fact that the perpetrators, Michael Adebolajo and Michael Adebowale, remained
on the scene after the attempted beheading, continually talking
to members of the public who recorded what was happening
on their smart phone devices. What was also striking here was
that even before all the facts were established, politicians and
media alike were quick to declare that the violence "looked like
Terror." This justification was made on two counts. First, it was
presumed that the target for the violence was military personnel. The second rationale, more compelling at the time, was the
footage of one of the assailants stating without remorse for the
action: "We swear by almighty Allah we will never stop fighting
you. The only reasons we have done this is because Muslims are
dying every day. This British soldier is an eye for an eye, a tooth
for a tooth. We must fight them."

He further added, as if to claim that the burden of history
left him with no option: "I apologize that women had to witness
this today, but in our land our women have to see the same. You
people will never be safe. Remove your government. They don't
care about you." British Home Secretary Theresa May immediately responded by declaring that the vicious assault on the
soldier was more than an individual crime but an "attack against
all of us." This justification, however, raised a number of serious
questions. Assuming that the violence was politically motivated,
did that necessarily imply that the attack was on the entire fabric
of our society? And what did it mean to collapse the military
with the civic so that no distinction can be established?

Like the violence witnessed at the Boston Marathon the
month previous, it was becoming increasingly evident that these
spectacles of violence were markedly different from the horrors
of 9/11 and 7/7 (the 2005 London bombings that killed 52 and
injured more than 700). When one is no longer purposefully

aiming for "mass casualty" shock appeal, the victims are much fewer in number. That does not demean the nature of the tragedy. It does however raise the question as to why these localized acts of violence can still be presented as part of a continuum of threat that endangers global security.

Michael Clarke, the director of the United Kingdom's far from impartial think tank known as the Royal United Services Institute (RUSI), speaking on the BBC, called the perpetrators of the attack "homicidal exhibitionists." They represented a handful of individuals—possibly lone—who crave the media spotlight and shock through the celebratory nature of violence as a public spectacle. This may well be true, but the question remains, why did these particular acts resonate while comparable events in other parts of the world are barely considered? Indeed, have we become so fixated in the contemporary period on these types of "media events" instead of the continual violence many suffer on a daily basis, which just so happen to occur outside of the spotlight?

Such events continue to be presented to us as random. This is not incidental. Random events strike without warning. In other words, they allow for no credible foresight. Some even reason that we need to accept their inevitability. Surely, however, if we accept that spectacles of violence are political, there is nothing random whatsoever about their occurrence. Political violence is always a process. It always has a history. Its spectacle as such cannot be divorced from the actual violence it serves to normalize. Nor can a solution be found unless it faces up to the altogether more difficult political task of questioning why we have become so fascinated by spectacles of violence. How else can we explain the extraordinary degree to which the digital recordings of the violence went viral? Let alone the real brutality and rage purposefully showcased for public consumption? This raises the question of our own complicity in such perverse and banalized media projections. It also asks us to consider, what might we do differently? That is to say, how might we conceive of a better ethics of violence such that its representations do justice to the horrors of the experience?

Counter-Fascist Aesthetics

Instead of outright rejecting the aesthetics of depravity as being exclusively tied to the pleasure of consumption and the spectacle of violence, if not fascism itself, Sontag modified Benjamin's position, arguing that it can have a more productive and pedagogical role. She championed images that were ugly, destabilizing, and shocking. Such images, argued Sontag, harbor a capacity to show great cruelties precisely in order to arouse compassion and empathy rather than mere titillation. She asserted that "for photographs to accuse, and possibly to alter conduct, they must shock."[31] Shock and rupture become the pedagogical registers of resistance in which the image might talk back to power, unsettling common-sense perceptions while offering "an invitation to pay attention, to reflect, to learn, to examine the rationalizations for mass suffering offered by established powers."[32] Sontag realized that poetic power is not always on the side of oppression when presenting images of suffering. Of course, she was just as aware that in a society that makes a spectacle out of violence and human suffering, images that attempt to shock might well reinforce a media-induced habituation to and comfort with "the horror of certain images."[33] In this regard, a counter-fascist aesthetic cannot simply be taken for granted; it needs to be produced and/or made explicit in those images that widely circulate and are available for public consumption.

We are drawn here to Arendt's notion of "instants of truth" that often come in the form of images, narratives, and stories that shock. They don't accommodate reality as much as they turn it upside down, eviscerating common-sense assumptions a culture has about itself while revealing an intellectual and emotional chasm that runs through established modes of rationality

and understanding. Such flash points not only rupture dominant modes of consciousness, they give rise to heated passions
and debates, sometimes leading to massive displays of collective
anguish and resistance, even revolutions. Among the notable examples is the horrifying image of the 14-year-old African-American boy Emmett Till, whose body was mutilated and tortured
by white racists after he allegedly whistled at a white woman in
Mississippi in 1955. The image of his disfigured body helped to
launch the Civil Rights movement in the United States. There
are also the four-decades-old iconic images taken at My Lai that
revealed the slaughter of at least 500 innocent South Vietnamese
women, elderly men, and children by American soldiers during
the Vietnam War. These photographs, like the ones that surfaced at Abu Ghraib more recently, served as a tipping point
in reinvigorating a more powerful and consolidated anti-war
movement by culturing revulsion and disgust.

Art and culture can and should play critical roles in emancipatory politics. Photographers, as Mieke Bal points out, "can
deploy art not only as a reflection but also as a form of witnessing that alters the existence of what it witnesses." Bal also insists that art can be used "to reconquer beauty [when] mobilized
as a weapon *against* suffering," as represented by Nan Goldin's
deeply personal photographs displaying the violence and aggression that marked her relationship with her lover. What is at stake
is the perversion of a formative culture that increasingly deters
democratic society and enforces that deterrence both through
coercive violence and through modes of visual depravity that
debase the political subject. This latter line of thought raises a
different set of questions. What forms of responsibility and what
pedagogical strategies does one invoke in the face of a society
that feeds off spectacles of violence and cruelty? What forms of
witnessing and education might be called into play in which the
feelings of pleasure mobilized by images of human suffering can
be used as "a catalyst for critical inquiry and deep thought"? Re-

sponding to these questions entails recognizing, resisting, and transforming the pedagogical function of a cultural apparatus that seriously limits and undermines any viable notion of aesthetics that might extend rather than shut down critical thought, agency, and action in the service of a democracy to come. Instead of reducing the populace to obedient spectators trained to experience pleasure and cathartic release in the degradation and negation of others' humanity, a society commercially indoctrinated to enjoy violence, aggression, war, and modes of masculinity must serve as an indictment, a source of memory, and evidence of the need to imagine otherwise and resist.

So how might we represent "war machines" with the due ethical care and political consideration they rightly deserve? We could spend an entire volume critiquing here the poverty of many mainstream representations whose narrative and cinematography are bereft of anything remotely resembling the type of qualities suggested. While Francis Ford Coppola's *Apocalypse Now* and Michael Cimino's *The Deer Hunter* continue to set an alternative standard for those who seek to open up more critically the violence so often debased in contemporary cinema, David Simon and Ed Burns's work stands apart in the contemporary period for its exemplary engagement with spectacles of violence. Our focus here is their compelling series *Generation Kill*. This series manages to frame the desiring war machine better than any cinematic exploration so far. It also provides a potent critique of the complexities and harrowing tragedy of warfare beyond the realm of military entertainment. Based on the U.S. Marine Evan Calder's personal account of the first three weeks of the invasion, it follows First Reconnaissance Battalion to dramatize the early violent stages. The focus on this period proves to be chaotic, intense, and fraught with political and strategic tensions. The story line is largely based on the inter-subjective relations between the lead Humvee group of Sergeant Brad "Iceman" Colbert (Alexander Skarsgård), Corporal Josh Ray Person (James

Ransone), Lance Corporal Harold James Trombley (Billy Lush), and "Scribe" Wright (Lee Tergeson), along with the higher chain of command including First Lieutenant Nathaniel Fick (Stark Sands), Captain Craig "Encino Man" Schwetje (Brian Wade), and First Recon's commander, Lieutenant Colonel Stephen "Godfather" Ferrando (Chance Kelly). These relations are wonderfully executed and benefit from the series format, which allows for a more thoughtful engagement with each character. Simon's ambition for this project was clear from the start:

> War is disorder and mayhem and brutality. . . . With all our technology, with all our precision, with all our rules of engagement, with all the good will and best intentions, it doesn't prevent the tragedies. No viewer should ever make the mistake of thinking that war will be like some Department of Defense film of a smart bomb going through the right window, which is what war is from a distance. . . . I would feel better about this war, personally, if I didn't believe that the people who ordered it did so with as callow a sense of what war is as adults can have. . . . Did they know what they were saying when they said "war"? And I just get the impression, since they didn't serve, since they went out of their way not to serve, that maybe they didn't know.

Generation Kill purposefully disrupts the simple and uncritical binaries often associated with war movies. It brings the vexed question of agency directly into the production, thereby allowing for the complexities of the soldiers' personal stories to be given the attention they require. As Simon further explains, "I want to have ideas that are challenging and worth being challenged. A substantial story is one that has two sides to it. And if you don't cheat, and stumble into one side and stick up the other one as a straw man, you've got something that's actually worth thinking about." While *Generation Kill* offers a number of compelling scenes made all the more memorable with some extraordinary dialogue, including the capturing on the airstrip that evidences the extreme-sports mentality of the higher chain of command, it is the final scene that offers the most potent critique of violence. Much of the violence in the series happens in the instant. It is shot as moments of high drama, with a violent intensity that is made all the more believable due to the lack of precision and strategic thought beyond the level of killing itself. Throughout the mission, these moments of violence, some reactionary, many desired, are captured by the marine-turned-cinematographer Captain Jason Lilley (Kellan Lutz). The final scene consists of a screening of a montage from his footage, which is played back to the company as testimony to their exploits. It also promises a way for the marines to achieve certain closure as they are distanced from the action to assume the position of the spectator.

Johnny Cash's "When the Man Comes Around" provides a perfect musical score to the unfolding drama. It begins as a celebration of violence as each frame is rejoiced in and the camaraderie is evident, with the group huddled around the screen. Only Sergeant Colbert has his back symbolically turned to the performance. Slowly, however, as the spectacles of violence are replayed back to the marines, the atmosphere changes. For the audience, the spectacle confronts the spectacle to forceful critical effect. This has a profound bearing on the marines' behavior. As they are encouraged to confront as a matter of entertainment the violence and terror they have wrought upon insurgents and innocent people alike, what begins as a sequence of intensive violence, interspersed by all too familiar masculine gestures, subtly begins to operate at a slower temporality to permit thoughtful reflection. Gradually, in marked silence, they appear embarrassed by their own company. As star leads they are now shamed by what they are forced to witness with this new angle of vision. No longer is there the exuberant "Ooh Rah" battle cry so often associated with their masculine expressions. Instead the desire for violence turns into disgust as one by one each marine walks away from the screening. Leaving Colonel Pearson, Captain Lilley left with Lance Corporal. Trombley who oblivious to the critical response reviews "it's fucking beautiful"! As they both leave Trombley, who pauses then showing his disappointment clenches his rifle before making an ambiguous exist as to his further intentions, the words of Cash echo a poignant and poetic narrative to the spectacle of violence which can no longer be tolerated.

SEVEN

BEYOND ORWELL

Violence and the Surveillance State

The revelations of government lawlessness and corporate spying by whistle-blowers such as Chelsea Manning, Jeremy Hammond, and Edward Snowden give new meaning—if not revitalized urgency and relevance—to George Orwell's dystopian fable *1984*. Orwell offered his readers an image of the modern state that has become dystopian, one in which privacy is no longer valued as a civil virtue and a basic right, nor perceived as a measure of the robust strength of a healthy and thriving democracy. The right to privacy in *1984* comes under egregious assault, and such ruthless transgressions of privacy point to something more sinister than the violation of individual and collective rights. As important as Orwell's warning was in shedding light on the horrors of mid-twentieth-century totalitarianism and the endless regimes of state spying imposed on citizens, the text serves as a brilliant but limited metaphor for mapping the expansive trajectory of global surveillance that has come to consolidate neoliberal power through a grid of financial and police-state mechanisms. As Marjorie Cohn has indicated, "Orwell never could have imagined that the National Security Agency (NSA) would amass metadata on billions of our phone calls and 200 million of our text messages every day. Orwell could not have foreseen that our government would read the content of our emails, file transfers, and live chats from the social media we use."[1]

In a Christmas message videotaped in 2013, Edward

Snowden references Orwell's admonition of "the dangers of microphones, video cameras and TVs that watch us," allowing the state to regulate subjects within the most intimate spaces of private life.[2] But these older modes of surveillance, Snowden elaborates, are nothing compared to what is used for social control today. For Snowden, the threat posed by the new surveillance can be measured by its reach and use of technologies that far outstrip anything Orwell envisioned and pose a much greater threat to the privacy rights both of citizens and of sovereign powers. He reiterates this point by reminding his viewers that "a child born today will grow up with no conception of privacy at all—they will never know what it means to have a private moment to themselves, an unrecorded, unanalyzed thought."[3] Snowden is correct about the danger to privacy rights, but his analysis fails to go far enough in linking together the question of surveillance with the rise of "networked societies," global flows of power, and the emergence of oppressive state regimes.[4]

The democratic ideal rooted in the right to privacy under the modernist state in which Orwell lived out his political imagination has been both transformed and mutilated, almost beyond recognition. Just as Orwell's fable has morphed over time into a combination of "realistic novel," real-life documentary, and a form of Reality TV, privacy has been radically altered in an age of permanent, "non-stop" global exchange and circulation. So, too, in the current period of historical amnesia, privacy has been redefined through the material and market-fundamentalist registers of a neoliberal order in which the right to privacy has succumbed to the seductions of a narcissistic culture and capitalism's unending necessity to turn every relationship into an act of commerce and to make all aspects of daily life visible and subject to data manipulation.[5] In a world devoid of ethical care, compassion, and protection, privacy is no longer connected and resuscitated through its connection to public life, the common good, or a vulnerability born of the recognition of the frailty of human life. In a world in which the worst excesses of capitalism are unchecked, privacy is nurtured in a zone that organizes forgetting, indifferent to its transformation and demise under a "broad set of panoptic practices."[6] Consequently, culture loses its power as the bearer of public memory in a social order where a consumerist-driven ethic "makes impossible any shared recognition of common interests or goals" and furthers the collective indifference to the growth of the surveillance state.[7]

Surveillance has become an accepted feature of daily life. In fact, it is more appropriate to analyze the broader regime of surveillance, rather than address exclusively the violations committed by particular surveillance states. If there is state authoritarianism to speak of, it must be addressed within a wider frame of reference that understands its connection to wider capitalistic flows, along with the manipulation of desires that hallmark twenty-first-century fascism. Hence it is not that an authoritarian state allows fascism to develop; on the contrary, global forms of neoliberal fascism demand the construction of authoritarian enclaves to police the masses and discipline the recalcitrant. In this instance, the surveillance and security state is one that not only listens, watches, and gathers massive amounts of information through data mining necessary for identifying consumer populations, but also acculturates the public into accepting the intrusion of surveillance technologies and privatized commodified values into all aspects of their lives. Personal information is *willingly* given over to social media and other corporate-based websites and gathered daily as people move from one targeted website to the next across multiple screens and digital apparatuses. As Ariel Dorfman points out, "social media users gladly give up their liberty and privacy, invariably for the most benevolent of platitudes and reasons," all the while endlessly shopping online and texting.[8] This collecting of information might be most evident in the video cameras that inhabit every public space from the streets, commercial establishments, and workplaces to the schools our children attend, as well as in the myriad scanners placed at the entry points of airports, stores, sporting events, and the like.

Yet the most important transgression may be happening not only through the unwarranted watching, listening, and collecting of information but also in a regime that normalizes surveillance by upping the pleasure quotient and enticements for consumers who use the new digital technologies and social networks to simulate false notions of community and to socialize young people into a regime of security and commodification in which their identities, values, and desires are inextricably tied to a culture of private addictions, self-help, and commodification.

Surveillance feeds on the related notions of fear and delusion in the interests of producing particular subjects, modes of identification, and desires that accept intrusion as an overarching power wedded to the normalization of terror that is comparable to a state of war.[9] Forms of tyranny and oppression, in their contemporary manifestations, as evidenced so grippingly in Orwell's text, no longer depend on the raw displays of power but instead have become omniscient in a regime of suppression and surveillance in which the most cherished notions of agency collapse into unabashed narcissistic exhibitions and confessions of the self for the gaze of power. The self has become not simply the subject of surveillance but a willing participant and object. Operating off the assumption that some individuals will not willingly turn their private lives over to the spying state and corporations, the NSA and other intelligence agencies work hard to create forms of micro-tyrannies in which the "electronic self" becomes public property. Every space is now enclosed within the purview of a society that attempts to govern the entirety of social life. As Jonathan Schell points out:

Thanks to Snowden, we also know that unknown volumes of like information are being extracted from Internet and computer companies, including Microsoft, Yahoo, Google, Facebook, PalTalk, AOL, Skype, You-Tube, and Apple. The first thing to note about these data is that a mere generation ago, they did not exist. They are a new power in our midst, flowing from new technology, waiting to be picked up; and power, as always, creates temptation, especially for the already powerful. Our cell phones track our whereabouts. Our communications pass through centralized servers and are saved and kept for a potential eternity in storage banks, from which they can be recovered and examined. Our purchases and contacts and illnesses and entertainments are tracked and agglomerated. If we are arrested, even our DNA can be taken and stored by the state. Today, alongside each one of us, there exists a second, electronic self, created in part by us, in part by others. This other self has become de facto public property, owned chiefly by immense data-crunching corporations, which use it for commercial purposes. Now government is reaching its hand into those corporations for its own purposes, creating a brand-new domain of the state-corporate complex.[10]

Social cynicism and indifference accelerate a culture of conformity in which the values of critical agency have been replaced by consumer-fed hallucinatory hopes.[11] Surveillance and its accompanying culture of anxiety now produce subjects that revel in being watched, turning the practice if not the threat posed by surveillance into just another condition for performing the self. Every human act and behavior is now potential fodder for You-Tube, Facebook, or some other corporate-controlled social network. Privacy has become a curse, an impediment that subverts the endless public display of the self. Zygmunt Bauman echoes this sentiment in arguing thus:

These days, it is not so much the possibility of a betrayal or violation of privacy that frightens us, but the opposite: shutting down the exits. The area of privacy turns into a site of incarceration, the owner of private space being condemned and doomed to stew in his or her own juice; forced into a condition marked by an absence of avid listeners eager to wring out and tear away the secrets from behind the ramparts of privacy, to put them on public display and make them everybody's shared property and a property everybody wishes to share.[12]

Everything that moves is monitored, and information is endlessly amassed and stored by both private and government agencies. No one, it seems, can escape the tentacles of the NSA or the spy agencies that are scouring mobile phone apps for personal data and intercepting computer and cell phone shipments in order to plant tracking devices and malware in them.[13] Surveillance is now global, reaching beyond borders that no longer provide an obstacle to collecting information and spying on governments, individuals, prominent politicians, corporations, and pro-democracy protest groups. The details of our daily lives are not only on full display but are also being monitored, collected, and stored in data banks waiting to be exploited for purposes of marketing and social control. At the same time, the right to privacy is eagerly given up by millions of people for the wonders of social networking or the varied seductions inspired by consumer fantasies. The loss of privacy, anonymity, and confidentiality has also had the adverse effect of providing the basis for what Bauman and David Lyons call the undemocratic process of "social sorting," in which different populations are subject to differential treatment extending from being protected by the state to being killed by drone attacks launched under the auspices of global surveillance and state power.[14]

Under neoliberalism, the security regime works in tandem with a growing number of individuals and groups ranging from immigrants and low-income communities to the chronically un-employed, who are considered disposable. Precarity, mobility, flexibility, and deregulation all work to disempower large seg-ments of the population who now have to be controlled, if not contained. Fear, harassment, the crushing of dissent, and mass incarceration become part of a catastrophic politics in which the new forms of violence expand their reach in order to justify a whole new range of injustices and an accompanying culture of cruelty, largely driven by those who have long since signaled the death of the political. The right-wing notion that the govern-ment should be used largely to punish rather than nurture or protect its citizens has now been amplified and normalized. How else to explain that at least "36 states have passed state terrorism statutes, essentially mini–PATRIOT ACTs," used to criminal-ize various forms of dissent?[15] The purpose of using repressive legislation to quell and punish peaceful protests is on full display in Oklahoma where XL pipeline opponents are facing state ter-rorism charges for "dropping glitter inside a building during a peaceful banner drop."[16]

Privacy is no longer a principled and cherished civil right. On the contrary, it has been absorbed and transformed within the purview of a celebrity- and market-driven culture in which peo-ple publicize themselves and their innermost secrets in order to promote and advance their personal brand. Or, it is often a prin-ciple invoked by conservatives who claim their rights to privacy have been trampled when confronted with ideas or arguments that unsettle their notions of common sense or their worldviews. It is worth repeating that privacy has mostly become synony-mous with a form of self-generated, non-stop performance—a type of public relations in which privacy makes possible the un-earthing of secrets, a cult of commodified confessionals, and an infusion of narcissistic, self-referencing narratives, all of which serve to expand the pleasure quotient of surveillance while normalizing its expanding practices and modes of repression that Orwell could never have imagined. Where Orwell's characters loathed the intrusion of surveillance (thereby instilling some form of hope into the dystopian narrative), according to Bauman and Lyons, today,

> *We seem to experience no joy in having secrets*, unless they are the kinds of secrets likely to enhance our egos by attracting the attention of researchers and editors of TV talk shows, tabloid front pages and the . . . covers of glossy magazines. . . . Everything private is now done, potentially, in public—and is potentially available for public consumption; and remains available for the duration, till the end of time, as the internet "can't be made to forget" anything once recorded on any of its innumerable servers. This erosion of anonymity is a product of pervasive social media services, cheap cell phone cameras, free photo and video Web hosts, and perhaps most important of all, a change in people's views about what ought to be public and what ought to be private.[17]

Orwell's *1984* looks subdued next to the militant financial-carceral police state grid that seamlessly connects new forms of slow violence, abandonment, and social control with corporate-sponsored governance and the terror wars. Surveillance has not only become more pervasive, intruding into the most private of spaces and activities in order to collect massive amounts of data, it also permeates and inhabits everyday activities so as to be taken for granted. Surveillance is not simply pervasive, it has become normalized. Orwell could not have imagined the intrusive capabilities of the new high-powered digital technologies of surveillance and display, nor could he have envisioned the growing web of political, cultural, and economic partnerships between modes of government and corporate sovereignty capable of collecting almost every form of communication in which human beings engage. What is new in the post-Orwellian world is not just the development of new and powerful technologies used by governments and corporations to spy on people and assess personal information as a way to either attract ready-made customers or to sell information to advertising agencies, but the emergence of a widespread regime of surveillance to deter and criminalize dissent, as was the case with the nationally coordinated repression of the Occupy movement. In that case alone, authorities, with help from anti-terrorism resources, arrested more than 7,000 people.[18]

Intelligence networks now inhabit the world of major corporations such as Disney and the Bank of America as well as the secret domains of the NSA, the FBI, and fifteen other intelligence agencies. As Edward Snowden's revelations about the prism program revealed, the NSA also collected personal data from all of the giant high-tech service providers, who, according to a senior lawyer for the NSA, "were fully aware of the surveillance agency's widespread collection of data."[19]

Quentin Skinner is right in insisting that surveillance is about more than the violation of privacy rights, however important that may be. Under the surveillance state, the greatest threat one faces is not simply the violation of one's right to privacy, but the fact that the public is subject to the dictates of arbitrary power it no longer seems interested in contesting. And it is precisely this existence of unchecked power and the wider culture of political indifference that puts at risk the broader principles of liberty and freedom, which are fundamental, as Skinner writes, to democracy itself:

> The response of those who are worried about surveillance has so far been too much couched, it seems to

me, in terms of the violation of the right to privacy. Of course it's true that my privacy has been violated if someone is reading my emails without my knowledge. But my point is that my liberty is also being violated, and not merely by the fact that someone is reading my emails but also by the fact that someone has the power to do so should they choose. We have to insist that this in itself takes away liberty because it leaves us at the mercy of arbitrary power. It's no use those who have possession of this power promising that they won't necessarily use it, or will use it only for the common good. What is offensive to liberty is the very existence of such arbitrary power.[20]

The dangers of surveillance far exceed the attack on privacy and warrant much more than simply a discussion about balancing security against civil liberties. The latter argument fails to address how the growth of surveillance states is connected to the rise of the punishing state, the militarization of neoliberal societies, secret prisons, sanctioned torture, a growing culture of violence, the criminalization of social problems, the depoliticization of public memory, and one of the largest prison systems in the world, all of which "are only the most concrete, condensed manifestations of a diffuse security regime in which we are all interned and enlisted."[21] The authoritarian nature of the surveillance and security system with its "urge to surveil, eavesdrop on, spy on, monitor, record, and save every communication of any sort on the planet"[22] can only be fully understood when its ubiquitous tentacles are connected to wider cultures of control and punishment, including security-patrolled corridors of public schools, the rise in super-max prisons, the hyper-militarization of local police forces, the rise of the military-industrial-academic complex, and the increasing labeling of dissent as an act of terrorism in the United States and beyond.[23]

Virginia Eubanks argues that the practice of surveillance should be seen as a civil rights issue, because its practice is separate and unequal. Moreover, as she points out, for "most people privacy is a pipe dream. Living in dense urban neighborhoods, public housing, favelas, prisons, or subject to home visits by case workers, poor and working people might wish for more personal space but they don't make Snowden's mistake of assuming that privacy is 'what allows us to determine who we are and who we want to be.'"[24] Regimes of surveillance must be held accountable for their violation of deep-held human rights and democratic values, including "internationalism, active citizenship, access to information, freedom of expression, democratic governance, civic participation, multilateralism, inclusivity and non-discrimination, plurality, cultural diversity, freedom of speech. . . . Seeing privacy as the cornerstone for democracy is a kind of naïveté we can no longer excuse nor afford."[25]

The point of no return in the emergence of the corporate-state surveillance apparatus is not strictly confined to the practice of archiving immense pools of data collection to be used in a number of illegal ways.[26] It is in creating a *regime* in which surveillance becomes trivialized, celebrated, and legitimated as reasonable and unquestioned behavior. Evidence that diverse forms of public pedagogy are sanctioning the security state is on full display in post-Orwellian America, obvious in schools that demand that students wear radio chips so they can be tracked.[27] Such anti-democratic projects are now also funded by billionaires like Bill Gates who push for the use of biometric bracelets to monitor students' attentiveness in classrooms.[28] The normalization of surveillance is also evident in the actions of giant Internet providers who use social messaging to pry personal information from their users. The reach of the regime of surveillance can also be seen in the use of radio chips and GPS technologies to track a person's movements across time and space.

At the same time, regimes of surveillance work hard pedagogically to trivialize the importance of a massive surveillance environment by transforming it into a source of entertainment. This is evident in the popularity of Reality TV shows such as *Big Brother* or *Undercover Boss*, which turn the event of constant surveillance into a voyeuristic pleasure.[29] The atrophy of democratic intuitions of culture and governance is evident in popular representations that undermine the meaning of democracy as a collective ethos that unconditionally stands for social, economic, and political rights.[30] One example can be found in Hollywood films that glorify hackers such as those in the *Matrix* trilogy, or TV programming like *Homeland* that celebrates professionalized modern spying and government agents' use of drones to exterminate people accused of evil. What is lost in the regime of surveillance is that spying and the unwarranted collection of personal information from people who have not broken the law, in the name of national security and for commercial purposes, is a procedure often adopted by totalitarian states.

The surveillance state's immense data-mining capability represents a historical rupture from traditional notions of modernity with its emphasis on the social contract. The older modernity held up the ideals of justice, equality, freedom, and democracy, however flawed. The investment in public goods was seen as central to a social contract that implied that all citizens should have access to those provisions, resources, institutions, and benefits that expanded their sense of agency and social responsibility. Late liberalism and its expanding surveillance net subordinates human needs, public goods, and justice to the demands of commerce and the accumulation of capital, at all costs. The contemporary citizen is primarily a consumer and entrepreneur wedded to the belief that the most desirable features of human behavior are rooted in a "basic tendency toward competitive, acquisitive and uniquely self-interested behavior which is the central fact of human social life."[31]

Modernity is now driven by the imperatives of an uncom¬promising neoliberal political and economic system that em¬brace what Charles Derber and June Sekera call a "public goods deficit" in which "budgetary priorities" are relentlessly pushed so as to abandon the security of welfare and drastically reduce social provisions as part of a larger neoliberal class warfare that leads to the death of the commons both as an idea and a reality.[32]

Debates about the meaning and purpose of the public and social good have been co-opted by a politics of anxiety at every stage of life, relegating notions of the civic good, public sphere, and even the very word "public" to the status of a liability, if not a pathology.[33] In addition, since 9/11 there has been an intensification of the fear of dissent, matched by a fear of others, especially those non-white populations who are poor and non-Christian. Those regimes benefiting from massive concentrations of wealth, power, and income harbor a deep fear and suspicion of their people. This is a fear that demands social exclusion and containment, promotes widespread religious and racial discrimination, fuels the expansion of the punishing state, and has become a unifying thread of the secret regimes of surveillance.

Fear has lost its social connotations and no longer references fear of social deprivations such as poverty, homelessness, lack of health care, and other fundamental conditions of agency. Fear is now personalized, reduced to an atomized fear that revolves around crime, safety, catastrophe, and survival. In this instance, as the late Harvard economist John Kenneth Galbraith once warned, modernity now privileges "a disgraceful combination of 'private opulence and public squalor.'"[34] This is not surprising given the basic elements of neoliberal policy, which as Jeremy Gilbert indicates, include the privatization of public assets, contraction and centralization of democratic institutions, deregulation of labor markets, reductions in progressive taxation, restrictions on labor organization, and active encouragement of competitive and entrepreneurial modes of relation across the public and commercial sectors.[35]

Under the regime of neoliberal capitalism, the expansion of government and corporate surveillance measures becomes synonymous with new forms of governance and an intensification of material and symbolic violence.[36] Rather than wage a war on terrorists, the neoliberal security state wages a war on dissent in the interest of consolidating class power. How else to explain the merging of corporate and state surveillance systems updated with the most sophisticated shared technologies used in the last few years to engage in illicit counterintelligence operations, participate in industrial espionage,[37] and disrupt and attack pro-democracy movements such as Occupy and a range of other non-violent social movements protesting a myriad of state and corporate injustices.[38]

This type of spying in the interest of stealing industrial secrets and closing down dissent by peaceful protesters has less to do with national security than with mimicking the totalitarian abuses and tactics used by the Stasi in East Germany during the Cold War. How else to explain why many law-abiding citizens, including "those with dissenting views within the law can be singled out for surveillance and placed on wide-ranging watch lists relating to terrorism"?[39] Public outrage seems to disappear, with few exceptions, as the state and its corporate allies do little to protect privacy rights, civil liberties, and a culture of critical exchange and dissent. Even worse, they shut down a culture of questioning and engage in forms of intellectual violence. Brutality in this case becomes the preferred antidote to the demanding work of reflection, analysis, dialogue, and imagining the points of view of others. The war against dissent waged by secret counterintelligence agencies is a mode of domestic violence in which, as David Graeber has argued, violence is "often the preferred weapon of the stupid."[40]

Liberal modernity in this instance has been updated, wired, and militarized. No longer content to play out its historical role of a modernized panopticon, it has become a multilayered grid of militant financialization, entertainment, and police-state social control. In addition, this new stage of modernity is driven not only by the need to watch but also the constant threat of criminalization. Phone calls, emails, social networks, and almost every other vestige of electronic communication are now being collected and stored by corporate and government organizations such as the NSA and numerous other intelligence agencies— just in case. Snowden's exposure of the massive reach of the surveillance state with its biosensors, scanners, face-recognition technologies, miniature drones, high-speed computers, massive data-mining capabilities, and other stealth technologies made visible "the stark realities of disappearing privacy and diminishing liberties."[41] But the NSA and the other sixteen intelligence agencies are not the only threat to privacy, freedom, and democracy. Corporations now have their own intelligence agencies and data-mining offices, and use these agencies and new surveillance technologies largely to spy on those who question the abuses of corporate power.

The emergence of fusion centers exemplifies the way power is now a mix of corporate, local, federal, and global intelligence agencies, all sharing information that can be used by various agencies to stifle dissent and punish pro-democracy activists. What is clear is that this combination of gathering and sharing information often results in a lethal mix of anti-democratic practices in which surveillance now extends not only to potential saboteurs but to all law-abiding citizens. Within this sinister web of secrecy, suspicion, state-sanctioned violence, and illegality, a new culture of authoritarianism thrives and poses a dangerous threat to democratic freedoms and rights. It also poses a particular threat to those outside the United States who in the name of national security are subject to "a grand international campaign with drones and special operations forces that is generating potential terrorists at every step."[42] Behind this veil of concentrated power and secrecy lies not only a threat to privacy rights but the very real threat of violence on both a domestic and a global level.

As Heidi Boghosian argues, the omniscient state in George Orwell's *1984* is "represented by a two-way television set installed in each home. In our own modern adaptation, it is symbolized by the location-tracking cell phones we willingly carry in our pockets and the microchip-embedded clothes we wear on our bodies."[43] While such devices can be used for a number of useful applications, they become dangerous in a society in which corporations and government have increased power and access over every aspect of our lives. Put simply, "the ubiquity of such devices threatens a robust democracy."[44] Particularly dangerous, as Boghosian documents in great detail, is this:

> As government agencies shift from investigating criminal activity to preempting it, they have forged close relationships with corporations honing surveillance and intelligence-gathering techniques for use against Americans. By claiming that anyone who questions authority or engages in undesired political speech is a potential terrorist threat, this government-corporate partnership makes a mockery of civil liberties. . . . As the assault by an alignment of consumer marketing and militarized policing grows, each single act of individual expression or resistance assumes greater importance.[45]

The dynamic of neoliberal modernity, the homogenizing force of the market, a growing regime of repression, and an emerging police state have produced more sophisticated methods for surveillance and mass suppression of the most essential tools for dissent and democracy: "the press, political activists, civil rights advocates and conscientious insiders who blow the whistle on corporate malfeasance and government abuse."[46] Neoliberalism has also created a social order in which surveillance becomes self-generated, aided by a public pedagogy produced and circulated through a machinery of consumption that encourages transforming dreams into data bits. Such bits then move from the sphere of entertainment to the deadly serious integrated spheres of capital accumulation and policing as they are collected and sold to business and government agencies that track the populace either for commercial purposes or for fear of a possible threat to the social order and its established institutions of power.

Absorbed in privatized orbits of consumption, commodification, and display, Americans in particular vicariously participate in the pleasures of consumer culture, relentlessly entertained by the spectacle of violence in which, as Graeber, suggests, the police "become the almost obsessive objects of imaginative identification in popular culture [with people] watching movies or viewing TV shows that invite them to look at the world from a police point of view."[47] It is worth repeating that Orwell's vision of surveillance and the totalitarian state looks tame next to the emergence of a corporate-private-state surveillance system that wants to tap into every conceivable mode of communication, collect endless amounts of metadata to be stored in vast intelligence storage sites around the country, and use that data to repress any vestige of dissent.[48] Whistle-blowers are not only punished by the government; their lives are also turned upside down in the process by private surveillance agencies and major corporations that increasingly work in tandem. These institutions both share information with the government and do their own spying and damage control. For instance, Bank of America assembled fifteen to twenty bank officials and retained the law firm Hunton & Williams in order to devise "various schemes to attack WikiLeaks and Greenwald whom they thought was about to release damaging information about the bank."[49]

Some of the most dreadful consequences of neoliberal modernity and cultures of surveillance include the elimination of those public spheres capable of educating the public to hold power accountable, and the dissolution of all social bonds that entail a sense of responsibility toward others. Politics has not only become dysfunctional and corrupt in the face of massive inequalities in wealth and power, it has also been emptied out of any substantive meaning. At the same time, under neoliberal regimes of surveillance, citizenship has become depoliticized, reduced to an act of producing, consuming, and discarding without pause, hastening the exhaustion of life and the depletion of resources.[50] Or, even worse, the political identity of citizens loses its public character as it becomes a function of new digital technologies with optical scanners that reduce all citizens to suspects and objects of state control. Rather than being defined through one's relations to others and the larger society, citizens are increasingly defined under regimes of surveillance through an amalgam of unlimited biometric information including fingerprints, retina scans, genetic codes, and other biological data assembled from technologies once "conceived for criminals."[51] Giorgio Agamben argues that in a post-9/11 world "biological identity" takes primacy over political identity and "the unspoken principle which rules our society can be stated like this: every citizen is a potential terrorist." The war on terrorism has become terrifyingly normalized, turning every social space into a war zone and every member of society into a potential future suspect. *If you see something, say something.*

As surveillance and fear become a constant condition of neoliberal culture, there is a growing indifference, if not distaste, for politics among large segments of the population. This distaste is purposely manufactured by the ongoing operations of political repression against intellectuals, artists, non-violent protesters, and journalists on both the left and the right. Increasingly, as such populations engage in dissent and the free flow of ideas, whether online or offline, they are considered dangerous and become subject to the mechanizations of massive global security apparatuses designed to monitor, control, and punish dissenting populations.

For instance, in England, the new head of MI-5, the British intelligence service, mimicking the U.S. government's distrust of journalists, stated that the stories the *Guardian* published about Snowden's revelations "were a gift to terrorists," reinforcing the notion that whistle-blowers and journalists might be considered equally dangerous.[52] Similar comments about Edward Snowden have been made in the United States by a number of members of Congress who have labeled him a traitor, including Senators Dianne Feinstein (Democrat-California), John McCain (Republican-Arizona), Saxby Chambliss (Republican-Georgia), and House Speaker John Boehner (Republican-Ohio) as well as former vice president, Dick Cheney.[53] Glenn Greenwald, one of the first journalists to divulge Snowden's revelations about the NSA's secret "unaccountable system of pervasive surveillance,"[54] has been accused by Representative Peter King of New York along with a number of others of being a terrorist.[55] More ominously, "Edward Snowden told German TV . . . about reports that U.S. government officials want to assassinate him for leaking secret documents about the NSA's collection of telephone records and emails."[56]

As the line collapses between corporate fascism, authoritarian power, and democratic governance, repression intensifies and increasingly engulfs the nation in a toxic climate of fear and self-censorship in which both free speech and even critical thought, itself are viewed as practices too dangerous to engage in. The NSA, alone, has become what Scott Shane has called an "electronic omnivore of staggering capabilities, eavesdropping and hacking its way around the world to strip governments and other targets of their secrets, all while enforcing the utmost secrecy about its own operations. It spies routinely on friends as well as foes."[57] Intelligence benefits are far outweighed by the dangers of illegal use of the Internet, telecommunication companies, and stealth malware for data collection and government interventions that erode civil liberties and target individuals and groups that pose no threat whatsoever to national security. New technologies ranging from webcams and spycams to biometrics and Internet drilling reinforce not only the fear of being watched, monitored, and investigated, but also a propensity toward confessing one's intimate thoughts and sharing the most personal of information. What is profoundly disturbing in this case is the new intimacy between digital technologies and cultures of surveillance, a profound an unseen intimate connection into the most personal and private areas of life as subjects publish and document their interests, identities, hopes and fears online in massive quantities.[58]

Surveillance propped up as the new face of intimacy becomes the order of the day, eradicating free expression and, to some degree, even thinking itself. In the age of self-absorption epitomized by the selfie, intimacy becomes its opposite and the exit from privacy becomes symptomatic of a society that gives up on the social and historical memory. In a world in which the struggle to resist is forcefully deterred and replaced with the need to comply in order to just get by, consuming, managing, and controlling data replaces the difficult task of cultivating solidarity, community, and real friendship. Computer "friends" and services are the new gateway to a debased notion of the social, a gateway in which there is "a shift of individual life to conditions in which privacy is impossible, and in which one becomes a permanent site of data-harvesting and surveillance."[59]

One of the most serious conditions that enable the expansion of the corporate-state surveillance grid is the erasure of public memory. The renowned anthropologist David Price rightly argues that historical memory is one of the primary weapons to be used against the abuse of power, and that is why "those who have power create a 'desert of organized forgetting.'"[60] For Price, it is crucial to "reclaim public memories as both a political and pedagogical task as part of the broader struggle to regain lost privacy and civil liberties."[61] Since the terrorist attacks of 9/11, neoliberal societies have succumbed to a form of historical amnesia fed by a culture of anxiety, militarization, and precarity. Relegated to the dustbin of organized forgetting were the long-standing abuses carried out by America's intelligence agencies and the public's long-standing distrust of the F.B.I., government wiretaps, and police actions that threatened privacy rights, civil liberties, and those freedoms fundamental to a democracy. In a post-9/11 world, security has become the dominant political category, installed under the pervasive incantations of fear and crisis, and has become the new normal, stripping the category of the political of any democratic substance. Agamben argues rightly that "the formula 'for security reasons' functions today in any domain, from everyday life to international conflicts, as a password in order to impose measures that people have no reason to accept. . . . The real purpose of the security measures is not, as it is currently assumed, to prevent dangers, troubles, or even catastrophes."[62] Hence the tragic irony, of course, that what is actually being produced here are systems which are fundamentally insecure by design.

In the present historical moment, it is almost impossible to imagine that wiretapping was once denounced by the F.B.I. or that legislation was passed in the early part of the twentieth century that criminalized and outlawed the federal use of wiretaps.[63] Nor has much been written recently to recall the lessons of the Church and Pike committees, which in the 1970s exposed a wave of illegal surveillance and disruption campaigns carried out by the F.B.I. and local police forces, most of which were aimed at anti-war demonstrators, the leaders of the Civil Rights movement, and the Black Panthers. And while a number of laws implementing judicial oversight for federal wiretaps were put in place, they were systematically dismantled under the Reagan, Clinton, Bush, and Obama administrations. As Price points out, although there had been a steady increase in federal wiretaps throughout the 1980s and 1990s, "in the immediate aftermath of 9/11, the American public hastily abandoned a century of fairly consistent opposition to govern wiretaps."[64] As the historical memory of such abuses disappeared, repressive legislation such as the USA PATRIOT Act and growing support for a panoptical surveillance and "homeland" security state increased to the point of dissolving the line between private and public, and tilting the balance between security and civil liberties largely in favor of a culture of anxiety and its underside, a managed emphasis on a one-dimensional notion of safety and security.

This violence of organized forgetting has another component besides the prevalence of a culture of anxiety that emerged after 9/11. Since the 1980s, the regime of neoliberalism with its emphasis on the self, privatization, and consumerism has largely functioned to disparage any notion of the public good, social responsibility, and collective action, if not politics itself. Historical memories of collective struggles against government and corporate abuses have been deposited down the memory hole, leaving largely unquestioned the growing inequalities in wealth and income, along with the increased militarization and financialization of societies, most notably in the United States. Even the history of authoritarian movements appears to have been forgotten as right-wing extremists in North Carolina, Wisconsin, Maine, Florida, and other states attempt to suppress long-established voting rights, use big money to sway elections, destroy public and higher education as a public good, and substitute emotion and hatred for reasoned arguments.[65]

Manufactured ignorance spreads through the dominant cultural apparatuses like wildfire, promoting the financialization of everything as a virtue and ethics as a liability. The flight from historical memory has been buttressed by a retreat into a politics of self-help and a culture of self-blame in which all problems are viewed as "evidence of personal shortcomings that, if left uncorrected, hold individuals back from attaining stability and security."[66] Within the crippling "affective and ideological spaces of neoliberalism," memory recedes, social responsibility erodes, and individual outrage and collective resistance are muted.[67] Under such circumstances, public issues collapse into private troubles and the language of the politics is emptied out so that it becomes impossible to connect the depredations visited on individuals to broader systemic, structural, and social considerations.

In a moving account of the use of surveillance by Pinochet under the Chilean dictatorship, Ariel Dorfman argues that surveillance was linked not only "to a legacy of broken bodies and twisted minds, the lingering aftermath of executions and torture," but also to an assault on the imagination itself, which under Pinochet's reign of terror lived in fear that no word, gesture, comment would be "immune from surveillance."[68] What is to be learned from this period of history in which surveillance became central to a machinery of torture and death? Dorfman answers with great clarity and insight, one that should serve as a warning to those so willing to sacrifice civil liberties to security. He writes:

> Who was to guarantee that someday, someone might not activate a network like this one all over again? Someday? Someone? Why not right then and there, in democratic, supposedly post-atrocity Santiago in 2006? Were not similar links and nexuses and connections and eyes and ears doing the same job, eavesdropping, collecting data and voices and knowledge for a day when the men in the shadows might be asked once again to act drastically and lethally? And why only in Santiago? What about America today, where, com-

pared to the data-crunching clout of the NSA and other dis-intelligence agencies, Pinochet's [surveillance
state] looks puny and outdated—like a samurai sword
noticed by an airman above, about to drop a nuclear
bomb on Hiroshima? What about elsewhere on this
planet, where democratic governments far and wide
systematically spy on their own citizens? Aren't we all
in harm's way?[69]

What Dorfmann makes clear is that surveillance is about
power and control, not just about privacy, and this abuse of power is often wielded most intensely against marginalized groups,
especially in "low-rights environments—poor communities, repressive social programs, dictatorial regimes, and military and
intelligence operations—where there are low expectations of
political accountability and transparency."[70] Not only are certain
groups such as low-income Americans, immigrants, and communities of color often targeted through different and unequal
forms of supervision, discipline, and surveillance but they are
"singled out for more aggressive scrutiny."[71] As historical memory recedes, so does political consciousness, particularly the
danger that the surveillance state has posed to poor and working-class Americans who have been monitored for years and, as
Virginia Eubanks points out, "already live in the surveillance future."[72] She writes:

The practice of surveillance is both separate and unequal. . . . Welfare recipients . . . are more vulnerable to surveillance because they are members of a
group that is seen as an appropriate target for intrusive programs. Persistent stereotypes of poor women,
especially women of color, as inherently suspicious,
fraudulent, and wasteful provide ideological support
for invasive welfare programs that track their finan-

cial and social behavior. Immigrant communities are more likely to be the site of biometric data collection than native-born communities because they have less political power to resist it. . . . Marginalized people are subject to some of the most technologically sophisticated and comprehensive forms of scrutiny and observation in law enforcement, the welfare system, and the low-wage workplace. They also endure higher levels of direct forms of surveillance, such as stop-and-frisk in New York City.[73]

There is no excuse for intellectuals or any other members of the American public to address the existence, meaning, and purpose of the surveillance-security state without placing it in the historical structure of the times, or what might be called a historical conjuncture in which the legacy of authoritarianism is once again reasserting itself in new forms. Historical memory is about more than recovering the past; it is also about imbuing history with a sense of responsibility, treating it with respect rather than with reverence. Historical memory should always be insurgent, rubbing "taken-for-granted history against the grain so as to revitalize and rearticulate what one sees as desirable and necessary for an open, just and life-sustaining" democracy and future.[74] Historical memory is a crucial battleground for challenging a corporate-surveillance state that is motivated by anti-democratic legal, economic, and political interests. But if memory is to function as a witness to injustice and the practice of criticism and renewal, it must embrace the pedagogical task of connecting the historical, the personal, and the social. It is worth repeating that C. Wright Mills was right in arguing that those without power need to connect personal troubles with public issues, and that is as much an educational endeavor and responsibility as it is a political and cultural task.[75]

Obama's recent speech on reforms to the NSA not just

serves as a text that demands close reading but also as a model illustrating how history can be manipulated to legitimate the worst violations of privacy and civil rights, if not state- and corporate-based forms of violence.[76] For Obama, the image of Paul Revere and the Sons of Liberty is referenced to highlight the noble ideals of surveillance in the interest of freedom and mostly provide a historical rationale for the emergence of the massive spying behemoths such as the NSA, which now threaten the fabric of U.S. democracy and collect massive data on everyone, not just terrorists. Of course, what Obama leaves out is that Paul Revere and his accomplices acted "to curtail government power as the main threat to freedom."[77] Obama provides a sanitized reference to history in order to bleach the surveillance state of its criminal past and convince the American public that, in Michael Ratner's words, "surveillance is somehow patriotic."[78] Obama's surveillance state is just the opposite, and the politicians such as Representative Mike Ford and Senator Dianne Feinstein are more than willing to label legitimate whistle-blowers, including most famously Edward Snowden, Chelsea Manning, and Jeremy Hammond, as traitors while keeping silent when high-ranking government officials, particularly James Clapper Jr., the director of national security, lied before a senate intelligence committee.

President Obama's appeal to the American people to trust those in the highest positions of government and corporate dominance regarding the use of the mammoth power of the surveillance state makes a mockery out of the legitimate uses of such power, any vestige of critical thought, and historical memory. The United States has been lying to its people for over fifty years, and its deception extends from falsifying the reasons for going to war with Vietnam and Iraq to selling arms to Iran in order to fund the reactionary Nicaraguan Contras. Why should anyone trust a government that has condoned torture, spied on at least thirty-five world leaders,[79] supported indefinite detention, placed bugs in thousands of computers all over the

world, killed innocent people with drone attacks, enlisted the post office to log mail for law enforcement agencies, and arbitrarily authorized targeted assassinations?[80] Or, for that matter, a president who instituted the Insider Threat Program, which was designed to get government employees to spy on each other and "turn themselves and others in for failing to report breaches,"[81] including "any unauthorized disclosure of anything, not just classified materials"?[82]

What the American public does know is that the Obama administration has greatly extended the web of secrecy, has pursued a relentless attack on government whistle-blowers, and, in the face of egregious illegalities committed by the FBI, NSA, and CIA in the past, has instituted reforms that border on the laughable. Moreover, the Obama administration now promotes unmediated forms of violence most evident in indiscriminate drone attacks, suppression of civil liberties, and targeted assassinations that include Americans. In a move dripping with irony, the Obama administration points to the Foreign Intelligence Surveillance Court, created after the hearings held by Senator Frank Church into government abuse, as a much needed reform, when it fact today the court operates in secret and has proved to be a rubber stamp for just about any demand issued by the national security state. The message here for the American people is clear. Secrecy is a virtue for which there is no democratic accountability and the government can do whatever it wants in the name of "security" and waging the war on whatever is deemed threatening.

The incorrigibility of the politics of surveillance was on full display when the director of national intelligence assailed Edward Snowden before a senate intelligence committee hearing on late January 2014. James Clapper Jr. insisted that Snowden had done grave damage to the country and that his leaks not only damaged national security but aided terrorists groups. Clapper provided no evidence to support such a charge. Of course, what

he did not mention was that as a result of Snowden's revelations the American public is now aware that they are being spied upon by the government, in spite of the fact that they are not suspects in a crime and that governments around the world have condemned the indiscriminate and illegal spying of U.S. intelligence agencies. In a rather bizarre comment, Clapper also accused Snowden of "hypocrisy for choosing to live in Russia while making public pronouncements about 'what an Orwellian state he thinks this country is."[83] Recklessly, Clapper implied that Snowden is a Russian spy and that he had available to him a wide range of choices regarding where he might flee following his public revelations of NSA secret illegalities. By suggesting that Snowden's living in Russia somehow serves to cancel out his critique of the authoritarian practices, policies, and modes of governance, Clapper's comments reveal both a lack of self-reflection refarding the agency and the lies and innuendo the NSA will engage in to deflect or justify acts of criminality that are now a matter of public record. More chillingly, the NSA's scapegoating mechanisms come into full view when Clapper insinuated that "Snowden is conspiring with journalists, rather then acting as their source."[84] This is a serious accusation designed to ratchet up a climate of suspicion by suggesting that reporters such as Glenn Greenwald and others working with Snowden were participants in a crime and thus subject to criminal reprisals. In the end, such arguments are testament to how far the government will go in manufacturing a different truth in order to silence dissent.

Unfortunately, such legalized oppressions are not an Orwellian fiction but an advancement of the world Orwell prematurely described regarding surveillance and its integration with totalitarian regimes. The existence of the post-Orwellian state, where subjects participate willingly and surveillance connects to global state and corporate sovereignty, should muster collective outrage among the American public and generate massive in-

dividual resistance and collective struggles aimed at the development of social movements designed to take back democracy from the corporate-political-military elite that now control all the commanding institutions of American society. Putting trust in a government that makes a mockery of civil liberties is comparable to throwing away the most basic principles of constitutional and democratic order. As Jonathan Schell argues:

> Government officials, it is true, assure us that they will never pull the edges of the net tight. They tell us that although they *could* know everything about us, they won't decide to. They'll let the information sit unexamined in the electronic vaults. But history, whether of our country or others, teaches that only a fool would place faith in such assurances. What one president refrains from doing the next will do; what is left undone in peacetime is done when a crisis comes.[85]

History offers alternative narratives. Dangerous countermemories have a way of surfacing unexpectedly at times and, in doing so, can challenge the normalization of various forms of tyranny, including the mechanisms of a surveillance state defined by a history of totalitarian bigotry and intolerance. As the mainstream press recently noted, the dark shadow of Orwell's dystopian masterpiece was so frightening in the early 1970s that a group of young people broke into an FBI office in Media, Pennsylvania, stole as many records as possible, and leaked them to the press. No member of the group was ever caught.[86] Their actions were deeply rooted in an era when dissent against the Vietnam war, racism, and corporate corruption was running high, and also, it should be noted, an era in which the politics of fear was not a general condition of society and large groups of people were mobilizing in numerous sites to make power accountable on a number of fronts, extending from college campuses to the shaping of foreign policy. The 1971 burglary made it clear that the FBI was engaging in a number of illegal and criminal acts aimed primarily against anti-war dissenters and the African-American community, which was giving voice in some cities to the Black Power movement.

What the American people learned as a result of the leaked FBI documents was that many people were being illegally tapped and bugged, and that anti-war groups were being infiltrated. Moreover, the leaked files revealed that the FBI was spying on Martin Luther King Jr. and a number of other prominent politicians and activists. A couple of years later Carl Stern, an NBC reporter, followed up on the information that had been leaked and revealed a program called COINTELPRO, short for Counterintelligence Program, by which both the FBI and CIA were not only secretly harassing, disrupting, infiltrating, and neutralizing leftist organizations but also attempting to assassinate those considered domestic and foreign enemies.[87] COINTELPRO was about more than spying; it was an illegally sanctioned machinery of violence and assassination.[88] In one of the most notorious cases, the FBI worked with the Chicago Police to set up the conditions for the assassination of Fred Hampton and Mark Clark, two members of the Black Panther Party. Noam Chomsky has called COINTELPRO, which existed from the '50s to the '70s, when it was stopped, "the worst systematic and extended violation of basic civil rights by the federal government," and said it "compares with Wilson's Red Scare."[89] As a result of these revelations, Senator Frank Church conducted Senate hearings that both exposed the illegalities the FBI was engaged in and helped to put in place a number of polices that provided oversight to prevent such illegalities from happening again. Needless to say, over time these oversights and restrictions were dismantled, especially after the tragic events of 9/11.

What these young people were doing in 1971 is not unlike what Edward Snowden and other whistle-blowers are doing today, making sure that dissent is not suppressed by governments that believe power should reside only in the hands of government and financial elites, and that all attempts to hold power accountable should be repressed at almost any cost. Many of these young protesters were influenced by the ongoing struggles of the Civil Rights movement, and one of them, John Raines, was heavily influenced by the theologian Dietrich Bonhoeffer, who was killed by the Nazis. What is crucial about this incident is that it not only revealed the long historical reach of government surveillance and criminal activity designed to quash dissent, it also provides a model of civic courage by young people who acted on their principles in a non-violent way to stop what they considered to be machineries of warfare that led to the death of the political. As Glenn Greenwald argues, COINTELPRO makes clear that governments have no qualms about "targeting citizens for their disfavored political views and trying to turn them into criminals through infiltration, entrapment, and the like," and that such actions are "alive and well today in the United States."[90] Governments that elevate their own lawlessness to one of the highest principles of social order reproduce and legitimate violence as an acceptable mode of action throughout a society. Violence in American society has become its heartbeat and nervous system, paralyzing ideology, policy, and governance, if not the very idea of politics.

Under such circumstances, the corporate and surveillance state becomes symptomatic of a form of tyranny that has corrupted and disavowed the ideals and reality of a substantive democracy. More specifically, the government's refusal to prosecute government officials who torture; engage in illegal kidnappings; spy on Americans without due cause; dispatch secret operations forces wherever they want; and illegally gather intelligence on hundreds of world leaders, business executives, and foreign companies such as Brazil's Petrobras oil firm sends a clear and dangerous message to those who run the national security state. President Obama updates and "elaborates President George W. Bush's notions of preemptive strike by claiming the further privilege to order the killing of any citizen overseas who is believed to be a terrorist or a friend of terrorists."[91] In Obama's post-Orwellian state, the unifying message is that its lawlessness has become normalized and that whatever the national security state does, however horrific, nasty, and illegal, those who run it and carry out its policies and practices will not have to face a courtroom and be prosecuted in accordance with the rule of law.

Dissent is crucial to any viable notion of democracy and provides a powerful counter-force to the dystopian realities emerging increasingly in neoliberal societies, but dissent is not enough. It is crucial for everyone to find the courage to translate critique into the building of popular movements dedicated to making education central to any notion of politics. This is a politics that does the difficult work of assembling critical formative cultures by developing alternative media, educational organizations, cultural apparatuses, infrastructures, and new sites through which to address both the range of injustices plaguing our societies and the forces that reproduce them. The rise of cultures of surveillance along with the defunding of public and higher education, the attack on the welfare state, and the militarization of everyday life can be addressed in ways that allow people to see not only how such issues are interrelated with neoliberalism, but also what it might mean to make such issues critical and transformative. As Charlie Derber has written, "How to express possibilities and convey them authentically and persuasively seems crucially important" if any meaningful sort of resistance is to take place.[92] The regime of surveillance is reinforced through a new mass sensibility in which people surrender themselves to both the capitalist system and a general belief in its call for a security that never quite arrives. It does not simply repress subjectivity but constitutes it through a range of cultural apparatuses ranging from the schools and media to the Internet. The fundamental question concerns the educative nature of politics, that is, what people believe and how their individual and collective dispositions and capacities to be either willing or resistant agents are shaped. As Stanley Aronowitz argues,

> The fundamental question is subjectivity. How have people introjected or resisted domination and what are the fundamental influences on how they become social and political actors? The answer to these questions goes beyond the thesis of mass ignorance. It requires an exploration of the subjective, a journey that embraces, to be sure, an historical, geographic, and political economic analysis, but also requires plumbing the dimension of depth psychology to the regions of the political and cultural unconscious.[93]

To echo Spinoza's famous formulations: How do we learn to desire that which we should find patently oppressive? And in what ways is our servitude presented to us as though it were our salvation? Nothing will change unless the left takes seriously the subjective underpinnings of oppression in the world today. The power of the imagination, dissent, and the willingness to hold power accountable constitutes a major threat to contemporary forms of fascism and its authoritarian enclaves. Snowden's disclosures made clear that those in authority are deeply fearful of those intellectuals, critics, journalists, and others who dare to question authority, expose the crimes of corrupt politicians, and question the carcinogenic nature of a corporate state that has hijacked democracy: this is most evident in the insults and patriotic gore heaped on Manning and Snowden.

How else do we explain the concern on the part of both government and intelligence agencies that Snowden's disclosures about the NSA "have renewed a longstanding concern: that young Internet aficionados whose skills the agencies need for counterterrorism and cyber defense sometimes bring an anti-authority spirit that does not fit the security bureaucracy"?[94] Joel F. Brenner, a former inspector general of the NSA, made it very clear that the real challenge resulting from Snowden's revelations was to make sure that a generation of young people would not be taught to think critically or question authority. As Brenner put it, young people who were brought into the national security apparatus were selling not only their brains but also their consciences. In other words, they have to "adjust to the culture" by endorsing a regime that just happened to be engaging in a range of oppressive measures that threatened any viable notion of the democratic ideal.[95] What is clear is that the corporate-security state provides an honorable place for intellectuals who are willing to live in a culture of conformity. In this case, as Arthur Koestler said some years ago, conformity becomes "a form of betrayal which can be carried out with a clear conscience."[96] At the same time, it imposes its wrath on those who reject subordinating their consciences to the dictates of fascistic rule.

If the first task of resistance is to make the characteristics of the dominant power clear by addressing critically and meaningfully the abuses perpetrated by the corporate surveillance state and how such transgressions affect the daily lives of people in different ways, the second step is to move from understanding and critique to the hard work of building popular movements that integrate with one another rather than get stuck and fixated in single-issue politics. The left has been fragmented for too long, and the time has come to build national and international movements capable of dismantling the political, economic, and cultural architecture put in place by neoliberal forms of fascism and their post-Orwellian surveillance industries. As Aronowitz argues, the fragmentation of the left has made it dysfunctional in "generating a sustained movement against capital, or indeed, proposing a comprehensive, systemic alternative to the contemporary capitalism system."[97] Modern history is replete with such struggles, and the arc of that history has to be pressed forward before it is too late.

In a time of tyranny, thoughtful and organized resistance is not a choice; it is a necessity. Surely, as Fred Branfman argues, rolling back the surveillance state can take the form of fighting to end bulk collection of information; demand congressional oversight; indict executive branch officials when they commit perjury; give Congress the capacity to genuinely oversee executive agency; provide strong whistle-blower protection; and restructure the present system of classification.[98] These are important reforms worth fighting for, but they do not go far enough. What is needed is a radical restructuring of our understanding of democracy itself as well as what it means to bring it into being. The words of Bauman are useful in understanding what is at stake in such a struggle. He writes: "Democracy expresses itself in continuous and relentless critique of institutions; democracy is an anarchic, disruptive element inside the political system; essential, as a force of *dissent* and change. One can best recognize a democratic society by its constant complaints that it is not democratic enough."[99]

What cannot be emphasized too much is that only collective struggles will be capable of challenging contemporary forms of political oppression. If the first order of any abuse of power is unchecked secrecy, the first moment of resistance to such relations is widespread critical awareness of unchecked state and corporate power and its threat to democracy, coupled with a desire for radical change rather than reformist corrections. Democracy involves a sharing of political existence, an embrace of the commons, and the demand for a more democratic future that cannot arrive quickly enough. In short, politics in the United States in particular needs a jump start, because democracy is too important to be left to the whims of those in power who have turned the principles of self-government into an excuse for tyranny.

EIGHT

DYSTOPIAN REALISM

If You See Something, Say Something

The recent emergence of Islamic State (ISIS) seemed to catch the U.S. political system off guard. For weeks it was presented in the media alongside Ebola as the latest existential threat to neoliberal security and order. The real tragedy, however, is that the violent logics and dystopian outlook of this well-funded and heavily armed political formation do not represent a radical departure. In fact, ISIS evidences a certain mimicry of the system it seeks to supplant. Indeed, analyzed from the perspective of the spectacle, it becomes clear that the horrifying images projected from the chaos of our own creation, suggest a complex interplay of global forces wherein the idiom of violence used by the neoliberal system, and the production values used to mediate its narratives of subjugation and power, are also put in play by forces that are openly competing with it for regional domination and control—and beyond.

Neoliberalism's retreat from social responsibility, costs, and ethics, and its embrace of a kind of instrumental and technological fanaticism, have always contained a monstrous logic, and ISIS has seemingly adopted that logic and deployed it to the extreme as a political and military weapon. ISIS, in short, merely accentuates the logic of a system by using violence and massacre to the nth degree.

Dealing with the violence of ISIS requires political contextualization and serious engagement. However abhorrent we might find their actions, it is patently absurd for any leader involved with the ongoing acts of violence constantly recorded and made available on the Internet not to recognize that one strategic assault posed by ISIS is to deploy production values and aesthetics of entertainment used in Hollywood films and video games to project images of subjugation and power like those produced by U.S. military media operations in Guantánamo Bay at the outset of the terror wars. John Pilger ventures to take this a stage even further by noting the historical parallels with the Khmer Rouge, which terrorized Cambodia. As Pilger writes, this movement was the direct outcome of a U.S. bombing campaign: "The Americans dropped the equivalent of five Hiroshimas on rural Cambodia during 1969–73. They leveled village after village, returning to bomb the rubble and corpses. The craters left monstrous necklaces of carnage, still visible from the air. The terror was unimaginable."[1] The outcome was the emergence of a group made up largely of radical young men driven by a dystopian ideology, all dressed in black, sweeping the country in the most violent and terrifying of ways. The historical comparison is all too apparent: "ISIS has a similar past and present. By most scholarly measures, Bush and Blair's invasion of Iraq in 2003 led to the deaths of some 700,000 people—in a country that had no history of jihadism." In the Middle East, as in Cambodia, the U.S. and its allies foster the virulent spread of violence and political barbarity.

Within the United States the line between extreme violence and actual murderous rampages has blurred to the degree that one now informs the other in a kind of hallucinatory form of entertainment in which violence seems to offer the most adrenalized possibilities for feeling exhilaration, pleasure, and a sense of control. That is not in any way to justify the violence or to seek to rationalize its occurrence. But if you continually bomb a people, invade and occupy their land, appropriate their resources, harm their children, imprison and humiliate their families, and tear apart the fabric of the social order, there is direct responsibility for the inevitable backlash to follow.

The fact that the weaponry is "high-tech" and the soldiers privatized doesn't absolve the actor of any complicity. Such is the delusion of every form of imperium that enforces impunity for itself when it comes to the violence and coercion that it imposes, but not for those it allegeldy defends itself against. Is there any other way to understand ongoing killing of innocent people who find themselves too close to targets of U.S. drones in the ongoing terror wars?

David Carr, writing in the *New York Times*, captured the existential bleakness of the contemporary moment by commenting on the beheadings of U.S. journalists James Foley and Steven Sotloff. While following a familiar modernist diagnosis by noting the "medieval" contradictions of an organization whose spectacular budget, production capacity, editing prowess, and ideological intensity "serve as both propaganda and time machine, attempting to wipe away centuries of civilization,"[2] Carr was nevertheless appreciative of the importance of the spectacle, which he argues cannot be reduced to crude explanations. His observation is worth repeating here in some detail:

> ISIS clearly has a sophisticated production unit, with good cameras, technically proficient operators, and editors who have access to all the best tools. . . . The mastery of medium and message is evident in the careful crafting of the video. In the Sotloff clip, the enemy, in this case, President Obama, is shown through a video effects filter to make his visage in a news conference about ISIS appear distorted and sinister. An electronic buzz effect signals an interruption—a kidnapping, if you will—of the broadcast before a graceful typographical segue promises "A second message to America."

We are then in a desert, the horizon carefully situated at the midpoint of a two-camera shoot. There is thought put into the wardrobe selection; the victim is dressed in an iconic orange jumpsuit—a reference to detainees in American custody—and the killer costumed more as a ninja than a jihadist, all in black and his face obscured, holding a small knife and holster.

The actual murder is performed in the unflinching sunlight of the desert. (I thought more than once of the brutally clear morning of Sept. 11, 2001.) Because sound is difficult to capture on a windy expanse of arid land, the victim is wearing a lapel mike. Mr. Sotloff introduces himself in sober tones and begins to read a scripted statement off what seems to be a teleprompter. The executioner is cocky and ruthless, seemingly eager to get to the task at hand. When he does attack his bound victim, only the beginning is shown and then there is a fade to black. Once the picture returns, the head of the victim is carefully arranged on the body, all the violence of the act displayed in a bloody tableau. There is another cutaway, and the next potential victim is shown with a warning that he may be next.

Carr's depiction here offers a number of qualitative ways for interrogating the contemporary nature of the spectacle of violence. Specifically, it allows us to focus more directly upon what we might term the "violence of the medium" wherein the power of the global broadcast works to destroy the conditions of political possibility by ensuring that the spectacle perpetuates the cycle of violence; the "aesthetics of appearance" wherein the subjects themselves display certain characteristics; the "affective relations" wherein the atmosphere created between soldier and captive affects spectators at a visceral level by evidencing a notable level of emotional access and all too human responses; the "environmental framing" wherein localized topographies translate into questions of political (in)hospitability and endangerment; the "performative enactment" wherein the act of violence itself is subject to a complex assay that marks out legitimate versus illegitimate slaughter; the "temporal sequencing" wherein past/present/future collapse as the directed montage renders the act of killing but a momentary intervention in an unfinished production; and on to the "mediating strategy" wherein the decision for subsequent selective broadcast allows the imagery to function politically upon those exposed to it.

ISIS detainee James Foley and his executioner, ISIS broadcast, August 2014

Each of these qualities is significant, beginning with the violence of the medium. As Dexter Filkins wrote in the *New Yorker*, while ISIS soldiers make particular demands regarding intervention in the region, it is clear their ambitions will never be achieved; on the contrary: "Beheading an American hostage—and a bound, kneeling one at that—hardly seems likely to keep the United States out of the Middle East. Indeed, ISIS leaders couldn't have made the prospect of American air strikes more likely if they had sent a video to President Obama begging him to drop more bombs."[3] Winning the genuine freedom and localized bottom-up forms of local sovereignty necessary to abate violence is not a principal objective, nor has it ever been. As the terror wars and the spectacle converge, new modalities of indoctrination are enacted in which shock becomes the structuring principle in creating the necessary conditions for emotional lockdown, suspension of conscience, and total compliance with authority.

What is especially disturbing about the terror wars and the psychological weaponization of imagery is that they reveal how our societies are now programmed by a militant dystopian logic such that violence becomes a central indoctrinating force shaping not only the political terrain but the social as well. *If you see something, say something.* As novelist and cultural critic Marina Warner puts it, such representations matter most urgently since the images have "the power to lead events, not only [to] report them, [and] the new technical media have altered experience and become interwoven with consciousness itself."

The presentation of the two figures in each composition is particularly striking. From our initial witnessing, we are left in no doubt that their appearances are intended to inscribe a certain image consciousness. The deployment of an orange suit for the detainee corresponds with use of such garb in similar images of subjugation and dehumanization produced by the U.S. military in relation to its detainees at the onset of the terror wars.

U.S. detainees and their captors, U.S. military image, Guantánamo Bay terror war detention camp

The production and release of terror war images showing total subjugation of detainees dressed in orange suits originated not in ISIS's theater of operations, but in the U.S. military's. By speaking in the same visual codes, they reveal the horror common to them both. Taken together, the deliberate production and dissemination of such imagery illustrates how the terror wars are situated within a broader historical narrative, one whose visual component wages war on all who are exposed to its codes of total dehumanization and civilian death.

In the case of the ISIS imagery, the captor's appearance is similar to that of SWAT teams used in North American drug busts. His boots are not alien or exotic; they are familiar, used by paramilitary units everywhere and available in neoliberal societies at Walmart and Sears. The aesthetic appearances deployed in the images produced by both the U.S. and ISIS also accentuate particular features in ways that are consciously staged for the utmost affect. While ISIS chose to expose the faces of Foley and Sotloff to draw our attention to their all too visible terror as their forward-looking gaze confirms the sheer surrender to their predicament, the U.S. displays its detainees in a more helpless pose, letting the world see them cower in complete deference to accentuate the setting of total power.

Filkins also highlights another important point in his public commentary. Drawing connections between ISIS's latest broadcasts and Al Qaeda's "greatest hits" videos of suicide bombings in Iraq, he writes, "It's impossible to watch without concluding that those guys were enjoying what they did—that they were getting off on it. Videotaping a mass murder is not politics; it's pornography." While Filkins's attempts to divorce politics from desire represent an all too familiar reductionist maneuver, paving the way for us to have comfort in our more reasoned (hence politically astute) violence, neatly contrasted by their discreditable emotional outrage, he does nevertheless try to account for the affective relations at work as the spectacle panders to a multiplicity of libidinal vulnerabilities. Violent desires are part of a perverse economy of production/destruction that cannot be divorced from social and political processes. While questions of agency must account for individual desires, the social body as a whole is a vast experiment in assembling, controlling, and manipulating the affective dimension to human existence. Discourses of security, for instance, would have no traction whatsoever unless a threat could be substantively conveyed and anxiously felt. Or, as Brian Massumi writes, "it's enough for a threat to be felt to make it real. It needs no objective validation to have an effect as a future cause."[4]

Arguably what appears so disturbing regarding the productions disseminated by both the U.S. and ISIS is the *intimate portrayal of violence*. The situation depicts a human-to-human relationship in the most brutalizing of ways. It is tortuous in the clearest sense, as attention concentrates directly on the subjective stakes—and the spread of dehumanization—occurring through the perpetration of war. There is something profoundly phenomenological at work here as the detainees are completely denied any sense of agency and reduced to the level of an animal, or worse, a mere prop. Here we have a reworking of Giorgio Agamben's idea of "bare life," which on this occasion is no longer confined to the spatial figure of "the camp," but the *nomos* of the open plains. Even ISIS's victims' capacity of speech, which Aristotle famously argued sets the human apart from other species, becomes part of a complex drama that although permitted is done so on the basis that it will ultimately be muted by mediating forces. The U.S. images show its detainees gagged by medical masks; their voices, like their very identities, are fully controlled and denied. They are simply the enemy.

In the ISIS video production, speech is included in the last instants in order to transpose its very denial onto its spectators. Like the subjugated body, the word no longer registers as a person's own. It is an act of violence on spectators: those who view it become involved in the dehumanizing political ventriloquism both on display and *in progress* through exposure to the spectacle perpetrated through the images themselves. Through media, the terror wars' theater of operations spreads everywhere, and the violence is against consciousness and conscience themselves.

The complexity of this situation, however, cannot be fully grasped without comprehending how the spectacle is the generative force in the production of such violence in ways that perpetuate its occurrence. As Étienne Balibar writes, "it is not only a matter of describing the way in which extreme violence is *lived*, but more generally the way in which it is distributed between the poles of the individual and the collective, or of the subjective and the objective." That is to say, since extreme violence brings into question the integrity of "the body and the mind," it focuses our attention on "the mutual link of belonging between subjects and their historical and geographic environment."[5] To make sense of this broader picture, it is worth drawing comparisons here with the barbarity of the terror wars, which further reveal how the intimate connects to broader social morphologies and the most current forms of technology. As Adriana Cavarero writes on the grotesque violence of Abu Ghraib, which in a tragic rearticulating of history already served as a theater of cruelty during the totalitarian reign of Saddam Hussein:

> Although perpetrated in secret rooms, the actions of the torturers were in fact programmatically aimed, as regards both ends and means, at the realm of the eye. The setting did not prohibit photography, it allowed for and utilized it: both as an official tool of documentation for the Pentagon archives and above all as an instrument of humiliation for the victims. . . . The art of the digitized image—a technology born for the Web and destined for the Web—was recommended and encouraged at Abu Ghraib. Far from being an unforeseen contingency, the "souvenir photos" in their wretched banality, were just one of the variables, inevitable because embedded in the overall strategy, of the operations that were underway. . . . Torture in this case, materially perpetrated on bodies but no longer concealed, indeed acted out for a worldwide audience that the Internet guarantees, becomes spectacle[6].

Beyond the all too evident symmetrical relationships that history allows us to expose with shameful clarity, it is understandable from the perspective of the spectacle why state forces prefer to wage wars at a distance. High-tech violence allows for a near total control of imagery, information, and what remains of independent journalism. It strips out the intimacy of affective relations as the technological ability to distance the politics and killing, along with the ability to witness and create memory, thereby curating and censoring all human connections as is strategic for achieving "full spectrum dominance."[7] That is not to say we can neatly distinguish which is more ethical in terms of recognizing the victim's humanity. Whereas the intimate forces us to look directly at people's humanity, empathizing with a human form that appears not too dissimilar from our own, the spectacle of war waged today degrades that relatable condition in the most brutal and humiliating of ways; the fact that the violence to which we are exposed takes place at a distance already both denies the human in the frame and pre-conditions the spectator to comply with the projection of power and coercion. The images from Guantánamo Bay, for example, show few human features. Hence, as Judith Butler would explain, "If violence is done against those who are unreal, then, from the perspective of violence, it fails to injure or negate those lives since those lives are already negated."[8] These examples of dehumanization merely represent different sides of the same coin. And while the violence of ISIS appears as a perverse mimetic counter, it also serves as a painful reminder that such methods were until very recently standard operating procedure.

While paying his respects to James Foley, President Obama stated how his life stood in "marked contrast to his killers'," for while theirs was dedicated to "killing innocent, unarmed civilians in cowardly acts of violence," Foley had the courage to report from front lines to bear "witness to the lives of people a world away."[9] However, in our neoliberal system, it is the process of witnessing itself that is increasingly foreclosed from any ability to challenge power. Instead of valuing active witnesses capable of rendering political testimony and indictment, the system prioritizes itself, demanding all others be obedient and unquestioning spectators of how it curates justice, dissent, disobedience, and physical confrontation. The entire narrative from Ferguson, Missouri, to Staten Island, New York, presents a fresh domestic example. State authorities shoot Michael Brown, an unarmed black youth, to death and let him lie in the street for hours. No charges are brought. Community outrage is repressed by militarized police, resulting in more confrontation, criminalization of dissent, arrests. For communities of color, the terror wars are not new, they are 400 years old. Following the death of Michael Brown, Eric Garner was put in an illegal chokehold by a cop with a history of racial misconduct. Garner struggled to stay alive after the assault, shouting "I can't breathe." The police, paramedics, and other stood by and did nothing to come to Garner's assistance. This entire act of egregious violence was recorded on a bystander's cell phone and went viral on the Internet. In spite of the visual evidence, the cop, NYPD officer Daniel Pantaleo, walked free after the grand jury refused to indict him on any charges.

Imagery from today's terror wars enforces non-combatants' role both as pure spectators and as potential collateral damage, thus propelling the logic for increasing surveillance, militarization, lockdown, and violence. The spectacle is fully weaponized and the target on all sides is both civilian society and the humanity that animates it. Images of state terrorism now serve less to indict the perpetrators than to instill fear, to destroy the capacity for holding power accountable, and to send the message: "This could happen to you." As the military-police-surveillance grid gains in strength, digital technology reinforces the power of state and non-state barbarism rather than posing a threat to those who engage in terrorist acts. Within this ecology of coercion and control, images of horror are absorbed within a spectacle of violence that individualizes fear and functions as a terrorist's weapon of choice.

Beheading serves a very specific symbolic function that

brings directly to the fore the question of subjectivity. As Cavarero further writes, since the uniqueness of human form is concentrated in its facial expressiveness, what is being destroyed with the act of beheading is precisely the "singularity of each person."[10] This is what she refers to as being an "ontological crime" where the severed head becomes a symbol of a form of extreme violence, which "aims primarily not to kill but destroy its humanity, to inflict wounds on it that will undo and dismember it." For Cavarero, what is particularly disturbing about this performative enactment is the manner in which the severed head creates an interchange of gazes where the lines between victim and spectator enter into a more complex relationship. As we become forced spectators of the concentrated destruction of the most expressive qualities of the human condition, the singularity of the subject, so we are forced to internalize the trauma and connect with the vulnerability of the damned. As she writes, "the unwatchable is watching each one of us." Griselda Pollock offers a similar interpretation on the dehumanization of the singular, adding that as life is reduced to a situation of absolute helplessness, what is "torn away is the face, the site of figural unity of the human being, and the locus of the individual personality."[11] Is not the denial of the human equally apparent in the terror war photos released by the U.S. military depicting their control over their detainees in Guantánamo Bay?

Carr's description of the ISIS media operations notes their technical proficiency and sophisticated level of production. The montage format adopted by ISIS and its accompanying narrative also evidence an appreciation of the political importance of the medium, wherein the act of violence offers a certain historical transfer speaking to previous claims of power, while making visible the promise of violence to come. This is bargained against the violence of retribution, which is altogether expected. Spectacle thus begetting spectacle, in a self-perpetuating continuum of domination, conquest, dehumanization, murder, and war. Such temporal sequencing effectively collapses the past, the present, and the future as the memory of violence and the promise of violence-to-come places the recorded act at a point of intersection. What is forced upon its spectators doesn't offer anything that may break the cycle; like all torture pornography, it points instead to the *prequel* and the *sequel* of its occurrence.

The coercive threat of death has already taken life itself hostage. The time delay between the staging of the violence and its global witnessing ensures that its viewing is haunted by the knowledge that the subject has already suffered a terrifying fate. Such a situation acknowledges no resistance. It reduces everything to programming a Skinnerian response from its spectators. Still, yet, there is more to come. There is, as the video's closing sequence profiles, always the next body on the horizon of slaughter. The continuity in the characters here is notable. While the appearance of the same ISIS warrior in each production adds to the serial nature of the killing, the appearance of the next victims in the closing seconds adds to the anxiety as we are forced to build an ongoing picture of the people, like those shown forced to cower in the U.S. photos from Guantánamo Bay, whose lives and bodies are totally out of their own control.

Borrowing from Achille Mbembe, what is being produced in the ISIS videos are "necro-political celebrities," where the biographical details of both victim and killer (much effort has gone into such identification) reinforce the potency of the spectacle, while ensuring the images have subsequent political effect to perpetuate the cycle of violence *ad infinitum*. Everything changes, as Massumi might argue, so that everything remains the same. This brings us to that vexed question of what Butler terms "grievable life."

It is interesting to note, however, how the neoliberal system responds when a person from its ranks is forced to wear orange and is victimized as the subordinated enemy. Are not the narratives produced to document their lives presented to further convey the demonic qualities of the enemy and the "axis of evil" on which it pivots? We are not arguing here against the dignity of human memorialization. Too often this gets lost in the drama of violence. Our concern is to expose how the spectacle and its tragic mimeticism curates which lives are more important than others. How different might our politics be if all political leaders were required to pay the same biographical attention to each and every casualty of the terror wars—especially those victims, intentional or not, of violence inflicted in our names?

The default response programmed into political leaders follows a familiar pattern in which the subsequent public displays of outrage quickly lead to absolutist statements of righteous indignation that pave the way for unquestionable response. The discourse here is eerily familiar to the theology-infused outpourings that followed the 9/11 attacks (thereby adding layer upon layer to the mimetic nature of the violence and its ongoing dehumanization). The template is used time and time again, each time as if it were the first. Prior to the hard fast violence, the enemy must be named and demonized. ISIS is called a "monstrous" organization whose rampage through Syria and Iraq represents "act[s] of pure evil."[12] Pursuing such a strategy actually signals and directs media to present the matter in a variety of complex ways. While the message is expectedly uniform in terms of recognizing the depths of depravity, when it comes to the full reality of the violence, in the specific case of the ISIS assassination video, we are told that certain censorship is order, as exposure to the complete original would be just too much to take in. This is notable in a particular BBC digital broadcast in respect to Steven Sotloff. While the accompanying footage warns that the "video contains disturbing images," the content doesn't include anything more than what has been widely circulated.[13] Arguably, what is inferred as disturbing are the emotional words of his mother's plea for forgiveness; we could be disturbed by her loss, for it is also, due to familiarity, now our loss as well. He was one of the best of us. Hence moral absolutism connects here to the emotion of a social tragedy, partially seen, partially censored, ultimately to remind us that the U.S. and the Allies will never stand idly by and "watch the spread of evil"; they will enact great vengeance and fury to purge its presence from the world.[14]

We are not in anyway suggesting here that the spectacle of violence—or anything else—leads to uniform emotional responses. The public is not some docile mass that reacts in unison to the horrors of contemporary conditions. Some will invariably find the images intolerable to view. As rightly they should. Having said this, if we understand the spectacle to be a dominant form of political violence and ordering in the contemporary moment, one that seeks to steer the course of history in ways that affirm the continuous necessity for social control through coercion and subjugation, then the question of intolerability is not only contested in terms of emotional registers, it is colonized by the desire for violent retribution in the name of justice, peace, and security—the desire to win.

To that end, what might appear to be an intolerable reaction points more toward a *purer tolerance* for violence, which immediately connects to the spectacle as the retributive act must address the presumed trauma of witnessing throughout the social order. What is therefore required is a different concept of the intolerable that disrupts the spectacle while breaking free from it, and in so doing, allows us to reclaim collective agency and open up fronts of political practice as an art capable of resisting neoliberal mechanisms through aesthetic forms.

Workstations of Fear

The use of new digital technologies and social media by ISIS has drawn a great deal of attention from the dominant media not only because ISIS uses them as a form of visual terrorism to graphically portray the beheadings of captured American and

British civilians, but also because of its alleged sophistication as a marketing and recruitment tool. Examining ISIS's propaganda machine within a neoliberal frame of reference that responds to it in the language of the market does more than depoliticize the use of the media as a spectacle of terrorism; it also suggests that the new media's most important role lies in creating a brand, establishing a presence on Twitter, and producing a buzz among those individuals sympathetic to its goals. For instance, Dinah Alobeid, a spokesperson for the social analytics company Brandwatch, observes:

> Everyone needs a social media campaign today, even political movements in the Middle East it seems. The type of highly focused marketing and social media community building as exhibited by ISIS is something that brands strive for to get their message across. . . . Taking out the political and human rights implications of this situation, ISIS has a keen sense of how to attract their target demographics, keep them engaged, and spread their messaging and news via social media to highly interested individuals. ISIS's strength lies in the recognizability of its brand, the reach of its network, and its capacity to boost its Twitter presence through a combination of carefully crafted "official" messages, as well as the buzz and volume of fans sharing content across the globe.[15]

Power disappears in this analysis as social media are stripped of their diverse sites and complex usages, defined largely in terms of marketing. What is missing is the recognition that, as the link between the media and power becomes more integrated, the visual theater of combat increasingly uses neoliberal politico-military idioms to wage its terror wars. In almost the same way that multiple countries competing in Olympic ice skating competitions now use commercial music from the United States, not music unique to their own country, ISIS is increasingly using neoliberal visual modes to format its media operations.

Violence not only becomes performative, functioning as a kind of representational politics, but is also packaged so as to mimic the unbridled monopolization of pleasure now associated with images of killing, brutality, and cruelty. Moreover, representational shocks and outrages are now presented as either legitimate sources of entertainment or as part of an ethic of pure survival. It should come as no surprise that when mainstream media report on the bombing of ISIS targets in Syria and Iraq, they accompany their comments with images of the actual bombings, as if the viewer were looking at a video game.

Echoing the discourse of the "official" terror wars, the violence of politico-combat entities such as ISIS is produced almost exclusively within the vocabulary of moral absolutes pitting good against evil. Ironically, this is a binary discourse that mirrors a similar vocabulary used in the interest of the national security–surveillance state and the corporate-sponsored war machines of battle-ready domestic and global forces of repression. What is clear is that the spectacle of violence trades in absolutes, whether it makes such claims in the name of religion or of national interests. This friend/enemy distinction wipes out any sense of uncertainty, need for thoughtful debate, and reason itself. Whether it's George W. Bush's now infamous claim that "You are either with us or against us" or ISIS's insistence that its enemies are infidels for whom there will be no mercy, this is a repressive binary logic that suffocates debate, dissent, and autonomy of any substantive kind.

Hence it is all the more surprising to see this binary repeated in a September 29, 2014, *New York Times* op-ed by Roger Cohen titled "Here There Is No Why: For ISIS, Slaughter Is an End in Itself." In referring to the U.S. war against ISIS, Cohen states bluntly that "presented with the counter-human, the human must fight back." Surely, fighting "the inhuman" does not justify the indiscriminate killing of Syrian civilians by drones and high-tech fighter jets, among other heinous crimes? The human and inhuman too often bleed into each other, destroying this wretched, unreflective rhetoric. This is a dangerous binary, because it closes down questions of history, politics, power, justice, and the ethical imagination while legitimating revenge and militarism through the language of an unchecked moralism.

Just as the necessity of fighting terror has become the central rationale for war by the Obama administration and other governments, a visual culture of shock and awe has become ubiquitous thanks to the intensified and expanding presence of the Internet and 24-hour cable news shows devoted to representations of the horrific violence associated with terrorism—ranging from images of bombing raids in Syria to the countervailing imagery of grotesque killings of hostages by ISIS fundamentalists. The visual concussion of violence aestheticizes debate, celebrates a sacralization of politics as war, and stylizes raw violence as it is integrated into audio-visual spectacles that shock and massage the mind and emotions with the theatricality of power and a steady regimen of fear, extreme violence, and the drumbeat of a hyper-regressive masculinity. It gets worse. It is not unreasonable to assume that if the sheer brutality and barbarism of ISIS did not exist today, it would eventually and inevitably be produced by the United States. ISIS offers the United States a new enemy that fits right into its need to legitimate its own culture and apparatuses of fear, violence as spectacle, and machinery of militarism, regardless of its disingenuous appeal to human rights.

As the U.S. and Israel increase the intensity of their bombing of enemies in the Middle East, the official "workstations" of CNN and other news outlets engage in a kind of grotesque production of moral panics in their appeal to fear, insecurity, and imminent danger. Violence is something not to be condemned but to be appropriated as a methamphetamine stimulant for harvesting more spectators, higher Nielsen ratings, and more advertising revenue. The television and news reports read like scripts that have been written by ghostwriters from the National Rifle Association. Violence, coupled with a disingenuous appeal to peace, security, and national interests, becomes the only register to understand the conflicts in which countries like the United States and Israel are engaged.

The history, interests, and power relations behind such military actions, violations of international law, and global aggression that function almost exclusively in the service of violence, war, and global domination are obliterated from any official government reporting or the staged performances of the dominant media. Armed struggle feeds the call for more weapons to be sold across the globe, more guns to be used at home, the ever-expanding militarization of all aspects of social life, and the production of desires, identities, and modes of subjectivity conducive to living in a state of unending war. ISIS thus represents only one part of the dystopian imagination that now defines the political age in which we live.

Facing the Intolerable

Despite the daily spectacles of violence to which we are all continually subjected, never before has the selection and careful manipulation of violent aesthetics been so heavily policed, in terms of both their representation and their authenticating narratives. Some images are simply deemed too sensitive for public consumption due to the "raw realities" they force us to encounter. Such policing is not, however, about adhering to set principles or ethical standards concerning the circulation of violent imagery. As we have shown, our societies are flooded by images of violence, albeit in ways that serve to prioritize the spectacle over more complex compositions. Rather, regimes of mediated power and subjugation render certain images "intolerable" for the administration of neoliberal social control. When it suits its purposes, power uses spectacle to completely overlook the humanity of the people and communities victimized, and denies purposeful discussion about the broader political and historical contexts necessary to interpret events. What of the thousands of civilian children, women, and men inadvertently being killed, quietly rendered "collateral damage" of targeted assassinations? Would it not be intolerable if we were to learn of them and their lives? Could the killing continue if we did? Intolerability, therefore, pivots on conscience. For those in power, the intolerable is that which can catalyze people, networks, communities, and movements to challenge both the prevailing conditions and the brutalizing simulacrum that isolates and alienates as it entertains.

Spectatorship thus represents the veritable death of the witness, which Primo Levi and others show to be integral to both a somber reflection on the human condition and its capacity for political and social transformation. For the intensifying mediation of violence replaces reflective viewing by a militant consumerist ethos whose purpose is to harvest our attention, while foreclosing possibilities for diverse political reflection, collective response, dissent, and autonomous action.

That which appears intolerable must therefore be the site for rethinking the politics of visual communications, media, and aesthetics. For it is precisely the intolerable which allows us to defy the aesthetic regime of power and subjugation, along with the seductive nature of its spectacles of violence that are integral to normalizing the notion of disposable lives and to the imposition of disposable futures. This, however, requires a fundamental reworking of the concept of intolerance in a more politically astute way, so that we don't simply fall back upon the question of sovereign protectionism and the threshold between legal and illegal violence. We need to rethink the terms of intolerability in direct relation to both conscience and ethical claims on the future as imagined in the present. As Balibar warns:

To locate qualitatively what we call "extreme" in the register of violence is not to proceed to typologies or descriptions in the juridical sense, even given the development of jurisprudence and particularly the evolution of its definitions (for example, when it criminalizes rape or genocide). Rather, it is to problematize the very notion of threshold, above all because violence as such cannot be the object of undifferentiated anathema. Such anathema is vain; it would immediately mask, in the form of denial, that anthropologically fundamental fact that violence in its diverse forms (I would even say the social invention of diverse forms of violence), its very "creativity," pertains both to human experience and to history, of which it constitutes one of the "motors." Because violence and politics, violence and aesthetics, violence and moral experiences, and so on are inextricably associated, we feel the need to locate those thresholds associated with the idea of the intolerable. We place such thresholds in relation to a legal limit of the very possibility of politics. We might thus consider *thresholds of the intolerable* as manifestations of the *element of inhumanity* without which even the idea of *humanity* is meaningless.

Violence should be intolerable. That is the point. But in the age of the spectacle it needs a different registry beyond the juridical. If the task of ethical political discourse is to draw from both social imagination and social conscience in order to speak to the intolerable such that we might confront structural injustice and subjugation in the world, this needs to be connected to multiple political strategies that allow us to see through the darkness, challenge what remains hidden in plain sight, imagine better worlds, and make plans for manifesting them through transformed social relations free of dominance and coercion.

This places remarkable demands upon artists and critical ped-
agogues as facing the intolerable requires us to do more than
expose with greater ethical care and consideration issues of human disposability. It also requires rethinking the classical problem identified by Jacques Rancière, namely that the problem of
aesthetics has been to effectively draw a "straight line from the
intolerable spectacle to awareness of the reality it was expressing, and from that to the desire to act in order to change it."[16]
Facing the intolerable requires novel strategic alliances so we
might reimagine the art of living politically in the contemporary moment. Intolerable violence thus understood is markedly
different from fetishizing spectacles. It allows us to counter the
spectacle, exposing the limits of mediation that actually render
violence *tolerable* for public consumption. And it provides the
basis for reclaiming politics as an art form to meaningfully counter the banalization of violence so widespread today.

Our conception of the intolerable does not propose some
framework for understanding levels of individual tolerance to
exposure to violence. Every individual and community has different standards. It works instead by looking at what is being
occluded at the systemic level, locating within what is deemed
intolerable a particular ethical challenge and response to the
hidden order of political disposability. Approached this way, the
intolerable is akin to what Simon Critchley would identify as a
poetic intervention.

"Poesis," he explains, may be defined as "the creation of disclosure, the difficult bringing of things to birth through seem-
ings, through words or images or whatever. If there is a mystery
to things, it is not the mystery of the hidden, it is the mystery of
the absolutely obvious, what is under one's nose. The labor of
the poet or artist is the difficult elaboration of the openedness
within which we stand."[17]

There are alternative histories of the human experience—a
history of resistance and the fight for the liberation of politi-

cal subjectivities—which start from the presupposition that the political itself is a creative act dedicated toward the idea of what Jacques Derrida termed a "democracy-to-come." Genuine democracy is a social process, and when it is not deterred or denied by competing systems such as neoliberalism, it draws from and is driven by the social imagination: every act of social change begins with imagining a better world, imagining better conditions, imagining a better everyday life. One only has to look to the autonomous Zapatista communities in Chiapas, Mexico, to see evidence of one the most poetic of autonomous democracies, one that thrives on the imagination, memory, and dignity of its people and does so in open defiance of all forms of encroachment and neoliberal power.

If the spectacle is nothing but an entrancing sham, a soft violence waged through LED screens and mobile devices in order to embed consciousness with its own self-destructive malware that deters and subjugates the very agency that makes us creative, ethical, social, then poetics is all about reclaiming those powers and their unfettered exercise through social imagination, in the service of pioneering modes of living and relating that are free of violence and domination. At the crossroads between hope and despair, it is through poetics that we can begin to start thinking about politics as radical creation, as the possibility of what Rousseau called the "perfected act" . . . an art of politics capable of conceiving "new associations."[18]

The question is, by what means might social conscience be awakened, and how might its rousing lead to social formations that can catalyze widespread divestment from the spectacle and successfully challenge systems of subjugation and power dominating society today? Asking emphasizes the importance of rethinking the art of the political today.

In this regard, there is still much to be learned from the Zapatistas of Mexico, whose struggle for dignity and justice is full of imagination, theater, poetry, art, and the affirmation of otherness and difference. The indigenous Maya have been witness to 500 years of persecution and suffering. And yet, despite this continual history of persecution, they have embarked on a remarkable journey that has embraced non-violence as a political strategy. In doing so, they have sought to outlive the dialectical tides of history. This conscious decision was enshrined in their First Declaration of La Realidad, released on January 1, 1996. This declaration directly called for a new "image of the world" that is "not an image inverse to, and thus similar to, what is annihilating us." A sentiment later repeated by Zapatista insurgent Major Ana María, who, speaking at the opening ceremony of the "Intercontinental Encounter for Humanity against Neo-Liberalism," noted to many non-indigenous attendees:

> Behind our black face, behind our armed voice, behind our unnameable name, behind that, we see you . . . behind that we are the same simple ordinary men and women that repeat themselves in all races, that paint themselves in all the colors of the world. [Because in] this corner of the world we are equal because we are different.

Crucially, for the Zapatistas, this prioritization of difference has led to a reconceptualization and re-articulation of the concept of the political that is all about the affirmation of oppressed identities—those from below who have been subjugated and marginalized by power. Subcomandante Marcos elaborated:

> We are "other" and different . . . we are fighting in order to continue being "other" and different. . . . And what we are—far from wanting to impose its being in the "other" or different—seeks its own space, and, at the same time, a space of meeting. . . . That is why Power has its armies and police, to force those who

are "other" and different to be the same and identical. But the "other" and different are not looking for everyone to be like they are. . . . The "everyone doing their own thing" is both an affirmation of difference, and a respect for other difference. [Thus] when we say we are fighting for respect for our different and "other" selves, that includes fighting for respect for those who are also "other" and different, who are not like ourselves.

Beyond the Spectacle

While the subject matter of this book is concentrated in the bleakness of the contemporary condition, there are reasons to be optimistic. Despite such politically catastrophic times, spectacles of violence are only a particular (albeit dominant) vision of the world. They are driven by a failed political imagination whose ideas enslave and destroy us. And yet one has only to pay attention to the daily violence witnessed on our various mediated platforms to recognize that neoliberalism is exhausted and its modes of subjectivity increasingly revealing of its self-destructive nihilism. How else to explain the sheer brutality meted out against all forms of dissent, protest, and civic disobedience? Perhaps it is worth reminding ourselves here of Michel Foucault's observations in *Speech Begins after Death*. "Writing means," Foucault explains, "having to deal with the death of others, but it basically means having to deal with others to the extent that they're already dead. . . . I'm in the situation of the anatomist who performs an autopsy." To which he adds, "I also understand why people experience my writing as a form of aggression. . . . They feel there is something in it that condemns them to death." But as he further wittingly qualifies in a language most fitting: "In fact, I am much more naïve than that. I don't condemn them to death. I simply assume they're already dead. That's why I am so surprised when I hear them cry out. I'm as astonished as the anatomist who became suddenly aware that the man on whom he was intending to demonstrate has woken up beneath his scalpel. In short, I don't claim to kill others with my writing. I only write on the basis of the other's already present death."

Neoliberalism is intolerable. But in political terms, we can start to think about its already present death. What is more, we can take heart from the fact that people will always resist what they find patently intolerable. Despite the horrors, they will find reasons to believe in this world and that it can be transformed for the better. This alone is sufficient reason to continue to have faith in the human condition. As the Zapatistas show, those who are deemed disposable assert, time and time, again that resistance is a *creative act* that leads to new forms of perceiving, thinking, relating, and living. The globally dispossessed continue to challenge those who subjugate them. They face the intolerable with a dignified confidence. They continue to defy prevailing reason. And they refuse to get immobilized by the brutalizing simulacrum that is only capable of re-creating a mirror image of that which is violently experienced. In this regard, we might add that the greatest weapon in our political arsenal today remains *the power of the imagination*. As Chris Hedges has argued:

> It is through imagination that we can recover reverence and kinship. It is through imagination that we can see ourselves in our neighbors and the other living organisms of the earth. It is through imagination that we can envision other ways to form a society. The triumph of modern utilitarianism, implanted by violence, crushed the primacy of the human imagination. It enslaved us to the cult of the self. And with this enslavement came an inability to see. . . . Imagination, as Goddard wrote, "is neither the language of nature nor the language of man, but both at once, the medium of

communion between the two—as if the birds, unable to understand the speech of man, and man, unable to understand the songs of birds, yet longing to communicate, were to agree on a tongue made up of sounds they both could comprehend—the voice of running water perhaps or the wind in the trees. Imagination is the *elemental speech* in all senses, the first and the last, of primitive man and of the poets.[19]

Never have we more urgently required a new political imagination that can take us out of the poverty of contemporary forms of consciousness that prove to be politically catastrophic and lead to civil and social death. Power has always feared those who have dared to think differently. It has always banished the true poets of the age. It has always sought to pathologize or kill those who dared to imagine the alternatives instead of quietly conforming. This is not incidental, for it is precisely in the realm of the imagination that we can rethink the world. As Deleuze once noted, nobody has ever been put into prison for political reasons on account of their negativity and pessimism. Indeed, since neoliberalism cannot deny us the ability to imagine better worlds, for that is what ultimately defines the human condition, the power of the imagination as affirmatively conceived is by definition always and already engaged in forms of political resistance and struggle. To dare to imagine is always the start of a new form of politics that doesn't passively wait for historical forces to come to the rescue.[20] Knowing that it is possible to transform the world for the better, the power of imagination moves us to reclaim our collective futures.

ACKNOWLEDGMENTS

HENRY GIROUX thanks Susan Searls Giroux for her editorial help and the numerous conversations they had about many of the chapters in this book, all of which helped to improve the manuscript. His administrative assistant, Maya Sabados, patiently read every page of this book and offered invaluable insights and editorial suggestions. He also thanks Grace Pollock for her initial constructive edit of the manuscript. He thanks Brad Evans for his brilliance, friendship, and meticulous editing and writing in bringing this book to fruition. It has been a pleasure co-authoring this book with him. He further thanks the administration at McMaster University for providing him with the support necessary to work on this manuscript, along with Ryerson University for awarding him a Distinguished Visiting Professorship, which provided an office and some time to think through many of the ideas discussed in the book. Finally, he thanks Greg Ruggiero for the spirited dialogues with him during the editorial process.

BRAD EVANS would like to extend his friendship to and continued admiration for Henry Giroux. His generosity, courage, and commitment to the value of education and public pedagogy remain a source of inspiration. Brad Evans remains humbled by this collaboration. He extends his appreciation to colleagues at the University of Bristol. He is also thankful for the time spent with members of the Committee on Global Thought at Columbia University, New York, throughout 2013–14, during which a significant portion of this manuscript was initially drafted. His intellectual and personal debts of gratitude are far too numerous to acknowledge here, though particular mention is given to Ray Bush, Simon Critchley, Terrell Carver, Mark Duffield, Gregg

Lambert, Emma Murray, Adrian Parr, Julian Reid, Saskia Sassen and Michael Shapiro, whose continued support and guidance is always appreciated. He would like to join in the acknowledgment of Greg Ruggiero and Grace Pollock; their editorial contributions improved the text considerably. His family continues to remain the greatest source of inspiration and makes everything meaningful. And at the age of six, Amelie continues to amaze with her warmth, love, brilliantly inquisitive mind, and delightful spirit.

NOTES

CHAPTER ONE

1. Howard Zinn, "The Problem Is Civil Obedience," in Howard Zinn, *The Zinn Reader: Writings On Disobedience and Democracy* (New York: Seven Stories, 1997), p. 404.

2. On this, see Brad Evans and Julian Reid, *Resilient Life: The Art of Living Dangerously* (Cambridge: Polity, 2014).

3. Zsuza Ferge, "What are the State Functions that Neoliberalism Wants to Eliminate?" in Antole Anton, Milton Fisk, and Nancy Holmstrom, eds., *Not for Sale: In Defense of Public Goods* (Boulder: Westview, 2000), p. 183.

4. Lynn Parramore, "Exclusive Interview: Joseph Stiglitz Sees Terrifying Future for America If We Don't Reverse Inequality," *AlterNet*, (June 24, 2012). www.alternet.org/economy/155918/exclusive_interview%3A_joseph_stiglitz_sees_terrifying_future_for_america_if_we_don%27t_reverse_inequality

5. David Harvey, "The New Imperialism: Accumulation by Dispossession," *Socialist Register* (2004), pp. 63-87.

6. Chris Hedges, "Suffering? Well You Deserve It," *Truthout* (March 2, 2014). www.truthdig.com/report/item/suffering_well_you_deserve_it_20140302

7. Ibid.

8. Ibid.

9. Michelle Alexander, "The Age of Obama as a Racial Nightmare," *Tom Dispatch* (March 25, 2012). www.tomdispatch.com/post/175520/best_of_tomdispatch%3A_michelle_alexander,_the_age_of_obama_as_a_racial_nightmare/

10. Karen Garcia, "The Culling of the American Herd," *Truthout* (February 14, 2014). http://truth-out.org/opinion/item/22388-the-culling-of-the-american-herd

11. Eduardo Galeano, *The Open Veins of Latin America: Five Centuries of the Pillage of a Continent* (New York: Monthly Review Press, 1973), p. 2.

12. See, in particular, Zygmunt Bauman, *Modernity and the Holocaust* (Cambridge: Polity Press, 1989).

13. Hannah Arendt, *On Violence* (New York: Harvest Books, 1969).

14. Carlos Marighella, *The Mini-Manual of the Urban Guerilla* (Montreal: Abraham Guillen, 2002).

15. See Frantz Fanon, *The Wretched of the Earth* (London: Penguin Books, 1990).

16. On this, see Jennifer Abbott and Mark Achbar's insightful movie *The Corporation* (2003). Also see William Deresiewicz, "Capitalists & Other Psychopaths," *New York Times* (May 12, 2012). www.nytimes.com/2012/05/13/

opinion/sunday/fables-of-wealth.html

17. Paulo Freire's most famous book is *Pedagogy of the Oppressed*, 30th Anniversary Edition (New York: Continuum, 2006).

18. Ibid., p. 39.

19. Walter Benjamin, "Critique of Violence," in *Reflections: Essays, Aphorisms, Autobiographical Writings*, ed. Peter Demetz (New York: Shocken, 1986), pp. 277-300.

20. Steven Pinker, *The Better Angels of Our Nature: Why Violence Has Declined* (London: Viking, 2011).

21. See Evans and Reid, *Resilient Life*.

22. Michael Thomas, "There Will Be Violence, Mark My Words," *Newsweek* (December 28, 2011). www.readersupportednews.org/opinion2/279-82/9142-the-big-lie

23. Henry A. Giroux, "Between Orwell and Huxley: America's Plunge into Dystopia," *Tidal Basin Review* (in press).

24. Hannah Arendt, *The Origins of Totalitarianism* (New York: Harcourt, 1973).

25. Henry A Giroux, *The Twilight of the Social* (Boulder: Paradigm, 2012).

26. See, especially, Theodor W. Adorno, "Aldous Huxley and Utopia," *Prisms* (Cambridge: MIT Press, 1967), pp. 97-117.

27. Jacob Taubes, *Occidental Eschatology* (Stanford University Press, 2009).

28. On the issue of youth and the politics of disposability, see Henry A. Giroux, *Disposable Youth: Racialized Memories and the Culture of Cruelty* (London: Routledge, 2012).

29. João Biehl, *Vita: Life in a Zone of Social Abandonment* (Los Angeles: University of California Press, 2005).

30. Guy Standing, *The Precariat: The New Dangerous Class* (London: Bloomsbury Academic, 2011); and David Graeber, *The Democracy Project: A History, a Crisis, a Movement* (New York: Random House Publishing Group, 2013).

31. See Gilles Deleuze, "Post-Script on the Societies of Control," in Gilles Deleuze, *Negotiations: 1972-1990* (New York: Columbia University Press, 1990).

32. Fredric Jameson, "Future City," *New Left Review* (May-June 21, 2003). http://newleftreview.org/II/21/fredric-jameson-future-city

33. Jane Anna Gordon and Lewis R. Gordon, *Of Divine Warning: Reading Disaster in the Modern Age* (Boulder: Paradigm, 2009), p. 10.

34. See, for instance, Henry Giroux, *Zombie Politics*, 2nd edition; and John Quiggin, *Zombie Economics: How Dead Ideas Still Walk among Us* (Princeton University Press, 2010).

35. David Harvie and Keir Milburn, "The Zombie of Neoliberalism Can Be Beaten—Through Mass Direct Action," *The Guardian* (August 4, 2011). www.theguardian.com/commentisfree/2011/aug/04/neoliberalism-zombie-action-phone-hacking

36. See Evans and Reid, *Resilient Life*.

37. Wilhelm Reich, *The Mass Psychology of Fascism* (New York: Farrar, Straus & Giroux, 1970).

38. On this, see Brad Evans "Fascism & the Bio-political," in *Deleuze & Fascism: Security, War, Aesthetics*, ed. Brad Evans and Julian Reid (Abingdon: Routledge, 2013), pp. 42-63.

39. Gilles Deleuze and Félix Guattari, *Anti-Oedipus: Capitalism and Schizophrenia* (London: Continuum, 2003), p.31.

40. The relationship between the media and politics has been explored in far too many books to mention. Three different but useful texts are Robert McChesney, *The Problem of the Media* (New York: Monthly Review Press, 2004); Nick Couldry, *The Place of Media Power* (New York: Routledge, 2000); and Mark Poster, *The Second Media Age* (London: Polity, 1995). For a complex and brilliant analysis of the information society, see Scott Lash, *Critique of Information* (London: Sage, 2002).

41. Some important analyses of the relationship between the new media and aesthetics as well as critical commentaries on visual culture include: Lev Manovich, *The Language of the New Media* (Cambridge: MIT Press, 2001); Jessica Evans and Stuart Hall, eds., *Visual Culture: The Reader* (London: Sage, 1999); Hugh Mackay and Tim O' Sullivan, eds., *The Media Reader* (London: Sage, 1999); and Nick Couldry, *The Place of Media Power* (New York: Routledge, 2000).

42. Some classic works on the spectacle include: Guy Debord, *The Society of the Spectacle*, trans. Donald Nicholson-Smith (New York: Zone Books, [1967] 1994); Jean Baudrillard, *Simulacra and Simulation* (Ann Arbor: University of Michigan Press, 1995); Douglas Kellner, *The Persian Gulf TV War* (Boulder: Westview, 1992); Carol Becker, *Surpassing the Spectacle* (Lanham: Rowman and Littlefield, 2002); Jean Baudrillard, *The Spirit of Terrorism*, trans. Chris Turner (London: Verso, 2002); Slavoj Žižek, *Welcome to the Desert of the Real* (London: Verso, 2002); Douglas Kellner, *Media Spectacle and the Crisis of Democracy* (Boulder: Paradigm, 2005); and Retort, *Afflicted Powers: Capital and Spectacle in a New Age of War* (London: Verso, 2005).

43. Eugene L. Arva, "Life as Show Time: Aesthetic Images and Ideological Spectacles," *Perspectives on Evil and Human Wickedness* 1:2 (2003), p. 74.

44. Brian Massumi, "Preface," in *The Politics of Everyday Fear*, ed. Brian Massumi (Minneapolis: University of Minnesota Press, 1993), p. viii.

45. Debord, *The Society of the Spectacle*.

46. Retort (Ian Boal, T.J. Clark, Joseph Matthews, and Michael Watts), "Afflicted Powers: The State, the Spectacle and September 11," *New Left Review* 27 (May/June 2005), p. 8.

47. Debord, *The Society of the Spectacle*, p. 19.

48. Ibid., p. 12.

49. Ibid., p. 13.

50. Ibid., p. 12.

51. Ibid., p. 14.

52. Ibid., p. 24.

53. Retort, ibid., p. 9.

54. Retort, ibid., p. 8.

55. Debord, *The Society of the Spectacle*, p. 18.

56. Arva, "Life as Show Time," p. 70.

57. Debord, *The Society of the Spectacle*, p. 30.

58. Arva, "Life as Show Time," p. 76.

59. Lutz Koepnick, "Aesthetic Politics Today: Walter Benjamin and Post-Fordist Culture," in *Critical Theory: Current State and Future Prospects*, eds. Peter Uwe Hohendahl and Jaimey Fisher (New York: Berghahn, 2001), p. 108.

60. See Scott Lash, *Critique of Information* (London: Sage, 2002).

61. Stuart Hall, "The Kilburn Manifesto: Our Challenge to the Neoliberal Victory," *Common Dreams* (April 24, 2013). www.commondreams.org/view/2013/04/24-10

62. Mark Poster, *The Information Subject* (Amsterdam: Gordon and Breach, 2001), p. 127.

63. For a brilliant exploration of the new information technologies and their connection to war, terror, and new resistance movements, see Chris Hables Gray, *Peace, War, and Computers* (New York: Routledge, 2005).

64. Stanley Aronowitz, *Dead Artists, Live Theories, and Other Cultural Problems* (New York: Routledge, 1994), p. 42.

65. James Castonguay, "Conglomeration, New Media, and the Cultural Production of the 'War on Terror,'" *Cinema Journal* 43:4 (Summer 2004), p. 106.

66. Koepnick, "Aesthetic Politics Today," p. 95.

67. This issue is analyzed in detail in Corey Robin, *Fear: The History of a Political Idea* (New York: Oxford University Press, 2004).

68. These issues are taken up in more detail in Henry A. Giroux, *Public Spaces/Private Lives: Democracy Beyond 9/11* (Lanham: Rowman and Littlefield, 2003); *The Abandoned Generation: Democracy Beyond the Culture of Fear* (New York: Palgrave Macmillan, 2003); and *The Terror of Neoliberalism: The New Authoritarianism and the Eclipse of Democracy* (Boulder: Paradigm, 2004).

69. François Debrix, "Cyberterror and Media-Induced Fears: The Production of Emergency Culture," *Strategies* 14:1 (2001), p. 152.

70. See Jean Baudrillard, *The Spirit of Terrorism*, trans. Chris Turner (London: Verso, 2002); Slavoj Žižek, *Welcome to the Desert of the Real* (London: Verso, 2002); and Thomas Keenan, "Mobilizing Shame," *South Atlantic Quarterly* 103:2/3 (2004), pp. 435-449.

71. His most recent book on the subject is Douglas Kellner, *Media Spectacle and the Crisis of Democracy* (Boulder: Paradigm, 2005).

72. Rustom Bharacuha, "Around Adohya: Aberrations, Enigmas, and Moments of Violence," *Third Text* (Autumn 1993), p. 45.

73. Bigelow quoted in Slavoj Žižek, "It's Time to Be Dogmatic about Torture: Why *Zero Dark Thirty* Is Just Propaganda," *ABC Religion and Ethics* (January 29, 2013). www.abc.net.au/religion/articles/2013/01/29/3678722.htm

74. Naomi Wolf, "A letter to Kathryn Bigelow on Zero Dark Thirty's apology for torture," *The Guardian* (January 4, 2013). www.theguardian.com/commentisfree/2013/jan/04/letter-kathryn-bigelow-zero-dark-thirty

75. Bigelow quoted in Slavoj Žižek.

76. Ibid.

77. Susan Sontag, "Fascinating Fascism," *New York Review of Books* (February 6, 1975). www.nybooks.com/articles/archives/1975/feb/06/fascinating-fascism/

78. Nick Robinson, "Videogames, Persuasion and the War on Terror: Escaping or Embedding the Military-Entertainment Complex?" (*Political Studies*, Vol. 60, no. 3, 2012) p. 505

79. See http://lightbox.time.com/2014/09/15/war-photographer-video-game/#1

80. Berel Lang, *Holocaust Representation: Art within the Limits of History and Ethics* (Baltimore: Johns Hopkins University Press, 2000), p.19.

81. Primo Levi, *Survival in Auschwitz* (New York: Touchstone, 1996) p. 41.

82. Zygmunt Bauman, *Life in Fragments* (Malden: Blackwell, 1995), p. 3.

83. Theodor W. Adorno, *Can One Live after Auschwitz? A Philosophical Reader*, ed. by Rolf Tiedemann, trans. by Rodney Livingstone et al., (Stanford University Press, 2003), p. 252.

84. Ibid., pp. 252-253.

85. João Biehl, *Vita: Life in a Zone of Social Abandonment*, (Los Angeles: University of California Press, 2005), p. 20.

CHAPTER TWO

1. See, for instance, Henry A. Giroux, *Disposable Youth: Racialized Memories and the Culture of Cruelty* (London: Routledge, 2012); Charles Derber and Yale R. McGrass, *The Surplus American and How the 1% is Making Us Redundant* (Boulder: Paradigm, 2012); and Henry A. Giroux, *The Violence of Organized Forgetting* (San Francisco: City Lights, 2014).

2. Zygmunt Bauman, *Wasted Lives: Modernity and Its Outcasts* (Cambridge: Polity, 2004), p.97.

3. Ibid., p. 63.

4. Zygmunt Bauman, *Collateral Damage: Social Inequalities in a Global Age* (Cambridge: Polity, 2011)

5. On this, see in particular Gillian Wylie, ed., *Enacting Globalization: Multi-disciplinary Perspectives on International Integration* (New York: Palgrave, 2013).

6. See Brad Evans and Julian Reid, "The Promise of Violence in the Age of Catastrophe," *Truthout* (January 5, 2014). http://truth-out.org/opinion/item/20977-the-promise-of-violence-in-the-age-of-catastrophe

7. On this, see Brad Evans, *Liberal Terror* (Cambridge: Polity, 2013).

8. Naomi Klein, *The Shock Doctrine: The Rise of Disaster Capitalism* (New York: Picador, 2007).

9. João Biehl, *Vita: Life in a Zone of Social Abandonment* (Los Angeles: University of California Press, 2005), p. 4.

10. Ibid., p. 10.

11. See Robert B. Reich, "McCutcheon Took Us Back in Time, but It Might Just Birth the Next Occupy," *The Guardian* (April 6, 2014). www.theguardian.com/commentisfree/2014/apr/06/mccutcheon-conservative-supreme-court-next-occupy; Doug Henwood, "Our Gilded Age," *The Nation* (June 30, 2008), pp. 14, 17.

12. Robert Jay Lifton, *Death in Life: Survivors of Hiroshima* (Chapel Hill: University of North Carolina Press, 1987), p. 479.

13. Biehl, *Vita*.

14. Ibid. For a brilliant analysis of these zones, see also Chris Hedges and Joe Sacco, *Days of Destruction, Days of Revolt* (New York: Knopf, 2012).

15. As indicated by a report from the Corporation for Enterprise Development (CFED), "nearly half of Americans are living in a state of 'persistent economic security,' that makes it 'difficult to look beyond immediate needs and plan for a more secure future.' [The CFED report] finds that 44% of Americans are living with less than $5,887 in savings for a family of four." Quoted in Christopher Mathews, "Nearly Half of America Lives Paycheck-to-Paycheck," *Time Magazine* (June 30, 2014). http://time.com/2742/nearly-half-of-america-lives-paycheck-to-paycheck/

16. Zygmunt Bauman, *Liquid Times: Living in an Age of Uncertainty* (Cambridge: Polity, 2007), p. 14.

17. Robert O. Self, "The Antisocial Contract," *New York Times* (August 25, 2012). http://campaignstops.blogs.nytimes.com/2012/08/25/the-antisocial-contract

18. Joseph E. Stiglitz, *The Price of Inequality: How Today's Divided Society Endangers Our Future* (New York: W. W. Norton, 2013). See also Thomas Piketty, *Capital in the Twenty-First Century* (New York: Belknap, 2014).

19. See, for instance, Chris Hedges, *War Is a Force that Gives Us Meaning* (New York: Anchor, 2003); and Andrew Bacevich, *The New American Militarism: How Americans Are Seduced by War* (New York: Oxford University Press, 2013).

20. Radley Balko, *Rise of the Warrior Cop: The Militarization of America's Police Forces* (New York: Public Affairs, 2013).

21. Joseph Stiglitz, "In No One We Trust," *New York Times* (December 21, 2013). http://opinionator.blogs.nytimes.com/2013/12/21/in-no-one-we-trust/

22. Hannah Arendt, *The Last Interview and Other Conversations* (Brooklyn: Melville House, 2013), pp. 115-116. Aided, of course, by a right-wing dominated Supreme Court that is nothing more than an extension of the ruling

corporate elite. See for instance Mike Lofgren, "Can't We Just Say the Roberts Court Is Corrupt?" *Truthout* (April 7, 2014). www.truth-out.org/opinion/item/22942-cant-we-just-say-the-roberts-court-is-corrupt

23. The quote by Karl Jaspers is cited in Arendt, *The Last Interview and Other Conversations*, p. 37.

24. Ibid., p. 48.

25. See, for instance, Kristen Lewis and Sarah Burd-Sharps, *Halve the Gap by 2030: Youth Disconnection in America's Cities* (New York: Measure of America, 2013). www.measureofamerica.org/halve-the-gap-2030

26. Editor, "75 Economic Numbers from 2012 That Are Almost Too Crazy to Believe," *The Economic Collapse Blog* (December 20, 2012). http://theeconomiccollapseblog.com/archives/75-economic-numbers-from-2012-that-are-almost-too-crazy-to-believe

27. David DeGraw, "Meet the Global Financial Elites Controlling $46 Trillion in Wealth," *Alternet* (August 11, 2011). http://www.alternet.org/story/151999/meet_the_global_financial_elites_controlling_$46_trillion_in_wealth

28. Karen Garcia, "A Weaponized Human Refuse Dump," *Sardonicky: Musings on Politics and Popular Culture* (April 9, 2014). http://kmgarcia2000.blogspot.ca/

29. Zygmunt Bauman, "Downward Mobility Is Now a Reality," *The Guardian* (May 31, 2012). www.guardian.co.uk/commentisfree/2012/may/31/downward-mobility-europe-young-people. Bauman develops this theme in detail in *On Education* (Cambridge: Polity, 2012) and *This Is Not a Diary* (Cambridge: Polity, 2012).

30. Bauman, *Wasted Lives*, p. 76.

31. See Steve Fraser, "The Politics of Debt in America: From Debtor's Prison to Debtor Nation," *TomDispatch* (January 29, 2013). www.tomdispatch.com/dialogs/print/?id=175643. On the history of debt, see David Graeber, *Debt: The First 5,000 Years* (New York: Melville House, 2012).

32. Bauman, *On Education*, p. 47.

33. We are borrowing the term "zones of social abandonment" from Biehl, *Vita*. See also Giroux, *Disposable Youth* and Michelle Alexander, *The New Jim Crow* (New York: The Free Press, 2012).

34. Angela Y. Davis, "State of Emergency," in *Racializing Justice, Disenfranchising Lives*, eds. Manning Marable, Keesha Middlemass, and Ian Steinberg (New York: Palgrave, 2007), p. 324.

35. Biehl, *Vita*, p. 14.

36. See, for example, Lisa Marie Cacho, *Social Death: Racialized Rightlessness and the Criminalization of the Unprotected* (New York: University Press, 2012).

37. Steve Herbert and Elizabeth Brown, "Conceptions of Space and Crime in the Punitive Neoliberal City," *Antipode* (2006), p. 757.

38. Daniel Bell, *The End of Ideology: On the Exhaustion of Political Ideas in*

the Fifties (New York: Free Press, 1966) and Francis Fukuyama, *The End of History and the Last Man* (New York: Free Press, 2006).

39. See Evans, *Liberal Terror.*

40. Herbert Marcuse quoted in Peter Marcuse, "The Baran-Marcuse Letters: 'The Truth Is in the Whole,'" *Monthly Review Zine* (June 20, 2014). http://mrzine.monthlyreview.org/2014/marcuse200614.html

41. Quoted in Bruce Feiler, "The United States of Metrics," *New York Times* (May 16, 2014).

42. Max Horkeimer, *Eclipse of Reason* (New York: Martino, 2013), origi-nally published in 1947. For a discussion of the Frankfurt School critique, see Henry A. Giroux, *Theory and Resistance in Education* (New York: Greenwood, 2001), especially Chapter 1, "Critical Theory and Educational Practice."

43. Feiler, "The United States of Metrics."

44. John Steppling, "Sort of Awake," McMaster Centre for Scholarship in the Public Interest (December 15, 2013). http://mcspi.ca/posts/2013/12/sort-of-awake/

45. Zygmunt Bauman and David Lyons, *Liquid Surveillance* (Cambridge: Polity, 2013).

46. Zygmunt Bauman and Leonidas Donskis, *Moral Blindness: The Loss of Sensitivity in Liquid Modernity* (Cambridge: Polity, 2013), p. 7.

47. See Feffer, "Participatory Totalitarianism," *Common Dreams* (June 4, 2014). www.commondreams.org/views/2014/06/04/participatory-totalitarianism

48. Bauman and Donskis, *Moral Blindness*, p. 57.

49. C. Wright Mills, *The Power Elite* (New York: Oxford University Press, 2000), p. 222.

50. Chris Hedges, "Military Metaphysics: How Militarism Mangles the Mind," *Truthout* (February 3, 2014). www.truth-out.org/opinion/item/21624-military-metaphysics-how-militarism-mangles-the-mind

51. Bauman, *Life in Fragments*, p. 149.

52. Étienne Balibar, "Outline of a Topography of Cruelty: Citizenship and Civility in the Era of Global Violence," in Balibar, *We, The People of Europe? Reflec-tions on Transnational Citizenship* (Princeton University Press, 2004), pp. 125–126.

53. Ibid., pp. 149–150.

54. See www.youtube.com/watch?v=VOx3rpkMtY8

55. Max Silverman, *Disposable Life.* http://historiesofviolence.com/specialseries/disposable-life/full-lectures/

CHAPTER THREE

1. Mark Duffield, *Global Governance and the New Wars: The Merging of Development and Security* (London: Zed, 2001).

2. Tony Blair, *Prime Minister's Address to the Labour Party Conference Octo-ber 2001*, pp. 26–27. www.labour.org.uk

3. See in particular, Michael Ignatieff, *The Lesser Evil: Political Ethics in an*

Age of Terror (Princeton University Press, 2004);

4.   Theodor W. Adorno, "The Meaning of Working Through the Past," *Guild and Defense*, trans. Henry W. Pickford (Cambridge: Harvard University Press, 2010), p. 215.

5.   See Evans and Reid, *Resilient Life*.

6.   http://www.ussnewyork.com/ussny_about.html

7.   Zygmunt Bauman and Keith Tester, *Conversations with Zygmunt Bauman* (London: Polity, 2001), p. 63.

8.   Bauman, *Society Under Siege*, pp. 67, 68.

9.   Bauman and Tester, *Conversations*, p. 214.

10.   Jean Comaroff, "Beyond Bare Life: AIDS, (Bio)Politics, and the Neoliberal Order," *Public Culture* 19:1 (Winter 2007), pp. 197-219. This quote appeared in an early draft and is not in the published version of the article.

11.   This issue is taken up in great detail in Henry A. Giroux, *The Terror of Neoliberalism* and *Against the New Authoritarianism* (Winnipeg: Arbeiter Ring, 2005).

12.   Erich Fromm, *The Sane Society* (New York: Fawcett, 1965).

13.   Alex Kane, "Police Subject Man to 8 Anal Searches after Minor Traffic Violation," *AlterNet* (November 5, 2013). www.alternet.org/drugs/anal-searches-8-times-over-doctors-and-cops

14.   Often, only minor infractions of school policy can lead to police arrests. On "zero tolerance" in schools and the criminalization of students, see Mychal Denzel Smith, "The School-to-Prison Pipeline Starts in Preschool," *BillMoyers.com* (March 31, 2014). http://billmoyers.com/2014/03/31/the-school-to-prison-pipeline-starts-in-preschool/. Also see the American Civil Liberties Union's resource page, *School-to-Prison Pipeline*, at www.aclu.org/school-prison-pipeline. For more on the racist dimension of the school-to-prison pipeline, also see Jody Sokolower, "Schools and the New Jim Crow: An Interview with Michelle Alexander," *Truthout* (June 4, 2013). www.truth-out.org/news/item/16756-schools-and-the-new-jim-crow-an-interview-with-michelle-alexander

15.   See Henry A. Giroux, *America's Educational Deficit and the War on Youth* (New York: Monthly Review Press, 2013).

16.   Ethan Bronner, "Poor Land in Jail as Companies Add Huge Fees for Probation," *New York Times* (July 2, 2012), p. A1.

17.   Mark Duffield, *Development, Security and Unending War: Governing the World of Peoples* (Cambridge: Polity, 2007).

18.   On the issue of drone warfare, see Nick Turse, *The Changing Face of Empire: Special Ops, Drones, Spies, Proxy Fighters, Secret Bases, and Cyberwarfare* (Chicago: Haymarket Books, 2012); and Medea Benjamin, *Drone Warfare: Killing by Remote Control* (London: Verso, 2013).

19.   D. Gregory, "The Everywhere War," *Geographical Journal* 177:3 (2011), pp. 241-242.

20.   Amitai Etzioni, "The 'Secret' Matrix," *TheWorldToday.org* (July 2010),

p. 11.

21. Michael J. Boyle, "The Costs and Consequences of Drone Warfare," *International Affairs* 89:1 (2013), p. 3.

22. David Theo Goldberg, "Mission Accomplished: Militarizing Social Logic," in *Enrique Jezik: Obstruct, Destroy, Conceal*, ed. Cuauhtémoc Medina (Mexico: Universidad Nacional Autónoma de México, 2011), p. 187.

23. Tom Engelhardt, ""Washington's Militarized Mindset," *TomDispatch* (July 5, 2012). www.tomdispatch.com/blog/175564/

24. Michael Schwalbe, "Micro Militarism," *Counterpunch* (November 26, 2012). www.counterpunch.org/2012/11/26/mico-militarism

25. Adriana Cavarero, *Horrorism: Naming Contemporary Violence* (New York: Columbia University Press, 2013).

26. Personal correspondence with David L. Clark, McMaster University, May 23, 2014.

27. Michel Foucault, *Society Must Be Defended: Lectures at the Collège de France 1975-1976* (New York: Picador, 2003), p. 47.

28. Ibid., p. 256.

29. Ibid., p. 56.

30. On this, see in particular Zygmunt Bauman, *Society under Siege* (Cambridge: Polity, 2002).

31. Brad Evans and Mark Duffield, "Biospheric Security: How the Merger Between Development, Security & the Environment [Desenex] Is Retrenching Fortress Europe," in *A Threat Against Europe? Security, Migration and Integration*, ed. Peter Burgess and Serge Gutwirth (Brussels: VUB Press, 2011).

32. This critique of instrumental reason was a central feature of the Frankfurt School and is most notable in the work of Herbert Marcuse. See also Zygmunt Bauman's brilliant critique in *Modernity and the Holocaust* (Ithaca, NY: Cornell University Press, 2010), Reprint Edition.

33. Janet Allon, "7 Vilest Right-Wing Statements This Week: Laura Ingraham Hates Immigrants More than O'Reilly Does," *AlterNet* (July 5, 2014). www.alternet.org/print/tea-party-and-right/7-vilest-right-wing-statements-week-laura-ingraham-hates-immigrants-more-oreilly

34. See, for example, World Bank and Carter Centre, *From Civil War to Civil Society* (Washington, DC: World Bank & Carter Centre, 1997).

35. Cited in Matt Phillips, "Goldman Sachs' Blankfein on Banking: 'Doing God's Work,'" *Wall Street Journal* (November 9, 2009). http://blogs.wsj.com/marketbeat/2009/11/09/goldman-sachs-blankfein-on-banking-doing-gods-work/

36. C. Wright Mills, *The Politics of Truth: Selected Writings of C. Wright Mills* (New York: Oxford University Press, 2008), p. 200.

37. Stanley Aronowitz, *Against Schooling: Education and Social Class* (Boulder: Paradigm, 2008), p. xii.

38. Kate Zernike, "Making College 'Relevant,'" *New York Times* (January 3, 2010), p. ED16.

39. While this critique has been made by many critics, it has also been made recently by the president of Harvard University. See Drew Gilpin Faust, "The University's Crisis of Purpose," *New York Times* (September 6, 2009).

40. Harvey cited in Stephen Pender, "An Interview with David Harvey," *Studies in Social Justice* 1:1 (Winter 2007), p. 14.

41. Deleuze and Guattari, *Anti-Oedipus*, p. 215.

42. Eugene Holland, *Deleuze & Guattari's "Anti-Oedipus": Introduction to Schizoanalysis* (London: Routledge, 1999), pp. 77-78.

43. Paul Gilroy, "'After the Love Has Gone': Bio-Politics and Ethepoetics in the Black Public Sphere," *Public Culture* 7:1 (1994), p. 58.

44. The culture of cruelty is discussed in great detail in Henry A. Giroux, *Zombie Politics and Culture in the Age of Casino Capitalism* (New York: Peter Lang, 2011).

45. Geoffrey Hartman, "Public Memory and Its Discontents," *Raritan* 8:4 (Spring 1994), p. 25.

46. Terry Eagleton, *The Ideology of the Aesthetic* (Cambridge: Basil Blackwell, 1990), p. 344.

47. C. Wright Mills, "The Cultural Apparatus," in *The Politics of Truth: Selected Writings of C. Wright Mills* (New York: Oxford University Press, 2008), pp. 203-212.

48. Bauman, *Life in Fragments*, p. 151.

49. Sarah Lazare and Ryan Harvey, "WikiLeaks in Baghdad," *The Nation* (July 29, 2010). www.thenation.com/article/38034/wikileaks-baghdad

50. Jacques Rancière, *The Politics of Aesthetics* (London: Continuum, 2005).

51. Jacques Rancière, *The Emancipated Spectator* (London: Verso, 2009), p. 93.

52. Ibid., Rancière, p. 99.

53. Ibid., Rancière, p. 102.

54. Ibid., Rancière, p. 26.

55. Michael J. Shapiro, "The Presence of War: 'Here and Elsewhere,'" *International Political Sociology* 5:2 (June 2011), p. 118.

56. Gilles Deleuze and Félix Guattari, *What Is Philosophy?*, trans. Graham Burchell and Hugh Tomlinson (London: Verso, 1994), p. 76.

57. Michael Shapiro, *Cinematic Geopolitics* (Abingdon: Routledge, 2007).

CHAPTER FOUR

1. Robin D.G. Kelley, "Empire State of Mind," *Counterpunch* (August 16, 2013). www.counterpunch.org/2013/08/16/empire-state-of-mind/print

2. Joe Klein, "Despite Trayvon Martin's Death, America's Biracial Era Is Ending," *TIME* (July 29, 2013). http://content.time.com/time/magazine/article/0,9171,2147711,00.html#ixzz2v0A0qcvv

3. Bauman, *Wasted Lives*, pp. 92-93.

4. Erica Goode, "Many in U.S. Are Arrested by Age 23, Study Finds,"

New York Times (December 19, 2011), p. A15.

5. Reuters, "45% Struggle in U.S. to Make Ends Meet," *NBCNews.com* (November 22, 2011). www.nbcnews.com/id/45407937/ns/business-stocks_and_economy/#.T3SxhDEgd8E

6. Étienne Balibar, "Outline of a Topography of Cruelty: Citizenship and Civility in the Era of Global Violence," in *We, the People of Europe? Reflections on Transnational Citizenship* (Princeton University Press, 2004), p. 128.

7. Thomas Frank, "Lock 'em Up: Jailing Kids Is a Proud American Tradition," *Wall Street Journal* (April 2, 2009). http://online.wsj.com/article/SB123854010220075533.html

8. Henry A. Giroux takes up the ongoing militarization of higher education in *University in Chains: Challenging the Military-Industrial-Academic Complex* (Boulder: Paradigm, 2007).

9. Zenon Evans, "Ohio State University Gets Armored Military Vehicle, Repeatedly Dodges Questions about It," *Reason.com* (September 19, 2013). http://reason.com/blog/2013/09/19/ohio-state-university-gets-armored-milit

10. W.E.B. Du Bois, *The Souls of Black Folk in Three Negro Classics* (New York: Avon, 1965), p. 221.

11. It is important to note that while this may be true for anti-black racism, it is certainly not true for the racist policies being enacted by the United States against immigrants and nationals from the Middle East. The current moment of racial profiling, harassment, and outright use of unconstitutional means to intimidate, deport, and jail members of the Arab and Muslim populations in the United States represents a most shameful period in this country's ongoing history of state-sanctioned racist practices. While the focus of this chapter is on black-white relations, we are not suggesting that racism encompasses only the latter. Obviously, any full account of racism would have to be applied to a wide range of groups constituted by diverse peoples of color and ethnic origin.

12. For examples of the continuation of pervasive racism in American life, see Howard Winant, *The World Is a Ghetto: Race and Democracy since World War II* (New York: Basic Books, 2001); Manning Marable, *The Great Wells of Democracy: The Meaning of Race in American Life* (New York: Basic Civitas Books, 2002); David Theo Goldberg, *The Racial State* (Malden, MA: Blackwell, 2002); and Steve Martinot, *The Rule of Racialization: Class, Identity, Governance* (Philadelphia: Temple University Press, 2003).

13. Michael Omi, "Racialization in the Post-Civil Rights Era," in *Mapping Multiculturalism*, eds. Avery Gordon and Christopher Newfield (Minneapolis: University of Minnesota Press, 1996), p. 183.

14. Jack Geiger, "The Real World of Race," *The Nation* (December 1, 1997), p. 27.

15. Zygmunt Bauman, *The Individualized Society* (London: Polity, 2001), p. 205.

16. Zygmunt Bauman, *Globalization: The Human Consequences* (New York:

Columbia University Press, 2000), p. 47.

17. Amy Elizabeth Ansell, *New Right, New Racism: Race and Reaction in the United States and Britain* (New York University Press, 1997), pp. 20-21.

18. Goldberg, *Racial State*, p. 229.

19. Charles Gallagher, "Color-blind Privilege: The Social and Political Functions of Erasing the Color Line in Post-Race America," unpublished essay, p. 12.

20. Angela Davis, *Abolition Democracy: Beyond Empire, Prisons, and Torture* (New York: Seven Stories, 2005), p. 41.

21. The separation of power from politics in late modernity is taken up in detail in Zygmunt Bauman and Carlo Bordoni, *State of Crisis* (London: Polity, 2014).

22. David Denby, "Angry People–Crash," *The New Yorker* (April 25, 2005). www.newyorker.com/ critics/cinema/articles/ 050502crci_cinema

23. Ella Taylor, "Space Race," *Los Angeles Times* (May 6, 2005), p. 36.

24. Mahmood Mamdani, *Good Muslim, Bad Muslim: America, the Cold War and the Roots of Terror* (New York: Pantheon, 2004), p. 17.

25. Wendy Brown, *Regulating Aversion: Tolerance in the Age of Identity and Empire* (Princeton University Press, 2006), p. 16.

26. David Theo Goldberg, "Introduction," in *Multiculturalism: A Critical Reader* (Cambridge, MA: Blackwell, 1994), p. 13.

27. Stephen Hunter, "'Crash': The Collision of Human Contradictions," *Washington Post* (May 6, 2005), p. C01.

28. David Edelstein, "Crash and Fizzle," *Slate* (May 5, 2005). www.slate.com/id/ 2118119/

29. Gary Younge, "Like Michael Brown in Ferguson, to be poor and black renders you collateral," *The Guardian*, August 15, 2014. www.theguardian.com/commentisfree/2014/aug/15/michael-brown-ferguson-america-racism

30. Hannah Arendt, "Ideology and Terror: A Novel Form of Government," *The Origins of Totalitarianism*, (Houghton Mifflin Harcourt, New York: 2001), p. 464.

31. This issue is taken up in great detail in Henry A. Giroux, *Dangerous Thinking in the Age of the New Authoritarianism* (Boulder: Paradigm, 2015).

32. http://www.washingtonpost.com/news/post-nation/wp/2014/08/22/hands-up-the-ferguson-magazine-covers/

33. Slavoj Žižek, *Demanding the Impossible*, ed. Yong-June Park. (Cambridge, UK: Polity, 2013), p. 58.

34. Kevin Zeese and Margaret Flowers, "Ferguson Exposes the Reality of Militarized, Racist Policing," *Truthout* (August 18, 2014). http://truth-out.org/news/item/25645-ferguson-exposes-the-reality-of-militarized-racist-policing

35. Adam Hudson, "1 Black Man Is Killed Every 28 Hours by Police or Vigilantes: America Is Perpetually at War with Its Own People," *AlterNet* (March 28, 2013). www.alternet.org/news-amp-politics/1-black-man-killed-

every-28-hours-police-or-vigilantes-america-perpetually-war-its. See also the report titled Operation Ghetto Storm: http://mxgm.org/wp-content/up-loads/2013/04/Operation-Ghetto-Storm.pdf

36. See, especially, Radley Balko, *Rise of the Warrior Cop: The Militarization of America's Police Forces* (New York: Public Affairs, 2013), Michelle Alexander, *The New Jim Crow* (New York: New Press, 2010), and Jill Nelson, ed. *Police Brutality* (New York: Norton, 2000).

37. Foucault, *Society Must Be Defended* p.103

38. Mumia Abu-Jamal, "The Meaning of Ferguson," *The San Francisco Bay View*, September 29, 2014. http://sfbayview.com/2014/09/mumia-on-the-meaning-of-ferguson/

CHAPTER FIVE

1. Michel Foucault, *Discipline and Punish: The Birth of the Prison*, trans. Alan Sheridan (New York: Vintage, 1995). Originally published in 1975.

2. Judith Butler, *Gender Trouble* (New York: Routledge, 1990).

3. Judith Butler, *Precarious Life* (London: Verso, 2004).

4. Foucault, *Society Must Be Defended*, p. 247; Michel Foucault, *The History of Sexuality*, Vol. 1 (New York: Vintage, 1990), p. 138.

5. Judith Butler, *Frames of War: When Is Life Grievable?* (London, Verso: 2009), pp. 3, 4.

6. Ibid., p.4.

7. Rancière, *Emancipated Spectator*, p. 96.

8. For an example of utterly uncritical reporting on this type of over-the-top celebration of violence and the armed forces, see John Anderson, "On Active Duty for the Movies (Real Ammo)," *New York Times* (February 19, 2012), p. AR16.

9. Rancière, *Emancipated Spectator*, p. 96.

10. See, for example, A.O. Scott and Manohla Dargis, "Gosh, Sweetie, That's a Big Gun," *New York Times* (April 27, 2011), p. MT1.

11. Catherine Clement quoted in Hélène Cixous and Catherine Clement, *The Newly Born Woman*, trans. Betsy Wing, *Theory and History of Literature Series*, Vol. 24 (Minneapolis: University of Minnesota Press, 1986), p. ix.

12. See, for instance, Richard Terdiman, "Deconstructing Memory: On Representing the Past and Theorizing Culture in France Since the Revolution," *Diacritics* (Winter 1985), pp. 13-36.

13. Gerry Mooney and Lynn Hancock, "Poverty Porn and the Broken Society," *Variant* 39/40 (Winter 2010). www.variant.org.uk/39_40texts/Variant39_40.html#L4

14. Chris Hedges, "The Last Gasp of American Democracy," *Truthout* (January 6, 2014). www.truth-out.org/opinion/item/21052-chris-hedges-the-last-gasp-of-american-democracy

15. David Graeber, "The University Is Dead . . . and Cop Free Zones!" *Daily Struggles* (December 14, 2013). http://daily-struggles.tumblr.com/

post/69078097047/the-university-is-dead-by-david-graeber

16. Wendy Brown, *Regulating Aversion: Tolerance in the Age of Identity and Empire* (Princeton University Press, 2006), p. 16.

17. Zygmunt Bauman, "The London Riots: On Consumerism Coming Home to Roost," *Social Europe Journal* (August 9, 2011). www.social-europe. eu/2011/08/the-london-riots-on-consumerism-coming-home-to-roost/

18. Chase Madar, "Everyone Is a Criminal: On the Over-Policing of America," *Huffington Post* (December 13, 2013). www.huffingtonpost.com/ chase-madar/over-policing-of-america_b_4412187.html

19. Ibid.

20. Erik Eckholm, "With Police in Schools, More Children in Court," *New York Times* (April 12, 2013). www.nytimes.com/2013/04/12/education/ with-police-in-schools-more-children-in-court.html?ref=erikeckholm

21. Heather Vogell, "The Shocking Ways School Kids Are Being Restrained, Isolated against Their Will," *AlterNet* (June 23, 1014). www.alternet.org/education/ shocking-ways-school-kids-are-being-restrained-isolated-against-their-will

22. Alan Pyke, "Impoverished Mother Dies in Jail Cell Over Unpaid Fines for Her Kids Missing School," *ThinkProgress* (June 12, 2014). http:// thinkprogress.org/economy/2014/06/12/3448105/mother-dies-jail-cell-fines/

23. Ibid.

24. Achille Mbembe, "Necropolitics," *Public Culture* 15:1 (Winter 2003), p. 40.

25. Bauman, *Wasted Lives*, p. 13.

26. Zygmunt Bauman has brilliantly developed this insightful position in a number of books. See Bauman, *Wasted Lives; Globalization; Liquid Moder- nity*; and *Liquid Life* (London: Polity, 2005).

27. Bauman, *Wasted Lives*, p. 13.

28. Janet Pelz, "The Poor Shamed Us into Seeing Them," *Seattle Post-Intelligencer* (September 19, 2005). www.seattlepi.com/local/opinion/article/ First-Person-The-poor-shamed-us-into-seeing-them-1183193.php

29. Gayatri Chakravorty Spivak, "Can the Subaltern Speak?" in *Marxism and the Interpretation of Culture*, eds. Cary Nelson and Lawrence Grossberg (Urbana: University of Illinois Press, 1988), pp. 271-313.

30. Michael Shapiro, "HBO's Two Frontiers: *Deadwood* and *The Wire*," *Geopolitics* 00 (2014), pp. 1-21.

CHAPTER SIX

1. Susan Sontag, *On Photography* (New York: Picador, 1973).

2. Susan Sontag, *Regarding the Pain of Others* (New York: Farrar, Straus and Giroux, 2003).

3. Paul Virilio, *Art and Fear* (New York: Continuum, 2004), p. 28.

4. Peter Moskos, *In Defense of Flogging* (New York: Basic Books, 2011).

5. Peter Dale Scott, "Is One Muslim Man's Drug-

Crazed Rampage Terrorism?" *WhoWhatWhy* (November 25, 2014). http://whowhatwhy.com/2014/11/25/ will-one-mans-drug-crazed-rampage-change-canadas-history/

6.   Judith Butler, *Bodies That Matter: On the Discursive Limits of Sex* (New York: Routledge, 1993), p. 95.

7.   There is a long history of such abuses and racist violence being photographed by the perpetrators of Western colonialism. See, for example, Sherene Razack, *Dark Threats and White Knights: The Somalia Affair, Peacekeeping, and the New Imperialism* (University of Toronto Press, 2004). Equally relevant is the fact that many of the methods of abuse and torture used at Abu Ghraib prison have a long history and were "pioneered by the CIA in the 1950s and 1960s, [and] taught and used by American military, CIA, and police officials in Latin America from the 1960s into the 1980s." See Tom Engelhardt, "How Bush Took Us to the Dark Side," Tomdispatch.com (January 5, 2008). www. tomdispatch.com/post/174876/how_bush_took_us_to_the_dark_side. It is also worth noting that such techniques are used at home. In fact, the systematic torture of dozens of African-American males by Chicago police officers took place in a Chicago prison for nearly two decades beginning in 1971. See Amy Goodman, "Chicago's Abu Ghraib: UN Committee Against Torture Hears Report on How Police Tortured Over 135 African-American Men Inside Chicago Jails," *Democracynow.org*, (May 9, 2005). www.democracynow. org/2006/5/9/chicagos_abu_ghraib_un_committee_against. An excellent history of American torture can be found in Michael Otterman, *American Torture: From the Cold War to Abu Ghraib and Beyond* (London: Pluto, 2007).

8.   Since the release of the initial photos, new rounds of fresh photographs and film footage of torture from Abu Ghraib and other prisons in Iraq have emerged that "include details of the rape and ... abuse of some of the Iraqi women and the hundred or so children—some as young as 10 years old." See Ray McGovern, "Not Scared Yet? Try Connecting These Dots," *Common Dreams* (August 11, 2004). www.commondreams.org/views04/0809-11. htm. One account provided by U.S. Army Sergeant Samuel Provance, who was stationed in the Abu Ghraib prison, recalls how "interrogators soaked a 16-year-old, covered him in mud, and then used his suffering to break the youth's father, also a prisoner, during interrogation" (McGovern, 2004). Another *Washington Post* account cited an army investigation surrounding the Abu Ghraib practice of using unmuzzled military police dogs as part of a sadistic game designed to "make juveniles—as young as 15 years old—urinate on themselves as part of a competition." See Josh White and Thomas E. Ricks, "Iraqi Teens Abused at Abu Ghraib, Report Finds," *Washington Post* (August 24, 2004), p. A01. A new round of images also emerged in 2006. See Mark Oliver, "New 'Abu Ghraib Abuse' Images Screened," *The Guardian* (February 15, 2006). www.theguardian.com/world/2006/feb/15/iraq.usa

9.   Oliver, "New 'Abu Ghraib Abuse' Images."

10.   Editorial, "Outrage over Torture Video," *Gulf Daily News* (February

13, 2006). www.gulf-daily-news.com/NewsDetails.aspx?storyid=135297

11. Seymour M. Hersh, "The General's Report," *The New Yorker* (June 25, 2007). www.newyorker.com/magazine/2007/06/25/the-generals-report

12. Susan Sontag, "Regarding the Torture of Others: Notes on What Has Been Done and Why—To Prisoners, by Americans," *New York Times Sunday Magazine* (May 23, 2004). www.nytimes.com/2004/05/23/magazine/regarding-the-torture-of-others.html?src=pm&pagewanted=2

13. This issue is taken up with great insight and compassion in Robert Jay Lifton, *Super Power Syndrome: America's Apocalyptic Confrontation with the World* (New York: Thunder Mouth Press, 2003).

14. See Edward T. Pound and Kit R. Roane, "Hell on Earth," *U.S. News and World Report* (July 19, 2004). www.usnews.com/usnews/issue/040719/usnews/19prison.htm. Also see Editorial, "The Horror of Abu Ghraib," *The Nation* (May 24, 2004), p. 3; and Kate Zernike and David Rohde, "Forced Nudity of Iraqi Prisoners Is Seen as a Pervasive Pattern, Not Isolated Incidents," *New York Times* (June 8, 2004), p. A11.

15. See Henry A. Giroux, "Consuming Social Change: The United Colors of Benetton," a chapter in Giroux, *Disturbing Pleasures: Learning Popular Culture* (New York: Routledge, 1994), pp. 3-24.

16. Cited in Paul Virilio, *Art and Fear* (London: Continuum, 2000), p. 28.

17. Walter Benjamin, *Illuminations*, trans. Harry Zohn (New York: Schocken, 1969). See also Walter Benjamin, "Critique of Violence" in *Reflections: Essays, Aphorisms, Autobiographical Writings* (New York: Schocken, 1986).

18. Lutz Koepnick, "Aesthetic Politics Today: Walter Benjamin and Post-Fordist Culture," *Critical Theory: Current State and Future Prospects*, eds. Peter Uwe Hohendahl and Jaimey Fisher (New York: Berghahn, 2002), p. 95.

19. Ibid., p. 96. See also Susan Buck-Morss, "Aesthetics and Anaesthetics: Walter Benjamin's Artwork Essay Reconsidered," *October* 62 (Fall 1992), pp. 3-41.

20. Jim Frederick, "Anatomy of a War Crime: Behind the Enabling of the 'Kill Team,'" *TIME* (March 29, 2011). http://globalspin.blogs.time.com/2011/03/29/anatomy-of-a-war-crime-behind-the-enabling-of-the-kill-team/

21. Mark Boal, "The Kill Team," *Rolling Stone* (March 27, 2011). www.rollingstone.com/politics/news/the-kill-team-20110327

22. Ibid.

23. Ibid.

24. Ibid.

25. Seymour M. Hersh, "The 'Kill Team' Photographs," *The New Yorker* (March 23, 2011). www.newyorker.com/online/blogs/newsdesk/2011/03/the-kill-team-photographs.html

26. Luke Mogelson, "A Beast in the Heart of Every Fighting Man," *New York Times Magazine* (April 27, 2011). www.nytimes.com/2011/05/01/maga-

zine/mag-01KillTeam-t.html

27. Cited in Franco Bifo Berardi, *Precarious Rhapsody* (London: Minor Compositions, 2009), pp. 96-97.

28. David Carr, "War, in Life and Death," *New York Times* (April 24, 2011), p. B1.

29. David L. Clark, personal correspondence, May 15, 2011.

30. Shapiro, "The Presence of War," p. 112.

31. Sontag, *Regarding the Pain of Others*, p. 81.

32. Ibid., p. 81.

33. Ibid., p. 81.

34. Mieke Bal, "The Pain of Images," in *Beautiful Suffering*, eds. Mark Reinhardt, Holly Edwards, and Erina Duganne (University of Chicago Press, 2007), p. 107.

35. Ibid., p. 111.

36. Richard Beck, "Beyond the Choir: An Interview with David Simon," *Film Quarterly* 62:2 (Winter 2008), p. 47.

37. Ibid., p. 49.

CHAPTER SEVEN

1. Marjorie Cohn, "Beyond Orwell's Worst Nightmare," *Huffington Post* (January 31, 2014). www.huffingtonpost.com/marjorie-cohn/beyond-orwells-worst-nigh_b_4698242.html

2. See Costas Pitas, "Snowden Warns of Loss of Privacy in Christmas Message," *Reuters* (December 25, 2013). www.reuters.com/article/2013/12/25/us-usa-snowden-privacy-idUSBRE9BO09020131225

3. Ibid.

4. See Manuel Castells, *The Rise of the Network Society* (Malden: Wiley-Blackwell, 1996) and Zygmunt Bauman, *Collateral Damage: Social Inequalities in a Global Age* (Cambridge: Polity, 2011).

5. See Giroux, *The Violence of Organized Forgetting*.

6. Jonathan Crary, *24/7: Late Capitalism and the Ends of Sleep* (London: Verso, 2013), p. 16.

7. Ibid., p. 22.

8. Ariel Dorfman, "Repression by Any Other Name," *Guernica* (February 3, 2014). www.guernicamag.com/features/repression-by-any-other-name/

9. This theme is developed in Michael Hardt and Antonio Negri, *Declarations* (New York: Argo Navis Author Services, 2012).

10. Jonathan Schell, "America's Surveillance Net," *The Nation* (June 19, 2013).www.thenation.com/article/174889/americas-surveillancenet#axzz2YBvZWccM.

11. Jakob Augstein, "Once Upon a Time in the West," *Spiegel Online* (August 4, 2011). www.spiegel.de/international/world/0,1518,778396,00.html

12. Zygmunt Bauman and David Lyon, *Liquid Surveillance: A Conversation* (Cambridge: Polity, 2013), p. 28.

13. James Glanz, Jeff Larson, and Andrew W. Lehren, "Spy Agencies Scour Phone Apps for Personal Data," *New York Times* (January 27, 2014). www.nytimes.com/2014/01/28/world/spy-agencies-scour-phone-apps-for-personal-data.html?emc=edit_na_20140127&_r=0

14. Bauman and Lyon, *Liquid Surveillance*, pp. 13-14.

15. Christine Geovanis, "The *Chicago Tribune*'s War on Dissent," *Counterpunch* (February 17, 2014). www.counterpunch.org/2014/02/14/the-chicago-tribunes-war-on-dissent/

16. Ibid.

17. Bauman and Lyon, *Liquid Surveillance*, p. 33.

18. http://occupyarrests.moonfruit.com

19. Spencer Ackerman, "US Tech Giants Knew of NSA Data Collection, Agency's Top Lawyer Insists," *The Guardian* (March 19, 2014). www.theguardian.com/world/2014/mar/19/us-tech-giants-knew-nsa-data-collection-rajesh-de

20. Quentin Skinner and Richard Marshall, "Liberty, Liberalism and Surveillance: A Historic Overview" *Open Democracy* (July 26, 2013). www.opendemocracy.net/ourkingdom/quentin-skinner-richard-marshall/liberty-liberalism-and-surveillance-historic-overview

21. Hardt and Negri, *Declaration*, p. 23.

22. Tom Engelhardt, "A Surveillance State Scorecard," *TomDispatch.com* (November 12, 2013). www.tomdispatch.com/blog/175771/

23. Many of these issues are discussed at length in Henry A. Giroux, *The Violence of Organized Forgetting; The Twilight of the Social* (Boulder: Paradigm, 2012); and *Zombie Politics and Culture in the Age of Casino Capitalism*, 2nd edition (New York: Peter Lang, 2014).

24. Virginia Eubanks, "Want to Predict the Future of Surveillance? Ask Poor Communities," *American Prospect* (January 15, 2014). http://prospect.org/article/want-predict-future-surveillance-ask-poor-communities

25. Ibid.

26. There is a long history of surveillance being used to support illegal acts ranging from falsely accusing people of crimes, destroying social movements, and suppressing dissent to committing deadly crimes. See, for example, the literature on the FBI counter-terrorism program launched by J. Edgar Hoover that existed from the 1950s until it was dismantled in the 1970s. There are also the nefarious illegalities committed under the Clinton, Bush, and Obama administrations which have been well documented by a range of whistle-blowers and journalists from Daniel Ellsberg and Seymour Hersh to Jeremy Hammond and Edward Snowden. More recent resources include the following: Fred Branfman, "America's Most Anti-Democratic Institutions: How the Imperial Presidency Threatens U.S. National Security," *AlterNet* (Jun 9, 2013), www.alternet.org/print/news-amp-politics/executive-branch-threatens-us-national-security; Amy Goodman, "Glenn Greenwald on How Secretive DEA Unit Illegally Spies on Americans,

Covers Up Actions," *Truthout* (August 6, 2013), www.truth-out.org/video/item/18005-glenn-greenwald-on-how-secretive-dea-unit-illegally-spies-on-americans-covers-up-actions; and Christopher Calabrese and Matthew Harwood, "Nowhere to Hide: The Government's Massive Intrusion into Our Lives" *AlterNet* (September 22, 2013), www.alternet.org/civil-liberties/nowhere-hide-governments-massive-intrusion-our-lives

27. John W. Whitehead, "Is High-tech Surveillance in Schools a Security Need or a Money Scam?" *Huffington Post* (December 4, 2012). www.huffingtonpost.com/john-w-whitehead/the-fight-against-schools_b_2232112.html

28. Stephanie Simon, "Biosensors to Monitor Students' Attentiveness," *Chicago Tribune* (June 12, 2012). http://articles.chicagotribune.com/2012-06-12/news/sns-rt-us-usa-education-gatesbre85c018-20120612_1_gates-foundation-veteran-english-teacher-teachers-feedback

29. Hank Stuever, "TV Preview of 'Undercover Boss on CBS," *Washington Post* (February 7, 2010), p. E03.

30. Teddy Cruz, "Democratizing Urbanization and the Search for a New Civic Imagination," in *Living as Form: Socially Engaged Art from 1991-2011*, ed. Nato Thompson (New York: Creative Time, 2012), p. 57.

31. Jeremy Gilbert, "What Kind of Thing Is 'Neoliberalism'?" *New Formations* 55: 80/81 (Winter 2013), p. 9.

32. Charles Derber and June Sekera, "An Invisible Crisis: We Are Suffering from a Growing Public Goods Deficit," *Boston Globe* (January 22, 2014). www.bostonglobe.com/opinion/2014/01/22/the-hidden-deficit/LMvPwkE9tPmOQcezlCTFjM/story.html

33. Cruz, "Democratizing Urbanization," p. 58.

34. Cruz cited in Derber and Sekera, "An Invisible Crisis."

35. Gilbert, "What Kind of Thing Is 'Neoliberalism'?" pp. 11-12.

36. Todd Gitlin, "The Wonderful American World of Informers and *Agents Provocateurs*," *TomDispatch.com* (June 27, 2013), www.tomdispatch.com/blog/175718/; Ralph Nader, "Corporatizing National Security," *Counterpunch* (June 21, 2013), www.counterpunch.org/2013/06/21/corporatizing-national-security; and Tom Ferguson, Paul Jorgensen, and Jie Chen, "Who Buys the Spies? The Hidden Corporate Cash Behind America's Out-of-Control National Surveillance State," *The Next New Deal* (October 27, 2013), www.nextnewdeal.net/who-buys-spies-hidden-corporate-cash-behind-america%E2%80%99s-out-control-national-surveillance-state.

37. For a historical analysis of industrial espionage by the CIA and NSA, see David Price, "The NSA, CIA, and the Promise of Industrial Espionage," *Counterpunch* (January 28, 2014). www.counterpunch.org/2014/01/28/the-nsa-cia-and-the-promise-of-industrial-espionage/

38. This is clearly documented in Heidi Boghosian, *Spying on Democracy: Government Surveillance, Corporate Power, and Public Resistance* (San Franciso: City Lights, 2013).

39. Olivia Ward, "Inside the World of Big Data," *Toronto Star* (June 22, 2013), p. WD5.

40. David Graeber, "Dead Zones of the Imagination," *HAU: Journal of Ethnographic Theory* 2 (2012), pp.116-117.

41. Kate Epstein, "Total Surveillance *CounterPunch* (June 28-30, 2013). www.counterpunch.org/2013/06/28/total-surveillance/

42. Noam Chomsky, "Is Edward J. Snowden Aboard This Plane?" *Truthout* (August 1, 2013). www.truth-out.org/opinion/item/17923-is-edward-j-snowden-aboard-this-plane

43. Boghosian, *Spying on Democracy*, p. 32.

44. Ibid.

45. Ibid., pp. 22-23.

46. Mark Karlin, "From Spying on 'Terrorists Abroad' to Suppressing Domestic Dissent: When We Become the Hunted," *Truthout* (August 21, 2013). www.truth-out.org/news/item/18292-from-spying-on-terrorists-abroad-to-using-massive-surveillance-to-suppress-domestic-dissent-when-we-become-the-hunted

47. Graeber, "Dead Zones of the Imagination," p. 119.

48. Bruce Schneier, "The Public-Private Surveillance Partnership," *Bloomberg* (July 31, 2013). www.bloomberg.com/news/2013-07-31/the-public-private-surveillance-partnership.html

49. Arun Gupta, "Barrett Brown's Revelations Every Bit as Explosive as Edward Snowden's," *The Guardian* (June 24, 2013). www.theguardian.com/commentisfree/2013/jun/24/surveillance-us-national-security

50. Crary, *24/7*, p. 17.

51. Giorgio Agamben, "The Security State and a Theory of Destituent Power," *Philosophers for Change* (February 25, 2014). http://philosophersfor-change.org/2014/02/25/the-security-state-and-a-theory-of-destituent-power/

52. Amy Davidson, "When Journalists Are Called Traitors," *The New Yorker* (October 11, 2013). www.newyorker.com/online/blogs/closeread/2013/10/when-journalists-are-called-traitors-from-the-spiegel-affair-to-snowden.html

53. Brett Logiurato, "Snowden: 'Being Called a Traitor by Dick Cheney Is the Highest Honor,'" *Business Insider* (January 17, 2013). www.businessinsider.com/edward-snowden-dick-cheney-traitor-comment-guardian-chat-glenn-greenwald-2013-6

54. Edward Snowden, "Edward Snowden Letter to German Government in Full," *Guardian UK* (November 1, 2013). www.newstatesman.com/node/147614

55. David Weigel, "If It's Wednesday, Peter King Is Accusing the Media of Treason," *Slate* (June 12, 2013). www.slate.com/blogs/weigel/2013/06/12/if_it_s_wednesday_peter_king_is_accusing_the_media_of_treason.html

56. Erik Kirschbaum, "Snowden Says 'Significant Threats' to His Life," *Reuters* (January 26, 2013). http://uk.reuters.com/article/2014/01/26/

uk-security-snowden-germany-idUKBREA0P0DG20140126

57. Scott Shane, "No Morsel Too Minuscule for All-Consuming N.S.A.," *New York Times* (November 2, 2013), p. A1.

58. The range and scope of such technologies is made clear in Kevin Zeese and Margaret Flowers, "Confronting the Growing National (In)Security State," *Truthout* (June 26, 2013). www.truth-out.org/news/item/17208-confronting-the-growing-national-insecurity-state. See also Ronald J. Deibert, *Black Codes: Inside the Battle for Cyberspace* (Toronto: McClelland and Stewart, 2013).

59. Crary, *24/7*, p. 104.

60. David Price, "Memory's Half-life: A Social History of Wiretaps," *Counterpunch* 20:6 (June 2013), p. 14.

61. Ibid., p. 14.

62. Agamben, "The Security State and a Theory of Destituent Power."

63. Price, "Memory's Half-life," pp. 10-14.

64. Ibid., p. 10.

65. Alex Perene, "The Republican Plot to Kill Democracy: Why It Wants to Neutralize the Vote," *AlterNet* (January 27, 2014). www.alternet.org/republican-plot-kill-democracy. See the excellent documentary by Bill Moyers on North Carolina and the suppression of voting rights at Bill Moyers & Company, "North Carolina: Battleground State," *Truthout* (January 9, 2014). www.truth-out.org/news/item/21090-north-carolina-battleground-state

66. Chris Maisano, "Chicken Soup for the Neoliberal Soul," *Jacobin: A Magazine of Culture and Polemic* (January 21, 2014). www.jacobinmag.com/2014/01/chicken-soup-for-the-neoliberal-soul/

67. Ibid.

68. Ariel Dorfman, "Repression by Any Other Name," *Guernica* (February 3, 2014). www.guernicamag.com/features/repression-by-any-other-name/

69. Ibid.

70. Eubanks, "Want to Predict the Future of Surveillance?"

71. Ibid.

72. Ibid.

73. Ibid.

74. Roger I. Simon, "Forms of Insurgency in the Production of Popular Memories," *Cultural Studies* 1:1 (1993), p. 77.

75. C. Wright Mills, "On Politics," in *The Sociological Imagination* (Oxford University Press, 2000), pp. 185-186.

76. The text of Obama's speech on NSA reforms can be found at www.washingtonpost.com/politics/full-text-of-president-obamas-jan-17-speech-on-nsa-reforms/2014/01/17/fa33590a-7f8c-11e3-9556-4a4bf7bcbd84_story.html.

77. See Robert Scheer, "No Place to Hide: We're All Suspects in Barack Obama's America," *Truth-Dig* (January 21, 2014). www.truthdig.com/report/item/

no_place_to_hide_were_all_suspects_in_barack_obamas_america_20140121

78. Michael Ratner, "Obama's NSA Speech Makes Orwellian Surveillance Patriotic," *Truthout* (Januay 27, 2014). www.truth-out.org/opinion/item/21461-obamas-nsa-speech-makes-orwellian-surveillance-patriotic

79. James Ball, "NSA Monitored Calls of 35 World Leaders after US Official Handed Over Contacts," *The Guardian* (October 25, 2013). www.theguardian.com/world/2013/oct/24/nsa-surveillance-world-leaders-calls

80. See, for instance, Jonathan Turley, "10 Reasons the U.S. Is No Longer the Land of the Free," *Washington Post* (January 13, 2012), http://articles.washingtonpost.com/2012-01-13/opinions/35440628_1_individual-rights-indefinite-detention-citizens; Ron Nixon, "U.S. Postal Service Logging All Mail for Law Enforcement," *New York Times* (July 3, 2013), www.nytimes.com/2013/07/04/us/monitoring-of-snail-mail.html?pagewanted=all&_r=0, and note the listing by the *New York Times* of the surveillance crimes committed by the NSA, another agency we are supposed to believe acts in the best interests of the American people; and Editorial Board, "Edward Snowden, Whistle Blower," *New York Times* (January 1, 2014), www.nytimes.com/2014/01/02/opinion/edward-snowden-whistle-blower.html?hp&rref=opinion

81. Marisa Taylor and Jonathan S. Landay, "Obama's Crackdown Views Leaks as Aiding Enemies of U.S.," *McClatchy Washington Bureau* (June 21, 2013). www.mcclatchydc.com/2013/06/20/194513/obamas-crackdown-views-leaks-as.html#.Ucmuwmxzboo

82. RazFx Pro, "Hammer This Fact Home…," *News from a Parallel World* (June 22, 2013). http://lookingglass.blog.co.uk/2013/06/22/hammer-this-fact-home-16154325/

83. Mark Mazzetti and David E. Sanger, "Top Intelligence Official Assails Snowden and Seeks Return of N.S.A. Documents," *New York Times* (January 29, 20014). www.nytimes.com/2014/01/30/us/politics/intelligence-chief-condemns-snowden-and-demands-return-of-data.html?_r=0

84. Michael Calderine, "James Clapper Suggest Journalists Could Be Edward Snowden's Accomplices," *Huffington Post* (January 29, 2014). www.huffingtonpost.com/2014/01/29/snowden-accomplices_n_4689123.html

85. Schell, "America's Surveillance Net."

86. Amy Goodman, "'It Was Time to Do More than Protest': Activists Admit to 1971 FBI Burglary That Exposed COINTELPRO," *Democracy Now!* (January 8, 2014). www.democracynow.org/2014/1/8/it_was_time_to_do_more

87. Amy Goodman, "From COINTELPRO to Snowden, the FBI Burglars Speak Out after 43 Years of Silence (Part 2)," *Democracy Now!* (January 8, 2014). www.democracynow.org/blog/2014/1/8/from_cointelpro_to_snowden_the_fbi

88. For an excellent source, see Ward Churchill and Jim Vander Wall, *The*

COINTELPRO Papers: Documents from the FBI's Secret Wars against Dissent in the United States (Boston: South End, 2001). Also see *The People's History of the CIA.* www.thepeopleshistory.net/2013/07/cointelpro-fbis-war-on-us-citizens. html.

89. Chomsky quoted in Amy Goodman, "From COINTELPRO to Snowden, the FBI Burglars Speak Out after 43 Years of Silence (Part 2)."

90. Glenn Greenwald, "4 Points about the 1971 FBI Break-in," *Common Dreams* (January 7, 2014). www.commondreams.org/view/2014/01/07-9

91. Lewis H. Lapham, "Feast of Fools: How American Democracy Became the Property of a Commercial Oligarchy," *Truthout* (September 20, 2012). http://truth-out.org/opinion/item/11656-feast-of-fools-how-american-democracy-became-the-property-of-a-commercial-oligarchy

92. Charles Derber, private correspondence, January 29, 2014.

93. Stanley Aronowitz, "Where Is the Outrage?" *Situations* 5:2 (2014), pp. 9-48.

94. John M. Broder and Scott Shane, "For Snowden, a Life of Ambition, Despite the Drifting," *New York Times*, (June 15, 2013). www.nytimes. com/2013/06/16/us/for-snowden-a-life-of-ambition-despite-the-drifting. html?pagewanted=all&_r=0

95. Ibid.

96. Cited in Irving Howe, "This Age of Conformity," *Selected Writings 1950-1990* (New York: Harcourt Brace Jovanovich, 1990), p. 29.

97. Aronowitz, "Where Is the Outrage?"

98. Fred Branfman, "We Live under a Total Surveillance State in America—Can We Prevent It from Evolving into a Full-Blown Police State?" *AlterNet* (September 25, 2013). www.alternet.org/activism/we-live-under-total-surveillance-state-america-can-we-prevent-it-evolving-full-blown-police

99. Bauman, *Individualized Society*, p. 55.

CHAPTER EIGHT

1. http://johnpilger.com/articles/ from-pol-pot-to-isis-anything-that-flies-on-everything-that-moves

2. www.nytimes.com/2014/09/08/business/media/with-videos-of-killings-isis-hones-social-media-as-a-weapon.html?smid=tw-share&_r=0

3. www.newyorker.com/news/news-desk/death-steven-sotloff

4. Massumi, *Remains of the Day*, p. 19

5. Étienne Balibar, "Violence & Civility: On the Limits of Political Anthropology" (*A Journal of Feminist Cultural Studies* Vol. 20 Nos. 2 & 3, 2009) p. 10.

6. Cavarero, *Horrorism*, pp. 109, 111.

7. www.pipr.co.uk/wp-content/uploads/2014/07/jv2020-2.pdf

8. Judith Butler, "Violence, Mourning, Politics" (*Studies in Gender and Sexuality* Vol. 4 No. 1: 2003), p. 22.

9. www.whitehouse.gov/the-press-office/2014/08/20/statement-president

10. Cavarero, *Horrorism*, p. 16.

11. Griselda Pollock, *Visual Politics of Psychoanalysis: Art and the Image in Post-Traumatic Cultures* (New York: I.B. Taurus, 2013), p. 173.

12. www.independent.co.uk/news/world/middle-east/david-haines-british-hostage-david-haines-murdered-in-isis-beheading-9731691.html

13. www.bbc.co.uk/news/world-middle-east-29038217

14. www.aljazeera.com/news/americas/2014/09/kerry-islamic-state-iraq-2014910145016383660.html

15. Alice Speri, "ISIS Fighters and Their Friends Are Total Social Media Pros," *Vice News* (January 17, 2014). https://news.vice.com/article/isis-fighters-and-their-friends-are-total-social-media-pros

16. Rancière, *The Emancipated Spectator*, p. 103.

17. Simon Critchley, "The Infinite Demand of Art." www.artandresearch.org.uk/v3n2/critchley.php

18. Simon Critchley, *The Faith of the Faithless*, p. 92.

19. Chris Hedges, "The Power of Imagination," *Truthdig* (May 11, 2014). www.truthdig.com/report/item/the_power_of_imagination_20140511

20. On the radical imagination and the necessity to link it to everyday life and new forms of subjectivity, see Aronowitz, "Where Is the Outrage?"

INDEX

ABOUT THE AUTHORS

Brad Evans is a senior lecturer in international relations at the School of Sociology, Politics and International Studies (SPAIS), University of Bristol, UK. He is the founder and director of the histories of violence project. In this capacity, he is currently leading a global research initiative on the theme of "Disposable Life" to interrogate the meaning of mass violence in the twenty-first century. Brad's latest books include *Resilient Life: The Art of Living Dangerously* (with Julian Reid, Polity Press, 2014), *Liberal Terror* (Polity Press, 2013), and *Deleuze & Fascism* (with Julian Reid, Routledge, 2013). He is currently working on a number of book projects, including *Histories of Violence: An Introduction to Post-War Critical Thought* (with Terrell Carver, Zed Books, 2015).

Henry A. Giroux is a world-renowned educator, author, and public intellectual. He currently holds the Global TV Network Chair Professorship at McMaster University in the English and Cultural Studies Department and a Distinguished Visiting Professorship at Ryerson University. His most recent books include *The Violence of Organized Forgetting* (City Lights, 2014); *Zombie Politics and Culture in the Age of Casino Capitalism* (Peter Lang, 2011); *On Critical Pedagogy* (Continuum, 2011); *Education and the Crisis of Public Values* (Peter Lang, 2012); *Twilight of the Social: Resurgent Publics in an Age of Disposability* (Paradigm, 2012); *Disposable Youth* (Routledge, 2012); *Youth in Revolt* (Paradigm, 2013); *America's Education Deficit and the War on Youth* (Monthly Review Press, 2013); and *Neoliberalism's War on Higher Education* (Haymarket, 2014). A prolific writer and political commentator, he writes regularly for Truthout and serves on its board of directors. He currently lives in Hamilton, Ontario, Canada, with his wife, Dr. Susan Searls Giroux.